TRUE NORTH

Hunting Fossils Under the Midnight Sun

Lou Marincovich, PhD

Dream big!

Lou Marincovich

BERING
PRESS

PRAISE FOR *TRUE NORTH*

"This memoir is a can't-put-down page-turner, equal parts Jack London and Marincovich's idol Roy Chapman Andrews. But it is not just a rip-roaring adventure story; it also eloquently communicates both the intellectual thrill of scientific discovery and the emotional (and spiritual) energy derived from genuine exploration in some of the most challenging—and beautiful—environments on Earth."

— *Warren D. Allmon, PhD, Director*
Paleontological Research Institution, Ithaca, New York

"This book has so many of my favorite things—the romance of scientific adventure, a window into the mind of the explorer, the grit of the expedition, and the quest for nature's secrets that ends up revealing the depths of our own hearts and souls. It brings to mind the great science memoirs of Darwin, the transcendental writings of Thoreau, and the tales of Alaska and Everest told by Jon Krakauer. Read it, and be transported!"

— *Cassandra Vieten, PhD, President*
Institute of Noetic Sciences, Petaluma, California

"This is a story of adventure and high scientific accomplishment in the search for the most humble of fossils—seashells. We live on an ocean planet, and the bulk of the fossil record is found in ancient marine sediments, including those now found far from the present sea. Five hundred years ago Leonardo da Vinci first recognized the power of these shell fossils to reveal the dynamic history of the earth, and in particular, the ocean. Childhood reading about dinosaurs ultimately led Lou Marincovich down a path to a career as a paleontologist with the U.S. Geological Survey. Marincovich's global travels are highlighted by terrifying events along the African coast and in the wilds of Alaska and Siberia—along with personal revelation and great discovery. So you want to be a paleontologist? Buckle up, and read this book."

— *James C. Ingle, Jr., W.M. Keck Professor of Earth Sciences,*
Emeritus, Department of Geological Sciences, Stanford University

"For anyone who wants a life of adventure, Lou Marincovich makes a strong case that you should consider becoming a paleontologist!"

— *David J. Bottjer, PhD, Professor of Earth Sciences*
University of Southern California, Los Angeles, California

Printed in the United States of America.

ISBN: 978-0-9989485-0-8 (softcover)
ISBN: 978-0-9989485-1-5 (ebook)

Cover and interior design: dianarusselldesign.com

Publishing strategist: Holly Brady

Contact the author at: lou@loumarincovich.com

Address permission requests to Bering Press at: lou@loumarincovich.com

Cover photo shot on Kodiak Island, Alaska, 1978.

True North *is dedicated*

to my beloved wife and soulmate,

Karen Marincovich

1946-2009

CONTENTS

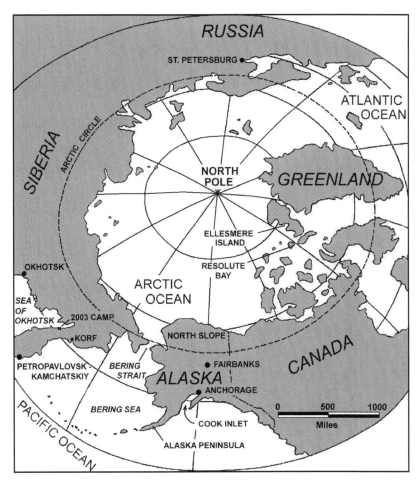

My field areas around the North Pacific and Arctic oceans.

My field areas in Alaska.

Era	Period		Epoch Start date (Ma)	
Cenozoic	**Quaternary**		Holocene	0.01
			Pleistocene	1.64
	Tertiary	Neogene	Pliocene	5.2
			Miocene	23.3
		Paleogene	Oligocene	35.4
			Eocene	56.5
			Paleocene	65
	Cretaceous			144

Cenozoic Era time scale. Ma = Mega-annum, or millions of years ago.

PROLOGUE

It was a rare sunny day in southwestern Alaska in July 2007 as the airliner rose from remote Popof Island. As we banked over the Pacific, the volcanic mountains of the Alaska Peninsula were arrayed before me like a museum diorama. I had spent much of my professional life there as a paleontologist researching fossil marine mollusks amid the forbidding peaks, wild animals and wilder weather. The rocky headlands, nameless beaches and desolate islands I had adventured over for the past thirty-four years stood out crisply, looking freshly painted in green, brown and snow white. Alaska was giving me a royal sendoff, as if the land knew I was returning to the "Lower 48," what Alaskans call "The Outside," for the last time.

Cold Bay, Cape Tachilni, Veniaminoff volcano and Unga Island, places named once then half-forgotten, passed below and faded away, all rich in memories to me, obscurities at best to the larger world. Probably no one else in history had been to every one of those places, and my heart strings tightened as I stared wistfully out the window. I was never again going to make fresh tracks through the dew-wet grass of a fog-rimmed valley that had no name, never again round a rocky corner and come across a caribou herd, wolf pack or grizzly, never again shelter under a rocky overhang from a punishing storm, smiling big because I was stormbound and alone yet powerfully and electrically alive.

The wilderness I reveled in, the lodestone for my heart and mind since childhood, where I had made scientific discoveries and been spared from death by sheer luck, was falling astern. Northward the Peninsula was sheathed in fog, its nearly constant companion, and I settled in for the 600-mile flight to Anchorage. I had come a long way from my boyhood in Southern California, but wilderness Alaska was exactly the destination fate had in mind for me. Leaving it forever was one of the most difficult decisions of my life. I could not have known that my departure ended a century-long era of Arctic exploration and research, that my boots had left the final tracks at Cape Aliaksin, Yellow Bluff Creek and Korovin Island for at least a human generation. ▲

COOK INLET, ALASKA

The shrieking alarm jolted me to full attention, as any sign of mechanical distress did on the oil-drilling platform miles from shore in the darkness of wintertime Alaska. The drill-rate indicator had plunged to zero, meaning that the antifreeze line running up to the derrick floor had accidentally been cut. Glancing out the window at brightly lit snow whipping sideways in the glaring industrial lights, and feeling my workroom rocked by gusts from the days-long storm, I shouldered on my parka and rainsuit as I grabbed my hard hat and tool bag while heading out into the frigid darkness.

Shielding my eyes from the blowing snow, I picked my way across the slippery steel deck amid standing puddles of diesel oil and drilling mud and climbed the grillwork stairway to the derrick floor. Greeting the crew of "roughnecks"—the men who operated the machinery that drilled the hole into the earth—I looked high up at the broken ends of a plastic antifreeze line that fed into the drill-rate gauge back in my workroom, the humbly named "mudshack."

On the widowmaker between the drilling tender J.W. Nickle and its platform. Finding privacy meant climbing to the top of the 142-foot derrick behind me.

"Looks like a nasty repair," commented Gene Inman the driller, a solidly built, moon-faced man with a ready smile and Texas drawl who headed the crew of roughnecks.

"No kidding," I replied. "I like you guys, but a 3:00 a.m. visit isn't what I had in mind."

"Well, you gotta expect problems even with an easy money job like yours," he said with a smile.

"Easy money, my ass! You roughnecks bullshit and smoke cigarettes here in a weather shelter with your eyes half closed, and tell lies about the last time you were ashore, but I have to stay alert all night and pay attention to alarms to keep your asses safe."

"Looks like *your* ass is gonna be up in the air real soon," said Gene as he directed his crew to rig up a bosun's chair, a simple canvas strap to sit on, like a children's playground swing, to winch me up to the broken line.

The ends of the torn quarter-inch antifreeze line taunted me from thirty feet up the drill pipe, as if knowing I was afraid of heights. I stuffed the repair tools into my rainsuit pockets, freeing my gloved hands for a death grip on the icy steel cable from which the bosun's chair hung. I took a deep breath, lifted my right arm and spiraled an index finder upward so the roughneck at the winch controls knew to launch me aloft.

Sheet metal walled the lower twenty feet of the oil derrick to shield the roughnecks from the worst of the winter weather. As I rose toward the 30-foot level, I popped above the weather shield and was instantly twirling at the end of a cable with a little piece of canvas under my ass, flying off to the side like a kite in the howling Alaskan winter storm. I could not repair the antifreeze line while spinning wildly, but there was nothing to grab on to. In desperation, I wrapped my legs around the Kelly hose, an 18-inch-thick black snake that carried hot chemical mud under high pressure down into the three-mile-deep drill hole. The hose bucked and jerked wildly as hot mud surged through it, driven by the pounding of 2,000-horsepower pumps.

The broken antifreeze line showed a ragged tear that needed to be trimmed and repaired with a small metal connector inserted between the broken ends. Effecting the repair was akin to standing in the back of a pickup truck speeding down a dirt road in a snowstorm while trying to thread a needle. Grasping the Kelly hose with my now-cramping legs and being jerked around like a rag doll, I trimmed the broken hose ends with wire cutters, but inserting the tiny connector and crimping small clamps over it was hopeless while wearing thick gloves. I removed my leather gloves one by one with my teeth while holding on to the steel cable that supported me, and stuffed them in my rainsuit pockets.

Feeling had quickly left my bare hands and the stiff gusts added an extra few degrees of wind chill to the -20°F temperature. I could *see* my fingers but I could not *feel* them as they grasped cutters, pliers and crimpers seemingly on their own. Several minutes of intent focus on my hands and tools crept by in increasingly painful slow motion, but I finally finished the repair.

Grateful to have gloves on again, I appraised my situation for a moment before signaling a roughneck to lower the bosun's chair. Between snow squalls I glimpsed gas flares from distant platforms, their light reflected on ice floes gliding outbound with the tide. I could not imagine a more miserable place to be at that stage in my young life. As a boy in Southern California, I had yearned more than anything else to become a paleontologist, but fourteen years later I was merely dangling from a steel cable at night in an Alaskan storm.

I blame it on Roy Chapman Andrews, the famous vertebrate paleontologist. My life was transformed on my tenth birthday when my mother gave me Andrews' children's book *All About Dinosaurs*, which described his adventures while discovering dinosaur bones in the unexplored Gobi Desert in the 1920s and 1930s. My previously unfocused mind was inflamed by his stories of hunting fossils in the wilderness, run-ins with bandits, supplies arriving by camel caravan, and fossil localities with names like the "Flaming

Cliffs." There was nothing in my boyhood to suggest that I would have an unusually exciting life filled with adventure, danger and scientific accomplishment, but my soul responded with fervor to Andrews' stories of wilderness paleontology, and this fed my dual drives for adventure and scientific order. Thanks to my mother's inspired gift, the greatest good fortune of my life was that I knew exactly what I wanted to be when I grew up. She had given me a dream I would hold on to for my entire life.

Dreams cost money, however, so there I was in Cook Inlet because I had spotted a summer job announcement on the University of Southern California's Geology Department bulletin board. It bore the eye-catching phrase "we pay one-third more than oil companies." Geologic Engineering Service would pay me $900 a month and living expenses for doing something called "mudlogging," which amounted to describing the rocks that the drill penetrated as it bored into the earth. All I had to do was commit to a few months working on an offshore drilling rig in Alaska.

I had just gotten my bachelor's degree, the first in my family to do so. Coming from a home environment where higher education was not appreciated, where one family member had tried to belittle me as "professor" when I was still in junior college, had made my educational slog harder than necessary. Steepening the educational trail, UCLA had an unwelcoming geology department during my stint there and lacked a decent paleontology program. I was too naive to apply for scholarships elsewhere, so I thought I was stuck in Los Angeles for grad school. The only other game in town was USC, where a nationally renowned paleontologist was on the faculty, but still I was reluctant to visit the campus and submit myself to yet another icy professorial encounter, the only kind I had known up until then. Eventually I set my fears aside and made an unannounced visit to USC Geology.

"Hello and welcome to USC," announced Dr. William H. Easton as he bounded up from his chair and warmly greeted me as soon as I knocked timidly on his open office door. "Please come in."

"Oh, thanks," I mumbled, stunned that a geology professor had greeted me warmly.

"My secretary called ahead and said you're interested in earning a doctorate here. What are your interests?"

"Cenozoic mollusks of the North Pacific, overall. But I was born just half an hour away in San Pedro (San PEA-dro), California, so I've always been interested in the famous Pliocene and Pleistocene faunas there."

"You've come to the right place, because my house in the Palos Verdes Hills is built on top of those deposits and I'm pretty interested in them myself."

I sighed in relief inwardly and probably grinned outwardly like an idiot. I immediately knew I would be going for my doctorate at USC. I got a clear sense that I would be a welcome addition to a community of senior and junior scholars, that the professors would be mentors instead of surly taskmasters. The feeling of relief at finding my intellectual home was immense, as if I were an orphan who had found his welcoming birth family. Dr. Easton's own specialty was rugose corals, a type of coral known only in the Paleozoic Era, the last one having died some 300,000,000 years ago, but despite our disparate specialties, we hit it off like I never had with a professor.

"I don't know much about rugose corals," I admitted.

"That doesn't matter," he replied, "since the principles are the same for studying any fossils." He would know, having authored the introductory paleo text used in every college in the country. He would become my friend and mentor as well as doctoral advisor.

I had found my welcoming intellectual home, but one I could not afford. The job announcement for mudlogging on the departmental bulletin board was a timely answer to my financial dilemma. If I worked on oil rigs in Alaska through the summer, I would earn enough to afford USC.

I was about to embark on an intermittent four years of hard, dangerous work where industrial accidents were the norm, my coworkers had grade-school educations and prison records, where opportunities for personal advancement were nonexistent, and boredom was interspersed with sharp episodes of terror. Roy Chapman Andrews had never worked on an oil rig, but I was following my own "adventure trajectory" and at that time needed a break from the world of education. Intellectuals are usually smart enough to avoid the sorts of situations and people I got to know from 1966 to 1970 in the worldwide oil exploration community known as "Oil Patch," but I was the exception.

▲ ▲ ▲

My young spirits rose as the drill ship *Wodeco* hove into view after a gut-churning seventy mile ride down a storm-tossed Cook Inlet from Anchorage; we passengers could hardly wait to depart that accursed little speedboat. My spirits sank just as fast when I saw that the only way to transfer to the drill ship was a knotted rope for Tarzaning across the churning waters of the Inlet.

"Grab the knotted rope and swing across to the drill ship," shouted the deckhand of the crew boat.

"Shit, that's really dangerous," I hollered back.

"That's all we got, your highness. Swing or jump," caustically bellowed the deckhand as men waiting behind me laughed. Now I had to swing across the frightening water gap.

The captain cautiously edged his speedboat closer, careful to keep his fragile vessel from being smashed and crushed by the hulking drill ship. One second our little boat's deck was five feet *above* the side rail of the *Wodeco*, and the next it plunged ten feet *below*. Having been raised around commercial fishing boats, I was fearful when the hulking tender loomed over our little speedboat, realizing we could be crushed flat and sunk in the next second.

A loud blast on the crew boat's horn interrupted me summoning up my courage to swing across.

"What's happening?" I asked the crew boat's deckhand, as I clung to a railing in the blustery rain.

"It's too rough to transfer you guys," he said. "Unless the weather lets off we're going back to Anchorage."

"Back to Anchorage?" I asked. "I'm already dying from being seasick. A trip back would kill me."

"There's nothing we can do, it's just too dangerous. Someone's going to get killed if we try to transfer you guys," he explained.

At that moment the crew boat lurched upward, twisted drunkenly, and crashed down on the side railing of the *Wodeco*, flattening it like tin foil. The captain immediately blasted his air horn and bellowed with authority, "Everybody inside, we're heading back to port." Nobody complained; crashing into the drill ship had jarred us off our feet. We swayed across the heaving, rain-lashed deck, back into the cabin and its airliner-style seats, and sat disconsolately for the next five hours, feeling sick as hell and getting up only to puke into the waves as we cursed them. After a hellish ten-hour round trip tour of Cook Inlet we tied up to the same Anchorage dock we had left at dawn. Nobody felt well enough to celebrate being alive and I simply went to the company apartment and slept, without eating.

The storm blew itself out overnight and my first enjoyable Cook Inlet crew boat ride was on a bright morning when the sea and land stood out in pristine detail. The glassy waters of the Inlet, made chocolate-milkshake brown by their load of glacial sediments, were backed by the immense Alaska Range to the west that featured 10,000-foot active volcanoes from which smoke and steam exploded. To the east lay the thickly forested Kenai Peninsula fronting the Chugach Mountains, whose lower slopes continued right into suburban Anchorage. The dreamlike landscape was a compelling sight for a geologist from the city and was the kind of rich emotional experience I had dreamt about as a youth. I felt myself drawn to that immense wilderness passing on both sides of the boat, where I knew almost no one lived and where undiscovered fossil beds must lie.

Up close in the sunlight, the *Wodeco* was a pretty homely affair, built in a time that predated concerns about safety or basic comfort. An oil derrick and all its machinery had been stuffed into the middle of the small coastal freighter, leaving precious little space for people to work and live. An unmuffled 2,000-horsepower engine that powered the rotary drill sat in the middle of the tiny ship and blasted out brain-melting noise around the clock. Men could not make themselves heard unless they shouted and their lips were actually touching the ears of the other guy.

Veteran mudlogger Sig Erson, a man of average height and built with a saggy face and graying widow's peak, showed me the galley, where three or four guys in hardhats were watching a small television they could not hear. We all nodded in greeting but, understandably, nobody tried to say hello. Beside the galley was a small sleeping compartment for us mudloggers that held only a metal-frame bunk bed with a bare, pinstripe mattress and musty pillow on the lower bunk. Whichever of us was not working could "relax" in the thunderously loud galley or lie down in the equally earsplitting bunkroom. There was nowhere else on the small, machinery-packed ship that was safe to snooze, but falling asleep in the bunkroom verged on the impossible. Not only was the noise deafening, but the bed's iron frame was not bolted to the deck, so the entire bed moved around the darkened compartment from the vibrations of the huge drilling engine thundering a mere 50 feet away. As I labored to fall asleep before my first twelve-hour work shift, referred to as a "tower" on oil rigs, the iron bed came to life and rotated randomly around the darkened compartment, roaming around like a modern robotic vacuum cleaner with my half-asleep body on top. When I awoke, my face was touching a bulkhead that had been on the other side of the room when I fell asleep. The moving bed was like something from a comedy skit, at least seen from the perspective of time.

My workroom, the mudshack, was a claustrophobic, gray compartment where I monitored a hydrogen-flame chromatograph and drill-rate chart and, most importantly, collected and described a sediment sample for each ten feet we drilled into the seafloor. I kept a running log—literally the "mud log"—that described the type and thickness of each rock layer we drilled through. The chromatograph continuously sampled the man-made drilling mud circulating out of the well for signs of hydrocarbons and set off an alarm if we encountered a "show" of gas or oil. The last thing I did with each sample was to squirt it with an industrial solvent and observe it under a microscope. Any traces of oil floated to the top of the solvent and showed up under ultraviolet light. After showing me the ropes, Sig left the operation in my newbie hands and went to crash in our Vibra Bed bunkroom.

My first mudlogging tower went from midnight Friday to noon Saturday and almost ushered me into eternity: one of the gallon solvent tins had a pinhole leak from which deadly liquid slowly seeped, and during the night fumes overcame me despite the din and vibration of the drilling machinery next door. The next thing I knew, Sig was duck-walking me around an outside deck to revive me in the night air. I had almost died my first day in Oil Patch! We tossed the leaking container overboard and aired out the compartment; the rest of my first mudlogging stint was uneventful. Fortunately, I worked on the hellish *Wodeco* for only two days before I went ashore for assignment to another rig. Mudlogging had appeared out of nowhere as a way to make fast—if not easy—money for grad school. My work schedule of twenty-eight days of twelve-hour towers offshore followed by three days ashore for R&R was a grind, but a great way to save up for USC's costly tuition.

Alaska billed itself as the Last Frontier, and working on oil platforms in a wild and woolly place appealed to my adventurous nature. Unfortunately, Anchorage in 1966 was an especially bleak place, because the Good Friday earthquake had devastated the city only two years earlier, destroying whole neighborhoods and leaving cracked and askew buildings strewn across town. As a geologist I saw firsthand where the earth had flowed from under buildings like liquid, and where one side of the downtown shopping street of Fourth Avenue had dropped fifty feet and left the other side hanging high. The only entertainment was a string of seedy bars still open on the remaining high side of Fourth Avenue, so it was no hardship to be out in Cook Inlet where the oil platforms and drill ships clustered offshore over favorable geological structures.

The ship we approached in the crew-change speedboat, the drilling tender *J.W. Nickle*, was a small and homely affair. The platforms where we had stopped to drop off passengers earlier that morning as we plied our way down Cook Inlet were broad-shouldered, boxy giants perched high above the ocean on four massive legs that rested upon the seafloor. The *J.W. Nickle*, in contrast, was a drilling tender, a mere barge stuffed with machinery and living quarters, and it was anchored end-on to a spindly looking triangular platform. The platform was of the so-called jack-up variety; it could move up and down on its three legs to suit the ocean's depth at a given drill site. Bridging the sea between tender and platform was a ramp with walkway called the widowmaker. All in all the oil rig had the look of a quaint and overly large model toy.

The drilling tender J.W. Nickle and its three-legged jack-up platform. The mudshack where I worked is the white building with a window partly showing on the platform.

Once assigned a below-the-waterline bunkroom on the tender, which I shared with the other mudlogger, Sig Erson, I set to work immediately on a noon-to-midnight tower in a mudshack that was simply a trailer bolted to the platform near the derrick. I quickly settled down to the routine of collecting "cuttings" (ground-up rock) from an assembly called the "shaker screen," where chemical mud poured forth and brought the cuttings from miles deep in the earth. I analyzed the lithologies in the mudshack and drew up the mudlog as drilling proceeded. I enjoyed the physicality of the work and fit right in with the "roughnecks," who performed the drilling operation on the platform, and the "roustabouts," who kept machinery running and maintained the tender, because I had grown up in San Pedro among fishermen and stevedores, men who worked with their hands and backs.

In stark contrast to most sediments that we drilled through easily, after reaching nearly three miles deep in Cook Inlet we inevitably hit a rock layer called the Hemlock Sandstone, which contained car-size boulders of an extremely hard rock called quartzite. The quartzite quickly stripped the gear teeth off the drill bit and our drilling operation ground to a halt. The roughnecks pulled those miles of pipe out of the ground ninety feet at a time, then screwed on a diamond-studded bit that lacked teeth and looked like a mushroom cap. The diamond bit drilled very slowly, but it could stay rotating in the hole for a day or more, although it had some unpleasant characteristics. It induced a harmonic vibration in the drill pipe, so that the entire three miles of pipe bounced up and down several inches every couple of seconds. For the two days it took to penetrate through the Hemlock Sandstone, the entire platform, weighing hundreds of tons, bounded up and down like a demonic pogo stick. The herky-jerky up-and-down motion wore everyone down, and I took every opportunity to flee the platform for the drilling tender, ostensibly for a cup of coffee but really to escape the hated bouncing. The vertical pounding was accompanied by a clangorous mechanical cacophony as everything that was loose on the platform, and many things that were not supposed to be, smashed and banged together. Amid the din I had to remind myself that mudlogging was my ticket to geology grad school and the good life beyond.

My original plan was to work through the summer until the fall semester began at USC, then work future summers in Alaska to continue to pay for school. However, once in the swing of things on the *J.W. Nickle*, I decided to work through the upcoming fall semester and begin grad school in February 1967, so I would be done with Oil Patch in one episode and have enough money to work without interruption toward my PhD. Rig work in Alaska also appealed to my sense of adventure, as did the magnificent scenery, and not living in my mother's apartment in L.A. for a few months was a definite plus. I had wished for adventure, romance and a little danger when I was in high school, and I enjoyed getting a daily dose of each in Alaska along with $900 a month.

After my first month on the *J.W. Nickle* I went ashore for three days, or at least what I thought would be three days in Anchorage. Nobody had informed me that the crew boat rides were part of my "time off" until I boarded the twenty-passenger speedboat. After feeling outraged for the first couple of hours as we sped along, I was reconciling myself to the situation just as the thousand-horsepower boat stopped like a roped steer; the engine made a strangling sound and we settled to a dead stop. We had run over a large sheet of heavy plastic that had wrapped itself around the propeller so tightly that the boat was immobilized. We were stuck until help arrived hours later in the form of a spare crew boat that got us into Anchorage at dinnertime, the ride having started in the morning. I had not even stepped ashore by the time one of my three ashore days was shot.

I had not planned well enough for the absence of reading material on the *J.W. Nickle*, so I needed to stock up on books and magazines while in town. Anchorage lacked a bookstore, or maybe the earthquake had demolished it, so my search for reading material during my few remaining hours in town was in drugstores, supermarkets, tobacco shops and, best of all, the bus station. Unfortunately, beyond news magazines and car titles, there was precious little on offer, except for specialty titles related to women, men and guns. Why there were so many women's magazines for sale in a town with an acute shortage of women was a complete mystery. Also salient was a genre now extinct, which was men's magazines with names like *True, Ken, Male* and *Men*, which featured two-fisted stories, supposedly true, about good-looking, worldly men who led much more adventuresome lives than mine. World War II stories also loomed large. The biggest but least diverse category of magazines was devoted to firearms and ammunition, understandable in Alaska but not one of my interests. Every issue featured articles on "hot" handgun rounds, "killer" rifle loads, the fun of shooting with pre-modern black-powder weapons, and saving money by doing your own reloads. Still, I bought them all, since reading yet another comparison of .38-caliber handguns was better than reading nothing. Later on in my Alaskan adventures, when I worked as a field paleontologist and frequently encountered wildlife higher on the food chain than I was, firearms became of real interest, but not while I was on oil rigs. I bought every car magazine available, since cars have always been a passion, and at least I could bullshit enthusiastically about cars with the rig hands, something that split the difference between my stories about college and theirs about prisons. Mercifully, I *had* brought along from home my favorite collections of great poetry, by Louis Untermeyer and M.E. Speare, as well as *The Rubaiyat* and *Homer*.

A storm blew up overnight and the next morning the Inlet was sheathed in low clouds, fog and drizzle. The leaden skies poured down sheets of rain as our crew boat rolled and bucked in the storm swell. The captain would not slacken his speed just because a few of us were feeding the fish, or because there were floating logs the size of telephone poles in the Inlet that could punch a hole through the hull in a split second. On stormy days we wore life preservers even inside the cabin. But at least I had a bundle of fresh magazines in my duffel.

There was nothing attractive about the *J.W. Nickle* when I returned for a second twenty-eight-day stint and plenty that was ugly. Any warm and fuzzy feelings I may have once had about the source of my grad school funds faded quickly when I looked around and assessed what looked like a dilapidated offshore prison. Working the first month had been something of a lark and a learning experience, but the eight-month sentence that loomed ahead into the Alaskan winter was going to require real endurance. Still, laboring on an offshore oil rig in Alaska may have been Spartan and hazardous, but it appealed greatly to my adventurous nature, and the fact that it paid way better than any other "student" job meant that I was able to afford an education. The fact that geology doctoral students today at USC are fully supported does not diminish the fact that in my youth I was following a different path to my educational goal—one that included good pay, high adventure and a taste of danger.

Idle hours were a daily threat on the *J.W. Nickle*, given the four-hour gap between finishing my tower and sleeping eight hours before the next tower began. I did not dare play cards with my buddies who often tossed in their month's paychecks to up an ante, for fear of losing my tuition money. I did play thousands of dart games on a board nailed to a starboard bulkhead, and got so good at compensating for the side-to-side rolling of the tender that I severely overshot or undershot dart boards ashore, automatically adjusting for the rocking of waves that were not there. Old movies circulated weekly among the twenty or so oil rigs in Cook Inlet, and we used a portable projector with a scabrous gray bulkhead for a screen. Unfortunately, the movie lineup never changed. If we got the *Maltese Falcon* one week we were going to see it again in eight weeks. One week we were pleasantly surprised to get half a dozen reels at once, then disgusted to learn they were all anti-Japanese propaganda cartoons left over from World War II, showing scenes of leering, bucktooth aviators wearing thick glasses and bombing hospitals and schools. Even we rig hands, who expected so little in the way of entertainment and were grateful for nearly anything, were dumbfounded that our main entertainment that week was propaganda for a war that had ended more than twenty years earlier.

With Gene Inman and his drill crew of roughnecks on the J.W. Nickle. Gene is seated with his legs crossed and my practical-joking pal Putt-Putt is just behind him.

My main preparation for killing time in Alaska had been taking banjo lessons at the famous Troubadour Coffee House in Hollywood, picking and strumming my brand-new Sears banjo early Sunday mornings with other novices. I have always loved the sound of a banjo, but I was destined to advance in my abilities no farther than what I learned at the Trouba-dour. These first music lessons in my life confirmed what I already knew, that I had a tin ear. While other students mastered four or five songs, I labored to grasp the basics of the first song we tried, "Worried Man Blues." The good news in all this was that I would have a superabundance of time for banjo practice in my lonely little mudshack.

I was stolidly practicing my banjo one day in the mudshack, still trying to pick out "Worried Man Blues" acceptably a few months after I had first "learned" it at the Troubadour. As I glanced at the mudlogging instruments I noticed Gus, a roughneck, staring at me through the window in the mudshack door. As I continued plucking, he slowly reached up and stuck his fingers in his ears while his face exhibited great suffering. Out on the platform deck, where Gus was standing, a man could hardly hear himself think, due to the shriek of giant engines. I laughed at his implied jest and waved him in.

"What's that?" asked Gus.

"It's a banjo," I replied. "I'm practicing."

"Let's hear you play something," he commanded.

"Well," I said, "I'm not very good, but I'll give it a try." I then plucked out a ragged version of "Worried Man Blues."

"Wow," said Gus, "that's really something. How long did it take you to learn that song?"

"Uh, not long," I said.

"Can I try it?" he asked.

"No, you'll get my banjo dirty," I replied, hoping that Gus would go away and leave me to my musical career.

"No, I won't," he pleaded, "I just want to see how a banjo feels."

Feeling sorry for the guy, I handed him the banjo so he could at least tell his buddies that he had once held one. Gus relaxed into a chair, propped the banjo against his waist, and adjusted a couple of the strings. I was curious and started to worry; he almost seemed familiar with the instrument. He smiled at me benignly and proceeded to rip off tune after tune that sounded like Earl Scruggs in especially fine fettle. I was dumbfounded and could only shake my head and smile. I had swallowed Gus's story—hook, line and sinker.

"Where did you learn to play like that?"

"I was raised on a farm in Kentucky," he said. "I learned to walk and play banjo at the same time."

"That last tune I played was my biggest record," he boasted.

"You made records?" I asked, astonished.

"Yup," he said, "that one was more than two feet in diameter, my biggest record by far."

I smiled when I realized Gus was still kidding me.

"When I heard you playing from outside the mudshack I wished you would play the banjo ten-or," he admitted.

"Tenor?" I asked, "What's tenor banjo?"

"I wished," he continued, "you would play ten or eleven blocks away from me so I couldn't hear it." With that he handed me back what had been a fine instrument in his hands and felt like clay in mine, then turned around and stomped from the mudshack while laughing up a storm. I snapped the banjo in its case, slid it beneath the desk, and got back to reading *Of Human Bondage*. I knew I could *read* better than Gus.

Besides reading and my uphill struggle with the banjo, I listened to the only radio station we heard on Cook Inlet, KYAK, whose tagline was, "KYAK, your big country KA-YAK canoe, bringing you the best in country and western music every day from Anchorage, Alaska," followed by the jingle:

Way down South in the Indian Nation,
Everyone's talkin' 'bout a radio station
Listenin' is their only occ-u-PA-tion
Radio K-Y-A-K!

I had never liked country and western music much and was now bombarded by nothing but. I do not know if KYAK was the only radio station broadcasting from Anchorage in 1966, or if it was the only station powerful enough to be heard seventy miles away on the rigs, but I never heard any other station out there.

After two months on a small floater like the *J.W. Nickle*, I was delighted to be assigned to a large permanent platform, the *Grayling*. Even better, crew changes had been drastically speeded up by flying from Anchorage to Kenai, which was ninety percent of the way to the oil rigs, then taking a thirty-minute crew boat ride to the platforms, saving hours of transit time. I certainly did not miss spending most of a day in a crew boat pounding down (and sometimes back up) Cook Inlet, and this change alone doubled my monthly time ashore from one day to two.

As we drew close, I saw that the *Grayling* was by far the biggest rig I had worked on, because it had two oil drilling derricks atop it, kitty-corner across the blocky platform from each other. As it turned out, merely getting on to the *Grayling* was an adventure, since it had no dock, and we had to be hoisted aboard by a crane like so much cargo. Six of us stepped aboard an oversize life ring, which had coarse netting attached to its outer circumference that was then gathered together ten feet up at the crane hook. The netting was the sort used by World War II soldiers to clamber down the sides of troop ships. The ring was floored with canvas to hold our baggage, which freed up our hands for clinging to the outside of the net. As a lifelong acrophobe, I was petrified by this method of boarding the platform. It was crystal clear to my analytical brain that the skinny life ring would never support the weight of half a dozen men and their luggage, plus the weight of the netting, if we ever plunged into Cook Inlet, but what could I do? I reluctantly tossed in my duffel bag and banjo case and hugged the netting for dear life along with five other victims.

At a signal from one of the boat's crew, the crane driver abruptly jerked us off the deck for our 100-foot ride toward the clouds. We wretches hugging the net had no control over our fate, and my mind fixated on a vision of thrashing in the icy inlet waters in an entangling net amid bobbing luggage. Unfortunately, on this occasion the crane driver turned playful, like a fisherman who has solidly hooked a fish and wants to have some fun before landing it. He suddenly stopped our ascent and let us swing back and forth for a few eternal seconds, which was, as the more-experienced men shouted to me, an unspoken warning to hang on even tighter. The crane driver suddenly unspooled a yard or two of cable and we dropped like a stone toward the sea before coming to a jerking halt amid yells and curses from the netted victims. My body may have stopped, but my stomach kept going as I lapsed into hyperventilation. I was paralyzed into a mute acceptance of imminent death, eyes closed, jaw clenched, hands curled into claws and turning white on the ropes. My whole body was shaking by the time we were hoisted over the rail and plopped onto the platform, but after taking a few moments to recover I retrieved my duffel and banjo and made my way to my four-man bunk-room. I never got used to boarding the *Grayling* that way, but it was never as terrifying again. On one occasion after we landed at Kenai I got my first helicopter ride out to a platform, on a Korean War-vintage Sikorsky S-55. It was loud as hell and painted bright yellow, so we called it Ole Yeller. It was worrisome to be in such a loud, shaky contraption but thrilling to be flying without regular wings.

I arrived on the *Grayling* just as winter weather descended on southern Alaska and it was as cold and bleak as I imagined Siberia to be. One day during a particularly hard freeze, we were forbidden to leave the living quarters because the ambient temperature plus the howling storm combined for an incredible wind-chill factor of -110°F. Drilling was halted and the whole crew assembled in the galley, bullshitting and smoking over snacks and coffee for one whole midnight tower, midnight to noon. It was novel to see everyone together in one place, since our jobs normally kept us scattered all over the platform, but it felt a little like recreation hour in the prison yard because there were so many rough customers among the crew. Few intellectuals have lived at the bottom level of Oil Patch and in a sense I was a fish out of water, but perhaps because I had come from a working-class background I felt a certain kinship with the guys who were making their way through life in such tough jobs. My dad was the skipper of a tuna clipper in Peru and Chile for half of every year and had turned to stevedoring, loading and unloading freighters, at times when the fishing slowed. I remember his departures and arrivals at my boyhood home in San Pedro, and his absence at Christmas, but little else. Once he conceived me, he seems to have viewed his job as finished, never having taught me to toss a football, hit a baseball, work with tools, be resolute in the face of uncertainty, or negotiate any of the other stations of manhood.

Later in life I described this with some bitterness to my half-brother, who had grown up with our father home every day. I envied that he had had a father's guidance to rely on. "Dream on," he corrected me, "Dad didn't show me how to do a damn thing. He never took any interest in my growing up." So much for the grass being greener on the other side of the fence.

Shortly after the -110°F day, a real problem threatened the *Grayling* when the electricity died. A blob of water had somehow gotten into the diesel supply for the generators and froze somewhere in the miles-long maze of pipes and valves, so all operations on the platform ground to an abrupt halt. All of a sudden the lights winked out in the working and living spaces, machinery whined to a halt, and our heaters died. It is disorienting to be a human cog in the viscera of a gigantic machine, a small organic particle adapted to survive in a metal universe of gray bulkheads, shrieking motors and roaring, clanking machinery, and then to have it suddenly fall into silence and darkness. It was a late winter afternoon in the Arctic, so the sun had already gone down; we were left in complete darkness in a world crammed full of machinery, suddenly unable to see head-height pipes, walkways, stairs, gratings, passageways and compartments. Battery-powered emergency lights came on, but they were set high above the deck, so they cast a zigzag spiderweb of shadows in the workspaces due to the many pipes crisscrossing overhead. We were instructed to go to our bunkrooms, get under the covers with all our clothes on, and try to stay warm until the problem was fixed.

Lying in my bunk in the dark, trying to adjust to a silent platform, I heard a faint slithering or hissing sound, not mechanical or electrical, that at first was nearly imperceptible but became more distinct as I focused on it. I turned to Sig in the next bunk and asked, "What's that funny sound?"

"You mean the sort of scraping or dragging sound?" he asked.

"Yeah," I said, "it's more of a hissing or shushing, but it's nothing I've heard before."

"Maybe they're scraping the deck for some reason," he guessed.

"It's not a machinery sound," I said as I made my way over to a small window that looked onto the Inlet. The faint light given off by the platform's emergency lights reflected off thick sheets of ice surging in with the tide. It suddenly struck me with a chill what the hissing sound was: the grating of floating ice sheets as they ground and slithered their way past the *Grayling's* columnar steel legs. That sound must have been ever-present, but masked by everyday machinery noises. It was sobering to realize that the immense force of ice grinding against our steel island was at work all the time. Up until that moment, the *Grayling* had seemed invulnerable, planted solidly on the floor of Cook Inlet on elephantine legs, the massive platform solidly welded and bolted together upon them. Listening to the distinctly creepy sound, I imagined molecules of steel continuously being shorn off of the platform legs by the relentless conveyor belt of ice. I suddenly felt extremely vulnerable, like I was teetering on some fragile manmade artifact that did not stand a chance against nature. The platform legs were thick enough to last my lifetime, but one future day the *Grayling* platform would be no more than four stubs barely visible above the Inlet waters at low tide. All of a sudden the lights flickered into brightness, massive machinery whirred and roared to life again and pumps throbbed like beating hearts, the welcome vibrations coursing through our bodies; we were back online.

One morning we struck oil on the *Grayling* and I was the first to know, the good luck signaled by a shrieking gas alarm in the mudshack. I ran out to tell the drill crew to stop smoking, because a lighted cigarette has caused more than one oil rig to explode into a ball of flame. The roughnecks, chain smokers to a man, immediately switched to chewing tobacco, which I had never given a thought to.

"You ought to give it a try," said Gene Inman, the driller. "It won't hurt and it might help you."

"Help me how?" I asked.

"It'll make you feel more like a man instead of a mudlogger," he replied with a smile.

"Compared to your crew I already feel like Superman," I smiled back. "You guys probably have dresses for going ashore."

Gene pulled a well-used packet of Beech-Nut chewing tobacco from his coveralls, saying, "Have a chaw."

I bit off a tiny piece with the wariness bred of having tried haggis and poi. It tasted kind of sweet.

"Not that way," exclaimed Gene, grabbing the Beech-Nut. "Like this." He gnawed off a thumb-size chunk before pulling the chaw free. Then he conspicuously chewed it and inserted the wad in his cheek.

"Gotcha," I said, as I did my best to imitate a real man, and tried to ignore the thought of shared germs on the chaw. Chewing vigorously, my mouth instantly watered as if I had just sucked on cayenne pepper. Swallowing only spread the sickening sweetness farther into my body cavity. I felt my stomach lining curdle as the nauseating wave of Beech-Nut engulfed it.

"Not bad," I lied. "What flavor is this?"

"I only like the original flavor, not the others," he explained.

"Yeah, I can see why," I gasped as a rising blush of nausea and dizziness threatened to overwhelm me and I blinked back tears, trying hard not to gag aloud. "Well, I better get back to the mudshack; gotta keep an eye on the gas gauge. Thanks for the chaw."

"Anytime." replied Gene, who was wearing an ever-bigger smile than usual.

I hotfooted it down the grillwork stairway and spit the accursed wad overboard. Good God, what shit! I could not get the cloying sweetness out of my mouth until I had brushed my teeth twice and eaten a meal. Gene sometimes offered me a chaw from his Beech-Nut pouch with a knowing smile, but I never bit.

Whether they were razzing me for being a college boy, goading me to toss my paycheck into their poker pot, or trying to hook me on chewing tobacco, I loved the sense of camaraderie with the drill crew. I had spent my childhood in a silent world in which we children were admonished to be seen and not heard; my mother, Theresa Marie (Terry) Marincovich, was consumed by a perpetual migraine headache, and my father, Louie Nick Sr., was absent six months a year fishing in South America. Even when my father was around, dinnertime was as silent as a library and much of the conversation between my parents was in Croatian. Bantering and joking with the crew, along with the adventure of drilling for oil in Alaska, meant more to me than I could express to my rig buddies.

▲ ▲ ▲

During a telling moment at the end of high school, I lay atop my bed on a sunny day in Hollywood, musing about life and anticipating what lay ahead. "I want," I said—literally *said* aloud to myself—"a life of strong emotions." This heartfelt plea was an understandable reaction to a home life that had been unemotional in the extreme. I wanted more than the world of paleontology; I wanted my life to be an unfolding drama of breathless adventures. My young mind could not have known what it was asking for. I had not precisely meant "strong emotions," "strong *positive* emotions" being more what I had in mind.

Accompanying my plea for a rich emotional life, there flickered through my consciousness the pale vision of a woman standing in a room. Her shadowed, backlit features were hidden, but she was tall, slender and had short, dark hair. I sensed she was an artist. She was standing in a room filled with objets d'art, books and curios and seemed relaxed and at home, but resembled not at all my mother, a relative or even a movie star. I knew I was awake and not dreaming, as I lay staring up with my hands behind my head, but the clarity was remarkable before the vision faded, leaving me to wonder what the strange woman had to do with my plea for strong emotions. She would visit me again.

▲ ▲ ▲

For all of us on the crew, striking oil was a huge thrill. The discovery drill bit had been grinding away deep in the earth for several hours, and the oil company "toolpusher," or supervisor, decided to withdraw the drill pipe from the earth and put on a new bit before going any deeper. Three hours later, after pulling fifteen thousand feet of drill pipe from the ground ninety feet at a time, the roughnecks handed me the worn bit, which I was instructed to forward to the oil company's headquarters.

I was thrilled that we had struck oil on "my" tower, and that I had been the first to know of the discovery before the rest of the world, but the longer I glanced at the 6-1/4"-diameter Hughes X1G drill bit sitting on the mudshack floor, the more proprietary I felt. It seemed unfair that a manager somewhere in the Lower 48 would get to display the bit as a mere business trophy. With this in mind, my thoughts drifted to the pile of worn X1Gs out on deck waiting to be returned to the Hughes Tool Company for rebuilding. The bits were as alike as peas in a pod, but this particular *Grayling* Hughes X1G had a special meaning to me, so I pulled a switcheroo. I selected a not-too-badly worn X1G for the oil company to cherish and I kept the discovery bit as my proudest souvenir of Oil Patch; it sits chromed and resplendent by my fireplace to this day.

Oil strike or not, I became increasingly bored as the weeks crawled by, a feeling exacerbated by the close proximity of the same rough coworkers day in and day out. As much as I welcomed the camaraderie on the rig, the reality was that because of my emotionally unavailable family life, I had had lots of time to amuse myself alone growing up, and had become adept at it. Put simply, I needed to be alone at times. Many evenings as a boy I hid in a favored oak tree, out of sight of my mother or sister calling me to dinner from the corner across the street. I hugged the rough bark and smiled as I watched them eventually give up, and stayed in place for a few minutes before sauntering home. Solitude and independence were more important than food.

Fortunately, I always enjoyed language and I poured my energy into reading and winning spelling bees, the *San Pedro News Pilot* being the first answer to my voracious curiosity about the outside world. Later I discovered mom's Great Books series that she had stored away in the garage, and I absorbed everything from the short stories of Guy de Maupassant to Prescott's *History of the Conquest of Peru*, a breadth of literary discovery that served me well in life even as it set me off from most of my scientific colleagues. Spending so much time alone reading also presaged my adult profession while embracing the solitude of the wilderness.

Unfortunately, there were no trees to climb on an oil rig. I was mulling this problem one day when I suddenly realized that I was staring at the nearest substitute for my boyhood oak tree: the derrick itself, all 142 feet of it. The answer to getting away from everyone had been right over my head all along.

I could climb to the top of the derrick, called the "crown," on a series of fifteen-foot ladders that lacked any kind of safety enclosure. Getting there was the equivalent of scaling a fourteen-story building without safety gear, and a single misstep or gust of wind would be disastrous, but acrophobia and all, it was worth a try to be alone for a while. After gathering up my courage overnight, I started up the first ladder and discovered to my horror that the ladder was not firmly fastened to the derrick girders but rattled and shook when I put my weight on it. The bolts that held the ladders to the derrick were an inch thick, but they went through two-inch-diameter holes in welded brackets, which left a lot of room for the ladders to wiggle under my weight. In addition to the loose ladders, I felt the entire derrick vibrate and shake like a Brobdingnagian tuning fork under the assault of 2,000-horsepower engines that were rotating three miles of drill pipe hanging from a thirty-ton block and tackle at the crown, my objective. Suddenly afraid to climb another step, I looked back at the drilling tender, where a couple of guys were watching me, men of the sort I was tired of being around during every waking minute. I looked back up ladder #1 at the distant crown that was roofed by overcast. Time to get going.

Palms sweaty—I had forgotten gloves, but it was too late—feeling lightheaded and hyperventilating, I deliberately took one step at a time up the trembling, rattly ladder. Each sickening one-inch lurch away from the derrick, the first part of a potential fall to my death, was a nearly heart-stopping instant until I reached the top of the first ladder. I was fifteen feet, two-and-a-half body lengths, above my normal work elevation and felt as accomplished as Edmund Hillary cresting Mount Everest. The first run of four ladders got me sixty feet up to a walk-around deck where I could stand on the grated flooring and lean on the rail. I felt on top of the world, but I had eighty-two feet to go.

The next run of ladders went to the ninety-foot level, by which point the derrick had narrowed considerably and also vibrated more than at lower levels, just as a tuning fork vibrates more at its tip than at its base. I was nearly petrified with primal fear and bathed in sweat when I topped the final ladder and swung myself onto the walkway surrounding the crown. Grasping the vibrating railing with one trembling hand, the first thing I did was take several photos from this unique perspective as proof of my daring. Other than the *J.W. Nickle* there was nothing to see except flat, mud-colored ocean, the shores of Cook Inlet being veiled in mist. I took out my favorite pocket collection of great poems edited by Louis Untermeyer and gratefully sat down with my back against the inner railing at the crown, facing outward; leaning against the outer railing would have been a bit *too* daring. The two men on the tender had watched my whole climb and returned my hearty wave. I had gone to a lot of trouble and pushed through a lot of fear, but I was free! Three hours of delicious solitary reading brought me to bedtime, and I descended the derrick ladders with as much fear and loathing as I had climbed them, although once down, even while breathing hard and shaking, I felt like a new man.

On a day not long afterward, when the drilling was going slowly, I wandered up to the working floor where my favorite driller, Gene Inman, and his roughnecks were sitting around staring into space. Gene had supposedly spent hard time for manslaughter, but he was the most soft-spoken and pleasant man on the rig, even if he did sport a colorful full-length prison tattoo of the Virgin Mary on his backside, from his neck to his ankles, which had been done by a cellmate with a safety pin and ink.

"What's happening, Gene?" I asked.

"Just hanging around enjoying life," he said in his Texas drawl.

"When are you going to get this FUBAR operation up to full speed? Mudloggers are too valuable to just waste them sitting around," I declared with a smile.

"You looking for something to do?" he asked me.

"Anything would be better than hanging around," I answered.

"Well, I'm gonna show you how to hang around the right way so you'll enjoy it more," Gene smiled back devilishly.

"Yeah, what's that?" I was curious now, hoping for something, anything, to kill time.

Gene threaded a coil of 1" rope through a pulley hanging from a girder twenty feet above our heads, then made a big loop in one end. He removed his hardhat, then craned his head back and inserted it into the loop. With the rope firmly under the back of his neck, while staring straight up, he tugged hard on the free end of the rope. His body magically rose up twenty feet to the girder, which he smacked with one hand while letting out a whoop, then he smoothly played out the rope and descended to the deck, landing as gently as a stage angel.

Handing the looped rope to me, he said, "Now let's see you do that."

I could not let some Texas driller show me up, so I bragged, "I'll zoom up the rope and smack that girder twice as fast as you and come down twice as fast too."

"Big talk's cheap," he said, "Are you brag or fact?"

I set my hardhat on a fuel drum, backed into the noose, making sure it was seated firmly at the base of my skull as I craned my neck up, then gave the other half of the rope a mighty tug. I was younger and lighter than Gene and pulled hand over hand as fast as possible to beat his time, smacked the girder at the top twice, whooped twice, and prepared to lower myself. That was the hard part, as Gene well knew. I hung at the top of the rope for a few moments trying to figure out why I was not going down. I could not look anywhere but straight up; if I had been fool enough to straighten out my neck I would have fallen twenty feet and broken something. When I tried to unclench my top hand from the rope and let myself down a foot or so, my hand refused to obey my brain. I could barely even see my top hand by rolling my eyes down from my upward-staring face and forcefully *willed* my top hand to let go and move down the rope, but it did not move. My arms were now shaking, the muscles burning, the laughter and catcalls from below all too clear.

"Well, at least your valuable mudlogger's ass isn't wasting time now," called my former friend Gene Inman.

"You shoulda stayed in college," yelled up a roughneck.

In desperation, taking it one step at a time, I forced my hand to *slowly* let go and *slowly* move to grasp the rope below my other hand. I descended half a foot; only nineteen-and-a-half to go. The key was to move slowly, otherwise my brain thought I was falling and reflexively commanded my hands to stay on the rope. I slowly made my way down to the circle of hooting and laughing roughnecks.

Pulling myself up by the neck on a dare. Descending was the hard part.

"That was a fine demonstration," said Gene. "Did you learn how to rope-a-dope in college?"

"No," I replied, "I went to college so I wouldn't have to work on oil rigs with Texans, but it looks like I didn't study hard enough." Everyone had a good laugh over the rope trick and it was nothing I could have learned in college.

One of the drill crew roughnecks, nicknamed Putt-Putt, a rangy, dark-eyed, likeable nineteen-year-old figured into the next bit of intended fun, one that turned into a dreadful experience for me. He came by when I was collecting a sediment sample at the shaker screen, the vibrating mechanism that sieved rock cuttings from the hot liquid mud circulating out of the ground. We were drilling with a diamond bit, which was a smooth knob studded with hundreds of dark industrial diamonds the size of pencil erasers.

"You know," said Putt-Putt, "when we pull a diamond bit out of the hole all the diamonds are gone. Where'd they go?"

Sliding smoothly into my practical joke mode, I cautioned in a lowered voice, "Shh, nobody's supposed to know, but the diamonds come over the shaker screen and we get to keep them. It's a side benefit of mudlogging."

"No shit?" he said, "You get diamonds off the shaker screen?"

"Not so loud," I said, holding a muting hand in front of him, "If you don't tell anyone else, I'll cut you in."

Putt-Putt lowered his voice. "Okay, I can keep a secret." Then, after a thoughtful moment, he asked, "How do I get a diamond?"

"They're hard to spot, but I'll give you the next one I find. We just put in a new bit, so a diamond should be coming across the shaker screen pretty quick," I said cheerily, adding "If you spot one, don't tell a soul, just show it to me to make sure it's not some worthless rock."

Putt-Putt eagerly agreed, but I had not anticipated that he would tag after me for days whenever I collected a sample—which was each ten feet we drilled or about every hour—and avidly wait for "his" diamond to appear. I had created a pest named Putt-Putt and I needed to end the charade. On his next visit to the mudshack he handed me another valueless quartz grain, in which I showed exaggerated interest under the microscope.

"Wow," I exclaimed.

"Is it a diamond?" asked Putt-Putt.

"Yeah," I said, "a nice one."

"Oh, yeah? Uh, can I keep it?" inquired Putt-Putt with a note of uncertainty in his voice.

"Well," I said, "I don't know anymore about giving one away."

"Ah, come on," he said, "I've never even touched a diamond before; you can let me have it, I won't tell anyone."

"I'm still making money for college and have a long way to go," I explained.

"But there's hundreds of diamonds on each bit, you must have a lot already, and I just want one," he pleaded, his voice rising in desperation.

Sensing the potential for this to grow ugly, I replied, "Hell, you're right, it wouldn't be fair for me to have a bunch of diamonds and you get none. Okay, it's yours."

"That's freakin' great," he said and shook my hand. I placed the worthless quartz grain in a sample envelope I labeled "My very own diamond" and took Putt-Putt's photo. We were both pleased, at least for the moment.

A few days later Putt-Putt mentioned that he was soon to rotate ashore and wanted a *second* diamond for his girlfriend. With a tickle of worry at the back of my mind, I promised to keep my eye peeled for one. At my next midnight breakfast meal I noticed the galley hands cooking with coarse salt crystals and saw that some were clear cubes the size of a wooden match head. I grabbed a nice one, thinking it would make a convincing second "diamond."

Putt-Putt appeared in the mudshack at the very start of my tower, just in case I had come across a diamond in the past couple of minutes.

"Hey, Lou, what's new?" he opened.

"Nothing," I said, but a new thought formed even as I spoke. "I gotta go to the shaker screen to catch a sample. You can come too and we'll look for diamonds together. You never know."

"Yeah, that sounds great," he said enthusiastically as I picked my hardhat off the chromatograph and headed across the deck. I collected a quart of muddy cuttings then squatted down to appraise the rock chips coming across the screen by the ton from three miles underground. Putt-Putt squatted beside me like a boy mimicking his father and peered at the cuttings. I poked at the continuous stream of rock chips while palming the salt crystal from the galley. Trying hard to keep a straight face, I shouted, "There!" and seemingly plucked a diamond from the sediment rubble right before Putt-Putt's eyes. "Whoa!" I said, "This one's perfect," holding up the salt crystal to catch the glint of the overhead lights. Putt-Putt was stupefied; he had looked at the shaker screen a hundred times to no avail and I had just made a diamond appear like magic.

"Lucky you," I declared, "here's your second diamond," as he gazed in disbelief. I made him promise to put this diamond in the envelope with the first one, worrying that the soft salt crystal would round off if he handled it too much. At the same time I wondered if maybe this joke had gone too far.

It had. The end arrived like thunder when Putt-Putt and his overjoyed girlfriend went to a jeweler to have two diamond rings made. One of the "diamonds" dissolved in a drop of water in front of the amused jeweler and unamused couple, and the second crystal was just quartz. The jeweler laughed his head off and Putt-Putt felt like a fool under his girlfriend's angry glare, as I learned from a roustabout who returned to the rig ahead of Putt-Putt. A stab of fear penetrated my heart as I heard of

his humiliation. Putt-Putt was a basically gentle soul, but he had a legitimate reason to be angry, and I did not want to return to USC wearing
bridgework.

Putt-Putt exacted unique revenge when he snuck into the mudshack
and urinated into small metal pie tins I used for drying sediment samples;
he placed them under glowing red-heat coils and departed. I entered the
mudshack an hour later, was instantly overwhelmed by the stench and
retreated outdoors. I peered into the open door and saw the heat coils
glowing red above bubbling liquid-filled tins, then recognized the atrocious odor as urine. *Burnt* urine. I slammed my hardhat to the deck and
cursed a blue streak that included several "Putt-Putts." Gales of laughter
and raunchy catcalls erupted behind me, as Putt-Putt and the entire
drill crew of roughnecks were peering down from the derrick floor and
laughing at my expense. Just what I hated most, public ridicule. I turned
off the red-hot coils, opened the door and windows and listened to the pie
tins hiss and pop under cold water in the sink.

"You asshole, Putt-Putt, what the fuck did you do that for?" I shouted,
as the roughnecks' laughter redoubled.

"Because you gave me fake diamonds," he replied.

"That was a joke," I shrieked, "The fucking mudshack's gonna smell
like piss for days!"

They laughed harder and could hardly breathe as they collapsed
against each other. I struck a belligerent pose, fists on hips, hardhat
pushed up, jaw jutting forward as I looked up at them. Then the humor of
the situation struck me too and I joined the laughter.

"Okay, you got me," I said, "now let's call a truce."

"Fine with me," said Putt-Putt.

The putrid stench clung like paint to the mudshack's icy walls, even
though the door and windows were propped open for days in the subzero
temperatures. The mudlogger working the daytime tower was enraged
at the stench, since he had to breathe it for twelve hours a day too, while

bundled up in winter clothing indoors. I stayed on his shit list for weeks, but more importantly I was safely off of Putt-Putt's.

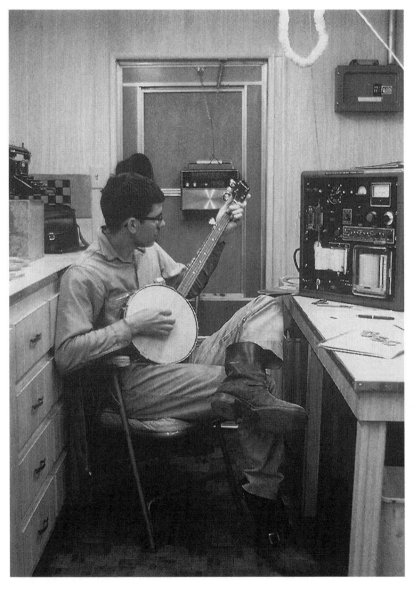

Killing time in the mudshack while keeping an eye on the hydrogen flame chromatograph.

Besides manufactured problems such as I had had with Putt-Putt, there were plenty of scary alarms and diversions on the *J.W. Nickle* to keep me on my toes. One involved a large industrial cylinder of hydrogen that powered the chromatograph we used in the mudshack to analyze the composition of gas or oil we drilled into. Every few weeks the tiny flame flickered as a sign that it was time to hook up a new hydrogen cylinder, which was lashed to a railing outside the mudshack. Trying to unscrew the steel cap that protected the fragile gas valve at the top of the tank, I discovered it was rusted tight even when I tried with a large pipe wrench. Putt-Putt and another roughneck saw my struggle, and brought over a comealong and two man-size chain wrenches to make sure we got the top off. We tightly lashed the cylinder to a girder with the comealong, then put one chain wrench on the body of the hydrogen cylinder and the second one on the recalcitrant steel cap. One guy leaned on the chain wrench to hold the cylinder clockwise while Putt-Putt and I leaned with all our weight on the other chain wrench to twist the cap off counterclockwise. The damned cap would have to give eventually and I thought I felt it move just a skosh. "I think it's giving," I said with a grunt.

At that moment Putt-Putt's ever-present cigarette as well as the other guy's flared up to preturnatural brightness. It looked like they were sucking on sparklers. We froze, suddenly aware that we were messing with a pressurized cylinder of explosive hydrogen gas, which was now leaking. Unfortunately, the cap itself was not turning off of the cylinder; however, a few inches below the cap was a seam between the main body of the cylinder and the top end of the cylinder. *That* was turning. We were twisting the heavy-duty hydrogen cylinder in two. I screamed, "It's leaking, toss it overboard!" Instantly undoing the chain wrenches and comealong, the three of us bodily arced the seventy-five-pound cylinder high and far over the platform railing and watched it spear into the muddy waters of Cook Inlet. Both guys still had their ciggie butts. That was my only spare hydrogen cylinder so I radioed ashore for a new one.

"I think there's a spare out on the platform deck," replied Sig Erson from Anchorage.

"I thought so too," I replied. "But it's not there now. Somebody took it or it got sent ashore or who knows what happened to it in this lash-up outfit. I looked around the tender and it's not there either."

Luckily, Sig was in Anchorage, so he bought a new hydrogen cylinder and sent it out that day on a crew boat. I could not admit to anything as stupid as almost leveling the mudshack and killing myself in a hydrogen explosion, since I needed a few more months of Oil Patch employment to build up my grad school fund.

I must have become wary of potential explosions, because a loud sound sent me running not long afterward. I had just collected a cuttings sample and was thinking how to best describe it in the mudlog while staring out the mudshack window. Suddenly, there was a fulsome "pop" sound and the view outside my window changed into a wall of flame, like an onscreen Hollywood gasoline explosion, but for real. I have no recollection of the next few seconds, but evidently I dropped my pencil, put on my hardhat, flung open the mudshack door, sprinted sixty feet across a deck so slick with diesel oil and drilling mud that I normally picked my way across it with great care, and threw myself behind a massive steel pier where I cowered with my head tucked into my shoulders, holding onto my hardhat with both hands. When I peeked around the pier I saw the undamaged mudshack and a dissipating cloud of black smoke. Standing up on the stairway of the derrick was my driller friend, Gene, laughing his head off at my expense. He explained that oily soot had accumulated in the exhaust stack of a diesel engine just outside the mudshack and that a spark had ignited the soot and shot a ball of flame right at the window I had been looking out of. Not being a fool, I had assumed a more drastic situation, and watching me haul ass across the slippery deck had made Gene's day, as he was happy to tell anyone within earshot during the next several meal times. I never did remember my duck-and-run drill, but my quick reactions to danger have always served me well.

Not long after the fireball episode I was leaning over the platform rail idly watching a chopper land on the helipad cantilevered from the platform. Some bigwig got out while the pilot snugly attached steel tie-down cables to his machine to keep it safely aboard ship in the blustery wind. I had ridden a helicopter once, during a crew change in a Korean War-vintage Sikorsky S-55 we called "Ole Yeller" and helicopters still seemed like magic. A few minutes later the pilot returned to the machine with a different passenger, an electrician I knew. The electrician was hopping a free ride ashore, rather than wait for a crew boat, while the bigwig stayed on the rig. After unhooking the tie-downs, the pilot fired up the machine and powered it up. The magic machine rose a few feet then abruptly slewed to one side, rolled upside down over the side of the rig and smashed hard with a tremendous crash and splintering of rotor blades. The pilot had forgotten to remove the last of four steel tie-down cables from the helicopter skids, so the rising machine quickly reached the end of its short tether and flipped over the platform like a rock swung overhead on a string. The pilot was killed instantly and the electrician was flung into the freezing waters of Cook Inlet. He was disappearing fast in the nine-mile-an-hour outgoing tide, but a radioed emergency call soon brought a passing crew boat to the rescue. When I saw him later he said he would wait a week for a boat ride ashore rather than get into a helicopter ever again. I did not blame him then, and years later had similar thoughts after I too went down in a chopper and survived.

By February the Alaskan winter was full on and I was sick of it. I had saved $7,000 for college in nine months and my financial motivation was fading, plus the dangers of rig life had begun to prey on my mind. The latest hazard to appear was thick slabs of ice in Cook Inlet that threatened to stave in the crew boat, especially when the tide was at full flood. I began to dream of sunshine, palm trees, intellectual pursuits and girls, none of which were available in Alaska. The vision of the pretty woman in the cozy room also continued to mystify me when it appeared, usually when I was slipping toward sleep in my bunkroom to the accompaniment of the pocketa-pocketa sound made by the water maker on the other side of the bulkhead from my bed. Whoever she was, I was not likely to meet her in offshore Alaska.

The final spur to head home was the episode described earlier when I hung thirty feet in the air in a bosun's chair with my legs wrapped around a jerking Kelly hose while repairing the antifreeze line during a vicious Alaskan winter storm at three in the morning. I had had enough of Oil Patch. Within a week I was aboard an airliner that lifted off from the pitch-dark morning of Anchorage and landed in the warm, clear, early evening in Los Angeles. In my pocket were seventy $100 bills.

I had become homesick for academia and could hardly wait to get in harness in graduate school. My initial impression of USC Geology and Prof. Easton had been spot-on. I would join a community of senior and junior scholars such as I had longed for since leaving high school. I ate up classwork, because each class was a step on the path toward researching fossils in the wilderness just like my hero, Roy Chapman Andrews. Gene, Putt-Putt and the others up in Cook Inlet were on a different path than I was and I wished them well, but I was destined for greater things, or at least I thought so.

My $7,000 from Alaska did not last through grad school, as I had hoped, because I bought a used Corvette in a rare instance of following my heart instead of my brain. Corvettes were a common site in Los Angeles, but they were expensive cars and I was an impoverished student. Make that a *formerly* impoverished student. My stash was burning a hole in my pocket one day when I spotted a fly-by-night used car dealer that specialized in Corvettes and Shelby Mustangs. I was smitten so hard by a dark green 1967 Corvette Sting Ray coupe that I did not even bargain with the salesman. I blew more than half of my hard-earned oil rig pay, but I was a very happy young man and the purchase was the start of a lifelong passion for early Corvettes that continues to this day.

I progressed steadily through my studies, and by my third year in grad school I had taken the required classwork for a PhD. Unfortunately, buying the Vette left me short of money to complete my educational journey. I felt ready for the final push in school, and was mentally gearing up for doctoral qualifying exams and dissertation work, but my soul needed a bit more adventure before buckling down to the last surge of scholarship. I needed more money to progress onward to a life of scientific research, and the path seemed to run right through the high-paying world of Oil Patch.

In retrospect it is puzzling that I did not apply for a scholarship of some kind. I was only the first in my family to go beyond high school, and I was not raised in an intellectual environment, so there was nobody to give me advice about college. I had to feel my way alone into terra incognita scholastica, missing some of the shortcuts that more clued-in students knew about. I was used to men working hard for a living, mostly on fishing boats or as longshoremen, and I had applied this model even in graduate school. Ultimately, I could have finished my doctoral work two years earlier if I had been awakened to scholarships, but I would have missed out on a lot of living along the way. ▲

CÔTE D'ORDURE, WEST AFRICA

Dahomey (Da-HO-mee; since renamed Benin, Beh-NEEN) is where good health goes to die, but I did not know that when I signed on to mudlog there for a year. June 1969 found me working in that West African country for $1,200 per month and expenses, with a $2,000 bonus for staying a year, but my lust for adventure was a bigger lure. My impatience with classwork arose from the fact that human beings did not evolve over millions of years only to stay in school into their late twenties, by which age our East African ancestors had been run down by hyenas and most residents of ancient Rome had died of old age. In my case, I finished up my master's degree on a Thursday and left for Dahomey on Friday, seeking enough adventure and cash to see me to the end of grad school.

With Duster in Cotonou, Dahomey.

43

As the airliner from Paris descended toward Cotonou (KOH-toh-NEW), the major city in Dahomey, the Gulf of Guinea flashed by in lovely dark blue on one side, with verdant rain forest on the other. Once over the city, the residential neighborhoods passing under the wings were decrepit, bare red-dirt streets lined with cinder-block and corrugated-metal shacks on weedy lots. Peering from the window of the landed plane, the Cotonou airport terminal was about the size of a Beverly Hills mansion. I straggled through the cabin door and passed into a sticky gel of heat, humidity, bacteria and fetid odors that make up the shared atmosphere of West Africa.

Lugging my bags to the Customs desk, I enunciated my prepared greeting to the uniformed agent: "Bonjour, monsieur."

"Bonjour, master," he replied.

I glanced behind me, expecting to find his uniformed supervisor, but saw only the few deplaning passengers. The agent stamped my passport and said, "Go that way, master," pointing inside with a lifted thumb. Casting a quizzical sideways glance at him, I bent down for my suitcases, but a young man grabbed them and said, "I will take your bags, master." Every Dahomeyan of whatever station, cops included, addressed me as "master" for the next year; protesting was pointless. Dahomey had become independent in the 1960s after French colonization, and I had assumed beforehand that its citizens would be proud of their new independence and maybe even a little prickly about it. I was wrong.

A Union Oil agent met us in the kitchen-size Customs area, a bribe conspicuously changed hands, and my luggage and I passed through unexamined, after which point my host handed over another bribe to allow us to get *out* of the airport. From the fetid-sauna weather, to becoming everyone's "master," to the Bribes-R-Us culture, signing up for a year in Dahomey was starting to look like a huge mistake. Had I been wiser than my twenty-five years allowed, I would have tuned in to the bad vibes and boarded a flight home within days instead of festering there for a year. It would have been the wisest decision of my life.

I was dropped off at the house of the Union Oil physician, Liam Strake, MD, who had been imported exclusively for the Oil Patch community of fifty or sixty men, women and children. Continuing the theme of unreality evident since I had set foot in Dahomey, Strake was an Irishman who dressed in white linen coat and pants, as if his last posting had been on *The African Queen*. In sync with his 1930s Hollywood tropical-doctor getup, a brilliantly florid, apple-doll face shouted out his alcohol addiction. He was a living, walking cartoon, so incompetent that twice during the year rig workers sincerely threatened to beat him to death if he did not sober up enough to fix their medical problems.

Dahomey is about the size of Tennessee, and its main city of Cotonou when I knew it was about the size of modern Boulder, Colorado. However, Cotonou suffers in comparison with Boulder, as it is made up mostly of rickety single-story buildings clustered on the low, swampy coastal plain, like a shantytown on the Mississippi River delta. The urban area is split into eastern and western halves by a river that drains a large lagoon just behind town and is a one- and two-story monument to shoddy cinder-block construction flavored with corrugated sheet iron and odd bits of wood and plastic. Running water and indoor plumbing were limited to the better parts of town, which were not extensive. A few streets were paved, but most were red dirt of the sort known to geologists as laterite. The main boulevards had names, including the touching Rue du President Kennedy, but most streets did not. The houses and businesses all lacked numbers; an AAA street map of Cotonou would largely lack text.

Dahomey had no tourist attractions with the possible exception of Ganvié, a village of huts pieced together from bamboo, reed mats, tree branches and plywood, perched on stilts over a lagoon outside of Cotonou. I took a dugout canoe tour of this atavistic suburb just once, and was so appalled to see people living like that in the late twentieth century that I never returned. Adults and children unsmilingly stared out of unglassed windows. Kids floated in the same water as turds. I could not imagine living a moment of their lives.

The pervasive poverty of Dahomey was difficult to comprehend; the worst neighborhood in Tijuana, Mexico, would be paradise compared to Cotonou. The average *annual* income of $80, or $6.67 a *month*, was unfathomable to anyone from the First World, but its effects were all too evident in human terms. Besides nearly no income, there was no indoor plumbing, running water, sewers, electricity or public transportation. Homes were lighted by kerosene lamps and meals were cooked over fires.

I discovered the local degree of desperation one day early in my stay along with Benoit Lafitte, the sturdily built, bellicose and proud Cajun mud engineer from the rig, when we encountered a beggar garbed in rags and missing one leg on a downtown street. I took out my wallet to give him some CFA francs, the French-backed money in former French African colonies, and masses of beggars instantly materialized, seemingly crystallized from the air, and converged on us. Benoit and I were enmeshed in a crowd of fifty or more shouting, diseased, filthy, jostling, deformed and desperate people, many waving stumps or showing disfiguring wounds. I was shocked, sickened and instantly felt endangered. I flung the CFA bills on the ground, turned around with Benoit and ran. We glanced back at what looked like a collapsed rugby scrum of wretches elbowing and kicking atop the money. From then on we gave money only to the Red Cross.

After a couple of weeks I moved from the soused doctor's house to my own one-bedroom apartment to accommodate my need for privacy. I got around town either on my German Zündapp moped, or a Volkswagen Beetle I shared with Duane, the other mudlogger—a tall, emaciated surfer dude who talked slowly and claimed that the metal plate at the back of his head, souvenir of a motorcycle accident, "didn't bother" him, although he was glad he had brought a year's supply of Ritalin from home.

Getting an apartment meant hiring a houseboy and a "guardian." Every foreigner employed a houseboy for $10 a month, fifty percent more than the average income in Dahomey, and the guy did everything from cooking, cleaning and mending to washing the car and shopping. My houseboy, Sam, was an English-speaker from Nigeria who had previously worked on American ships and knew how to cook the American dishes I preferred to the pervasive French fare. Building on the theme of unreality that had manifested itself from my first moment in Dahomey, on the advice of experienced expats I asked Sam to give me clippings of his hair and fingernails, Voodoo-based insurance that he would not steal from me when I was offshore, since I entrusted him with my apartment key. Sam was a Christian, but Voodoo, said to have originated in Dahomey, was the prevailing local belief, which Sam partly bought into. If he had stolen from me I theoretically would have given the clippings to a witch doctor, a ju-ju or gris-gris man, and had a curse put on him and his family. Sam turned out to be as honest as the day is long and in any case I lost track of his clippings.

Whenever I went offshore I gave Sam my perishable food, except for alcohol, and he was grateful for it in that starving country. Sam belonged to the Ibo tribe from next-door Nigeria, where the Biafran war was going on, and when Duane and I learned that Sam's wife and children were stranded in Nigeria for lack of money, Duane and I paid for his family to escape Nigeria and settle in Cotonou. Like all the Americans, and unlike most of the Europeans in Cotonou, especially the French, I treated Sam as an employee, not a lowly servant. Being a houseboy was a solid middle-class job that paid well at $10 a month and Sam enjoyed the side benefits of not only taking home any perishable food when I left for the rig, but also getting any of my used Made in America clothing, which was vastly superior to anything for sale in Cotonou. Sam sometimes had an assistant houseboy who paid Sam to teach him the ropes of working in a foreign household, so I was often ashore with two houseboys to tend to me and my apartment until they finished up in the midafternoon. Sam's only flaw was his penchant for lashing his assistant houseboy with a switch for any perceived mistake. I never interfered in these whippings, accompanied by much yelling on both sides, since I did not know the rules.

Houseboys preferred to work for Americans, because we treated them so much better than did the Europeans. Abuse of domestic workers was especially common among the French residents of Cotonou, whom I often witnessed beating houseboys with a large stick for some minor infraction. Even the Southerners and penitentiary-seasoned Europeans who made up most of our drill crew could not stomach mindless violence against fellow human beings, with the exception of bar fights among themselves.

"Guardians" were Dahomeyans who ostensibly protected one's house from robbery by sleeping beside it all night. When a foreigner first rented a house in Cotonou, potential guardians came by asking for a job and if you did not hire one they knew you did not have a guardian, so they might come back one night and rob your house. At least that was the story I got, so like all foreigners in town I was forced to hire a guardian to protect my apartment; it was a nice little racket that upped local employment and cost only $10 a month. To my surprise, despite the cloying heat and ghastly humidity, all guardians wore heavy U.S. Navy-style pea coats, sock caps and gloves. Where they bought clothing best suited to Labrador in equatorial Africa remained a yearlong mystery.

Getting along well with Africans helped me get to my apartment one night when a half dozen Dahomeyan roughnecks and I were unceremoniously dumped on the Cotonou dock around midnight along with too much luggage for me to carry to my apartment two miles away. The locals could walk home, but I was in a jam until the Dahomeyans talked among themselves and, unbidden, lifted my bags onto their heads and told me to lead the way to my house. I headed the column as we proceeded safari-style to my apartment and a sweaty hour later I thanked them profusely and invited them in for a cold beer. They demurred. The French had browbeaten them so severely when Dahomey was a colony that the Africans had a hard time being so familiar with a white man, even a friendly American. They would not cross my threshold, even when I tried to drag them in by main force, so we stood outside and drank a beer each, which is all they would permit themselves. I felt very comradely standing around drinking beer with my rig buddies in the hot night air after our brief "safari." It began to rain as we shook hands, then they walked off, waving happily.

I was disappointed to learn when I arrived in Dahomey that the drilling tender and platform were still two weeks away, under tow from Texas, and that the Union Oil honcho in Cotonou knew about the delay and could easily have gotten word to me in Europe, where I had spent two weeks on my way from America. Instead, he let Oil Patch's perennial philosophy guide his actions: if you can't eat it or screw it, piss on it. In place of a couple of extra weeks amid the glories of Paris, Munich and Vienna, I got fourteen more days in Cotonou, which conspicuously lacks glories. I was all too often accompanied in my wanderings by my mudlogging partner, Duane, and over time came to realize that a year in West Africa with Duane and his metal-plate head was like spending two years in West Africa alone. Even though the oil rig was absent, two German supply boats and a crew boat had arrived, and the jolly Germans were a welcome addition to the pool of Americans and Europeans, mostly criminal-class Brits, who made up the oil operation. The supply boats each carried 300 cases of Beck's beer, and the Germans were generous shipmates, so my first two weeks in Cotonou were marinated in free beer.

When the oil rig eventually arrived I was more than a little disappointed to see that the *G.L. Temple* was a clone of the *J.W. Nickel* on which I had spent nine months in Alaska. Before I boarded her, I already knew every nook and cranny of the 3,000-ton, 300-foot-long drilling tender and its accompanying triangular platform. Unique to the *G.L. Temple* was a raised helicopter pad that topped a whole new deck of white aluminum trailers fitted out as accommodations for the African workers. The oil company had hired as many locals as possible, but the tender had never been designed for so many people. The aluminum trailers atop the helipad relieved the crowding, but the *G.L. Temple* was overpopulated for the entire year.

French was the *lingua franca* of Dahomey and there were no newspapers, magazines or radio stations in English. TV had not yet reached Cotonou, so we were some of the few Americans on the planet who nearly missed the moon landing in July 1969. Several of us clustered around a BBC shortwave broadcast and heard snippets through the crackling static such as "... command capsule ...," "... Eagle has ...," "... step for mankind ..." and other fuzzy shreds that left us wondering if they had landed or crashed. Mercifully, some Dahomeyans listening to local French-language radio soon informed us that the Eagle had safely landed.

There was an epidemic of pink eye just after the moon landing, which Dahomeyans attributed to the arrival of moon dust on Earth. A few months later the United States sent a display of moon rocks to Cotonou and the line to see it was a mile long day after day. No Voodoo practitioner was going to miss eyeballing an actual piece of the moon.

Americans were more popular than ever after the moon landing, and for the next few weeks Dahomeyans in the street spontaneously shouted "Apollo Onze!" and saluted us with raised arms. We enthused back. Dahomey was at the small end of the world's regard, but even there Apollo 11 brought forth a warm surge of a common humanity, a feeling that we as a species, not Americans alone, had done it. The locals also shouted "Apollo Onze!" whenever our rig's Cajun mud engineer, Benoit Lafitte, hit a shot during pickup basketball games with Africans. To foster the spirit of shared humanity, Duane and I even had a typical Dahomeyan suit of clothes made by a local tailor for two dollars each, including the cloth. A shapeless top and baggy trousers belted with manila rope made up the "boubou." We were the only whites who wore boubous during the entire year, and the Dahomeyans loved it whenever we wore them around town.

Perhaps because of our boubou-wearing ways, Duane and I were the only foreigners from the oil rig invited to an African house party. We joined a festive group of about twenty young men and women who were dancing to slow music. I chatted a bit with the Dahomeyan who invited me, a tall and crafty-looking Union Oil employee with the unlikely name of Fletcher Christian, and danced with one of the young women. However, it was clear that our presence put the Dahomeyans a bit on edge. In a country with a French colonial past, the races did not always mix easily, even if we were easygoing Americans. I begged off after half an hour, feeling that my main contribution to the party was leaving behind a decent supply of liquor for the others to enjoy. Bottles of Jack Daniels and Tanqueray gin, plus a German-supplied case of Beck's were unaffordable luxuries for the partygoers. This high-class booze would have cost several months' pay for a Dahomeyan, and these brands probably were ones they had seen only in magazine ads. I had had this party donation in mind all along, and it is just possible that Fletcher Christian had too.

Good health was a major concern in Dahomey because we had so little of it. The very air was thick with microorganisms: when I departed West Africa after a year, the cool air in Santiago, Chile, seemed insubstantial, as if I could accidentally throw out a lung by breathing too hard. One visitor to that benighted coast has noted that West Africa is the only place on earth where one can *see* radio waves, so thick is the air with humidity, foul odors, dust and germs. As a result, we foreigners suffered from continual bouts of diarrhea, no matter how hygienic we tried to be. We called diarrhea "the wawas," from a British colonial acronym meaning "West Africa Wins Again." The wawas were a central fact of life, the state of one's guts being dinner table conversation, and it was commonplace for a guest to bolt up from dinner and cry out, "The wawas!" as they hurtled toward a bathroom, any bathroom, praying to get there before their guts exploded. The wawas were not ordinary intestinal upset, but sudden, explosive and painful to the point of passing out on a toilet. I have no idea how Dahomeyans dealt with this hideous affliction, but we foreigners lived on a steady diet of Lomotil, a little white pill that froze guts into blessed immobility. I was particularly cursed by the wawas, despite great attention to sanitation, and suffered from them off and on until 1995, twenty-five years after departing Africa.

Bad health did not end with the wawas. The fetid microbial stew we breathed, plus equatorial heat and sopping humidity meant that a simple cut or skin abrasion took weeks to heal, and bronchitis lasted two to three months. I suffered continual heat rash at every joint on my body, including places I did not normally think of as a joint. Malaria was rife, so like every Oil Patch inmate I swallowed an anti-malaria pill daily that had the bodily side effects of bruising easily and destroying short-term memory. Unfortunately, working in the all-steel environment of a drilling platform and a wave-rocked tender guaranteed regular bruises. I often discovered a major bruise on my thigh or arm with no recollection of how I had gotten it until my memory kicked in the next day.

Almost worse than the wawas was the ennui, French for "boredom." Far more than simple melancholy, the combined effects of the stultifying heat and humidity, cultural stagnation, and monotonous work devastated initiative. One victim of the lassitude was the rewrite of my master's thesis for publication. I fingered the gold lettering on the spine, turned the object over in my hand, and riffled through the pages, but my heat-addled mind could not function at a college level. The thesis I had slaved over for a year seemed like an artifact of another civilization, a curio only distantly related to my current life. I would get back to thinking when I returned to USC. I hoped.

Filth was unavoidable: like everyone, before going into my apartment kitchen I stamped my feet loudly to give the cockroaches time to hide before I entered, especially at night. If I neglected to do that, a dozen roaches clung to the counters and walls when I flipped on the light. I drank only water that had first been boiled, then poured through a diatomite filter, and before I ate a piece of fruit I first soaked it for half an hour in a bucket of potassium permanganate, a deadly poison, to kill surface germs. Still I got the wawas.

The poor sanitation was on full display one night in Maria's restaurant, one of the very few places where a foreigner thought to dine in Cotonou. Maria was a short, roly-poly Spaniard who ran what seemed to be a cleaner than average establishment that featured a simulation of continental cuisine. Benoit, Duane and I had just consumed our salads when Maria herself came over to boast about her new kitchen fixtures. Our congratulations earned us a private tour of her refurbished kitchen, but the only thing I remember of the tour is a gigantic rat perched on the tile counter beside the kitchen sink, vigorously ripping chunks from a head of lettuce, the very same head that had just supplied leaves for our dinner salads. Seeing the three of us frozen in versions of Edvard Munch's *The Scream*, Maria attempted to comfort us by saying, "Oh, he's always coming here!" as she shooed the portly *Rattus norvegicus* out the back door. Duane lost his cookies at the kitchen doorway, while Benoit and I retreated wordless and shaken to our table. The rest of the meal was consumed in contemplative silence, each forkful minutely examined for signs of recent varmint activity, along with a *lot* of beer and a follow-up cleansing alcohol purge at a bar. We eventually did eat at Maria's again but never ordered salads.

In addition to the enervating climate and shaky health of life in Cotonou, I soon learned that bribery or threats were the only way of getting anything done. A bribe was a "cadeau," French for gift, or "dash," as in, "You dash me, master?" Any African clerk worth his salt refused my cash payment for goods unless I added a cadeau. The official at the electrical company would not let me pay my household electricity bill each month unless I dashed him, on pain of cutting off my service. Everyone's hand was out, understandable in a country that is among the poorest

on the planet, but it was one more enervation among many that steadily
ground down foreigners in Dahomey.

At shaker screen to collect rock cuttings.

Another peculiarity of Dahomey was overt sex, as I learned soon
after my arrival when I went to a hardware store with Fletcher Christian.
The hardware was a mix of 1840s U.S. western frontier and current Third

World, basic but shoddy goods mostly blacksmithed locally. Fletcher conversed with the two young women clerks at the front counter while I browsed the aisles, something I enjoyed as a confirmed tool junkie. Fletcher and the girls gestured toward me and giggled a lot, while I occasionally smiled in their direction as I tried to figure out the purposes of the unfamiliar items they sold. Eventually I wandered back up front to join Fletcher and the young ladies.

"The ladies say you are the first American they've seen," said Fletcher.

"Great. Tell them I'm really enjoying their beautiful country," I fabricated. The ladies giggled louder when I tried to say the same thing in my budding French.

"They ask if you are living in Cotonou," continued Fletcher.

"Yes," I replied, "I just arrived."

"They want to go home with you," said Fletcher mysteriously.

"Go home with me for what?" I inquired, puzzled.

"The two ladies say they want to sleep with you," smiled Fletcher with a raised eyebrow.

"Both of them?" I asked.

"Yes," he said with a bigger smile.

I could not comprehend two young women openly offering sex, especially at the same time, since I had not bought them dinner and drinks beforehand. Compared to the elaborate courting rituals back home, this was a young man's dream come true: show up and get laid. However, like anything that seems too good to be true, I questioned what I might be getting into. I knew from living in the Union Oil doctor's house that the oil rig workers regularly caught social diseases from prostitutes. Some of the diseases were the normal ones and others were unique West African strains that the doctor could not treat, which was more than enough knowledge to give me pause at the girls' generosity. It was delightful for sex to be so freely offered, but the combo of the rig hands' infections and the hardware girls' forwardness was a big red flag, so I declined their offer. When Fletcher translated my answer, the girls looked genuinely deflated. Maybe I had made a mistake, but who could take the chance? Unfortunately, the very few single American women who passed through Cotonou that year never gave me a second look. Today the HIV rate for Dahomey is around 40%, so sexual openness has its risks.

The bars were filled with prostitutes, who I was told were mostly country girls spending time in the city to accumulate a dowry. That may have been so, because most of them walked awkwardly in heels and many had raised welts or geometric tribal scars on their faces. The majority wore long-haired wigs that they sometimes lifted off their short, natural hair for relief in the tropical heat. They charged 1,000 CFA francs a night, or U.S. $3.64, but if you waited until dawn and the woman was older, or had a kid in tow, the cost went as low as 100 francs, 36 cents. Buying an occasional beer for a lady of the night and chatting at the bar was as good a way as any to improve my French, but the roughnecks and roustabouts quickly learned that sleeping with a whore was a sure way to contract a venereal disease. Since our florid-faced Irish doctor in his white linen suit was unable to treat some strains of whatever in hell diseases my crew-mates contracted, some men were sent to Europe for treatment. This did not stop them from doing the same thing all over again their next time ashore, always hoping to catch a disease that our drunken doctor *could* cure. It was a long year for the rest of us unmarried men.

I drank socially in America, but needed vastly more anesthetic to endure life in Dahomey. Things got to the point where my houseboy, Sam, had standing orders to have *two* eight-ounce glasses of gin and tonic ready for me in the fridge for breakfast when I was ashore. Thus, when I staggered down to breakfast around noontime, after partying until dawn, I had something to wash my toast down with. My drinking was a worrisome development, but the combo of climate, illness, loneliness, a hazardous but boring job, and sexual frustration left me little choice.

Anesthesia got more interesting one day when I arrived home from a two-week stint offshore, and the inevitable door-to-door souvenir salesman came around with his wood carvings, painted monkey skulls, small ungulate horns and bronze statuettes. The statuettes always showed men and women fornicating, and we called these "difficiles," because so many of the sexual positions would be difficult if one's penis were shorter than one's torso. During one visit the trinket salesman said, "Voulez vous du tabac sauvage?" which seemed to mean, "Would you like some savage tobacco?" in my still-accumulating French. Hmm, "savage" tobacco? Marijuana was a rampant local weed that only needed picking and drying in the torrid sun, and for 500 CFA francs ($1.82 American) I got a bag of grass bigger than my head, which is where it was going to end up in any case. I had never smoked grass before, but it was a welcome addition to alcohol as my interface with Dahomey. I smoked a pipe to get as much of the cheap but weak weed into my bloodstream as possible, often while grasping a bottle of Flag beer in the other hand. Days ashore floated by in a haze of one or the other chemical, or both, but at the back of my mind was the thought that I was on a slippery moral slope.

Given the monotony of life in Cotonou, one would think that the small community of Americans banded together in mutual support. One would be wrong as far as American embassy officials went. The U.S. personnel had the best entertainment in Cotonou, first-run Hollywood movies flown in weekly and projected onto a bed sheet outdoors. Unfortunately, we Oil Patch denizens were denied entry to the Wednesday showings, because, as was crisply explained to us, we were not diplomatic personnel but mere U.S. citizens, the implication being that grubby oil rig ruffians were not welcome in their elevated company. Their attitude was ironic, considering how low one's status in the U.S. State Department must have been to score an admin job in Dahomey. Nobody in that embassy, a low cinder-block building with a drooping American flag on a too-short pole out front, could realistically have hoped that their next career step would be the Court of St. James or the Champs Elysées. They were small-minded, elitist pricks who would not let American citizens watch American movies at the American embassy. They were not good enough to work in Berlin or Tokyo, so denying us entry to their weekly movies was a power trip to prop up their bruised egos.

This galling standoff lasted until enough American oil rig workers had arrived in Cotonou with their families that Union Oil brought in an American teacher and started its own K-12 school. The embassy personnel were delighted, assuming that their own children would gladly be admitted, perhaps given preferred admission as the spawn of diplomats. The head of the Union Oil operation, Bill Elliott, a short and balding but crisp and forceful Texan, held a different viewpoint, since he and his wife and children were the most prominent of those excluded from movie nights. In sum, the snooty embassy folks had movies but no school and the entertainment-starved Union Oil folks had a school but no movies. Even the preening dunderheads at the embassy recognized when their bargaining position had eroded to nothing. Upon further consideration, the stingy government lifers were only too happy to have us over on movie nights, and once petty animosities were overcome combining forces greatly enlivened movie nights and social life overall. Everyone got along famously once the official snobbery was stripped away. My God, it was delightful to see an actual American movie once a week when I was ashore, and Hollywood escapism never had more devoted followers than us Oil Patch refugees in 1969 Cotonou.

We had one more run-in with the embassy folks, because a Union Oil communal residence house had a flagpole out front, as did many other buildings on that red-dirt street that housed foreign embassies. One day during a predawn drinking bout I suggested that our pole would look better with a flag on it like the embassies on that street displayed. As the motley of barflies pondered possible flag designs, I was looking at the bottle of Beck's beer in my hand and its key-on-shield label popped out as the perfect flag design. After all, we swilled beer continuously, and we had frequent parties at that house, so why not run a beer label up the flagpole? Someone else suggested making a flag that looked like a label of Cotonou's only locally brewed beer, appropriately called Flag. However, that brand's label simply said "Flag," with no design, and even for us, raising a flag bearing the single word "Flag" would have looked dumber than necessary. One of the rig wives sewed up the banner to my design, so within days our flagpole bore a large, green flag with a brilliant red and white Beck's logo. It looked terrific and became the residence's official party flag, to be saluted in mock solemnity with uplifted bottles and a shout of "Beck's!" at the start of every party. We regular party-throwers were proud of our flag, but huffy representatives from various embassies on our nameless red-dirt street whined that our flag was inappropriate, because it flew over a mere party house, not an embassy. I think they were mad because we never invited them to our parties. With the flag and the camaraderie, I sometimes felt like I was in a Third World-themed fraternity—if I squinted—that was somehow a continuation of my college experience.

Another flag-themed adventure was spawned one night when Duane and I were trying to think up an alternative to getting drunk in a bar. While sucking on a bottle of Flag beer, I mentioned that Dahomeyan flags had appeared around town that day, heralding some sort of national celebration and we somewhat too casually decided to steal a couple as souvenirs. Thinking ahead, I grabbed a kitchen knife as we piled into the VW. Duane drove and I rode shotgun toward downtown Cotonou and its flag-bedecked government buildings. He trolled slowly along the bumpy laterite streets, while I peered around for possible souvenirs between ironic gulps of Flag.

We wanted two decent-size flags that we could reach, but many were fairly small and hung high on a building, until I spied a 4-foot x 6-foot beauty drooping from a tall pole set among shadows in front of what looked like a fancy house; an ideal setup. Unstealthily approaching the crime scene in our misfiring VW with its rotted muffler, Duane pulled up next to the pole and I stepped out into the street, butcher knife at the ready. My plan was to cleanly cut the halyard and have the flag gently float down into my uplifted arms. Trying to appear nonchalant, I glanced sideways up at the limp flag and, taking a big breath, I raised the butcher knife with what I thought was cat quickness and sliced the rope. As I reached high with upturned face to receive the booty, a man with a big voice yelled loudly from the large house. Tearing my eyes from the flag, I saw a uniformed man with a rifle loping toward me. An outside light went on.

"Who in hell's that?" wondered Duane aloud. The light revealed that we had stupidly pulled up in front of a government office, and the flag now fluttering down was from an official flagpole. Fixated on the rifle-wielding guard, who was waving his weapon over his head and shouting at me in French, I had forgotten about the descending flag, which perversely avoided my uplifted arms and draped itself over my head. Suddenly blinded in tricolor purdah, I flailed around trying to gather up the large banner as I spun and lurched toward the erratically idling VW, which I could hear but not see. Duane's excited foot slipped from the brake to the gas, and the VW's corn-popping flatulence burst into a staccato roar that drowned out the uniformed guard's yelling. Thrashing around to gather up the flag, I forgot about the butcher knife I held and cleanly sliced my left arm from elbow to wrist. Squealing like a girl, bleeding like a stuck pig and swaddled like a festively attired tropical mummy in the blood-stained banner, I collapsed in a spinning heap through the passenger door, which Duane helpfully held open. The flag now tightly wrapped around my body, Duane gunned the engine and popped the clutch just as the angrily bellowing cop or soldier reached the car. With the bloody flag trailing in the red dirt, the passenger door banging painfully on my right leg, and myself screaming from the pain of my slashed arm, we fled all too obviously into the night.

Duane was afraid that the man would shoot at us, and I was terrified that the trailing lanyard would wrap around a wheel and compress my flag-wound body as tight as a hobo bundle at the end of a stick. A fleeting vision of the dancer Isadora Duncan, who was strangled by her trailing scarf when it got tangled in the spinning wheel of a 1920s Bugatti, flashed through my mind. Freeing my head from the flag, I pulled the lanyard and my leg into the car and shut the door. We felt lucky to be alive, the evening no longer lighthearted. There was no mention of looking for a second souvenir flag, and no debate about who would keep the blood-soaked banner we had. I was silent on the drive home, my mind pondering whether or not I was still grad school material; in addition, I had lost my only kitchen knife.

Life had slid far down the moral slope by this time, mostly due to drinking too much, beginning with my daily breakfast, when ashore, of sixteen ounces of gin and tonic with toast. Drinking was a worrisome development, but staying drunk and stoned was the only available relief from the daily wawas, atrocious climate, loutish and dangerous coworkers, boredom, a hazardous and boring job, and the manifold frustrations, especially sexual frustration, of life in Dahomey. Achieving insensibility was my main goal when ashore, at the almost nightly house parties, and in bars such as the Pam-Pam, Excelsior, Calebasse, Lido and Club du Plage.

I was blowing off steam in the worst possible way, with the worst possible people, mistaking moral degradation for adventure and cama-raderie. Like college freshmen throwing off the constraints of family life, I was cutting loose with my pals, except that my current "pals" were not other civilized if unfettered children, but knife-wielding low-lifes. The dictum that offspring should be seen and not heard had oppressed my life well into adulthood and now I was shedding its weight once and for all in the most spectacular way.

Visions of the elegant, artistic woman were fewer in West Africa. I was surviving in a previously unimagined kind of wilderness and perhaps my mind had less energy to project into a gentler future so unlike my present circumstances. Whoever she was, whatever she represented, she was waiting for the most turbulent and pointless year of my life to end.

My drinking life bottomed out in a dramatic encounter with two whores one night while tramping my way from bar to bar with Duane. We observed an Aussie roustabout from the rig lying on the red-dirt street and flailing around feebly while the whores grabbed for his wallet. We shouted at the whores to go away and walked toward them, but instead of retreating, the prostitutes snicked open switchblades and brandished them menacingly while shouting back at us. Unfortunately, my alcohol-drenched brain segued into a "crazier than thou" routine as I grabbed one of the many long-neck beer bottles littering the ground and smashed its bottom off against a wall. I leered dementedly at the whores, waved the jagged bottle in front of me and lunged. My mind flashed on an image of Burt Lancaster as Sergeant Warden in the bar-fight scene in *From Here to Eternity*, when he confronted the switch blade-wielding Ernest Borgnine with a broken beer bottle (like mine!) and growled, "OK, if it's killin' ya want, come on!" The whores' eyes grew big as I advanced on them and they lost heart and fled. Dusting off our Aussie buddy, we laid him unconscious in the Excelsior bar and ordered beers. In retrospect, I took an insane risk of personal injury for no gain. Worse was to come.

Halfway through my year in purgatory, selling my soul for cash, I got sick of spending time ashore with the same shabby men I worked with on the oil rig, and kept more and more to myself. The polyglot crew of the *G.L. Temple* were the roughest men I had run across in Oil Patch, making me think back almost wistfully to Gene, Putt-Putt and the drill crews in Cook Inlet three years earlier. The Americans and Europeans in Cotonou were from the bottom of the social heap, and I preferred my own company until I thought of a better idea, which was to pal up with the community dog.

Thus, out of my desire to spend less time with people, something I had valued since childhood, my favorite drinking companion became a dog, a mongrel named Belle Amie who lived with the Union Oil doctor. The almost constantly besotted Irishman, with his cartoonish florid complexion and white linen suit, was the very stereotype of a failed MD reduced to itinerant Third World employment. However, his clinic was a stable home for Belle Amie while the rest of us spent half our time on the offshore rig.

When I came ashore and felt like bar hopping, I picked up Belle in the beaten up VW I shared with Duane or wedged her in front of me on my Zündapp moped; she was always an excited passenger, barking at the few other vehicles on the road. I confidently bellied up to the bar even in a crowded drinking spot, because Belle always created a wide semicircle of space for me. If anyone came too close, Belle lowered her head and advanced a measured step or two, eyes locked on the offender, with a deep-throated growl, fangs exposed and hackles up. She was not kidding about protecting me, and inattentive barflies got bitten. When Belle was with me, I poured half of my first beer into a plate and she eagerly lapped it up before passing out in a few minutes, half a beer being plenty for her forty-pound body. Even asleep, she kept watch over me by the simple expedient of opening one red-veined eye, glaring at the offender and snorting; nobody was willing to wake her up. She looked no-shit serious even to me, and in truth she did not answer to commands well, so she definitely intimidated the inmates of Dahomey. What my rig buddies and the locals did not know was that Belle had been vaccinated for rabies by the Union Oil doctor. Probably no other dog in all of the Dahomeyan hellhole had received a rabies shot, so everyone was justifiably leery of any pooch. However, I was not about to display her vaccination papers to the surrounding sots, which would have meant less space for me at the bar.

I had a hard time carting Belle home on my moped when she passed out, which was nearly every time she drank. She was as limp as a seabag full of Jello, her head hanging over the Zündapp's handlebars and her flaccid body precariously balanced on the gas tank between my knees. I needed a gunny sack to stuff her into, but never found one. I usually was not feeling so well myself after hours of drinking gin and tonic with Flag chasers, and if she threw up I usually got sick too.

The moped suddenly got very loud during one of our dawn runs home when the muffler fell off. Turning around, I saw that a young boy was now clutching the hot muffler to his chest and looking a little afraid. He had been standing at the roadside when the part flew off, and the enterprising little twerp generously offered to *sell* my muffler back to me. Bleary with fatigue and the effort of propping up Belle, and hoping the kid would not run off with the only Zündapp muffler in all of West-freaking-Africa, I handed him 100 CFA francs, 36 U.S. cents or a day-and-a-half's pay for an adult. I was not sober enough to get off the moped and reattach the muffler, which by this time had cooled off, so I balanced it on Belle's limp body while she kept snoozing and we blatted home.

Belle Amie was central to an incident that developed when Benoit, Duane and I were bullshitting in my apartment. Benoit had a green Flag bottle tipped vertically to his lips when he happened to see tiny, white flatworms crawling up the *inside* of the bottle's neck, slithering toward his gullet. He instinctively flung the bottle away and blew a mouthful of beer onto the exact spot where Belle was snoozing. Startled awake in a blinding beer fog, Belle levitated off the tile floor like Wile E. Coyote and lit out through the multi-color plastic doorway streamers. She streaked into the front yard and—in her confusion—sank her fangs into my next-door neighbor, an attractive blonde woman my age who worked at the American embassy and was practicing her tennis swing. She screamed and ran into her own apartment, slamming the door before I could apologize. She had seemed to like me when I first moved next door, but once she learned I worked on the oil rig she regarded me as an untouchable, despite my master's degree. She thought all rig people were low-lifes, which—considering that my apparently demented, beer-soaked dog had just bitten her—seemed justifiable. My faint hope of ever getting into her pants winked out. Belle returned to stare into my eyes with a quizzical but sincere look, making sure that she had not screwed up and I reassuringly scratched her head. Just before she flopped down in a far corner of the room, safe from further alcoholic eruptions, she shook dry from nose to tail, thereby spattering the three of us with beer flecks. Belle was the genuine article, full of character. Duane and I minutely inspected our Flag bottles for interior worms, then continued drinking, while Benoit got a new bottle from the fridge and resumed drinking as if nothing had happened. Belle was already asleep, her rump defensively turned toward us.

Early in my year overseas, Belle Amie got knocked up and I named one of the puppies Rock, sharing her upkeep with Duane, since one of us was always ashore. I enjoyed Rock's companionship for a mere couple of months before he vanished from the front porch of my ground-floor apartment where I had improvised a low-walled playpen. I thought Rock had climbed out, but one of my neighbors had seen Rock being stolen from my front yard, so I knew he was gone for good. Dogs lived a tenuous life in Cotonou, being a dinner table item more often than a family pet.

Rock was gone and I was puppyless, but that soon changed by the turn of fortune's wheel. Another of Belle Amie's litter had gone to an American couple with a small son, but he tragically died of encephalitis and the couple returned to the States. They gave me Rock's littermate, which I gladly accepted to replace my stolen and cooked companion. I named Rock's successor Duster, after one of our dry holes. When a well is drilled and no oil encountered, the saying in Oil Patch is that "all you produced was dust"; in short, a dry hole is a "duster." Most of the wells we drilled in Dahomey were dusters, and I cannot recall which hole I named Duster after, but I had her for eight months in Cotonou and she added a lot of joy to my life in that otherwise cheerless purgatory.

Collecting seashells on platform leg.

After Duster had grown into a young adult, she was the spark for a memorable and disastrous event. Duane and I were driving into town when we passed a pack of dogs running in the same direction beside the coastal road.

"Hey, check it out," I said looking back at the happily frolicking hounds. "Duster's in that pack."

"No shit? I thought she hung around your place."

"Looks like she's out with her friends today."

"We'd better pick her up before somebody else does," said Duane, thinking of long-lost Rock as the clapped-out VW shuddered to a halt. I opened the door wide and looked back at the approaching mob of slavering mutts, beckoning Duster to leap into my arms.

"Come on Duster! Come on Duster!" I enthused while slapping my thigh. Spotting me, Duster sprinted to the front of the pack, her heart infused with doggie joy at seeing her master suddenly incarnate. She was now the leader of the mongrel pack, so what happened next was inevitable. She leaped into the VW, delirious with happiness and excitement, licking my face and wiggling up a storm.

A split second after Duster leapt into my arms, eight filthy mongrels followed her lead into the tiny car. Loud and smelly pandemonium engulfed us as I shielded my face and head from their slobber and fur. I did not dare leave my seat since I knew I would never force my way back into the jammed car through the canine Perfect Storm. The dogs were barking loudly and wildly jumping and worming their way back and forth between the back and front seats, wiggling across one another like a scrum of well-greased thirteen-year-old Olympic gymnasts. The overheated dogs soon discovered that our front windows were the only ones that opened in the crappy old VW and all nine hounds tried to force their heads around Duane and me into the outside air, while we protected our faces and nuts from being trampled. The snarling and barking rose to a crescendo along with our curses. The thought that only Duster had been vaccinated for rabies ran through my mind, but there was nothing I could do about having eight possibly rabid curs wrapped around me. I am not sure how Duane, buried in a squirming, deafening doggy scrum, kept the car pointed straight, but I am glad it was not me driving. I was having a hard enough time making a space with my arms where I could breathe without inhaling lethal amounts of dog hair and drool. We traced a wobbly path a few blocks to the center of Cotonou and pulled up next to a West African version of a farmers' market. Fifty or so older women gracefully strolled in their colorful skirts among tables and stands piled high with produce while delicately balancing large platters of fruit, vegetables, live snails, cooked monkey brains and raw meat on their heads.

Not one of those unsuspecting women ever imagined that a car would pull up and disgorge a pack of frenzied dogs. Neither Duane nor I had thought about it either. In our zeal to be rid of the dogs, we flung the car doors wide, and as the heaving ball of squirming, wild-eyed and yelping dogs tumbled from the canine clown car and spread among their bare feet, the shocked women panicked and disintegrated into a mob. Their stately and graceful balancing acts collapsed into wild disarray as shock and panic seized them. Everyone in Dahomey knew that dogs never had rabies shots; no native dog owner could afford such a luxury. In wild flight to save their lives, the women dropped and flung their wares willy-nilly. Fried monkey brains, pig parts, coconuts, live snails, raw meat, and a whole produce section of fruits and vegetables flew through the air. Shoppers scattered and stumbled on overturned platters and upended tables and crates, amid a rich stew of plant and animal parts, screaming in Fon and French. Duane and I were as stunned as the women vendors. "What the hell!" he said. "We're in trouble." "No shit, Sherlock," I replied. "Back this piece of shit out of here, and don't hit anyone," I yelled. I hugged Duster to my chest as Duane pointed us out of town. We felt terrible about exploding a doggie bomb in the market, but there was nothing to do but leave. Turning around to appraise the results of our spectacular arrival, I beheld what looked like a community food fight in a back lot by women and bystanders in colorful tropical garb. Duster wildly licked my face the whole while; she was nearly as much fun as her mother, Belle Amie, even though she was a teetotaler.

After we drilled four wells in Dahomey, the platform and tender were hauled by tugboats to Ghana, 200 miles west, to drill a couple of wildcat—exploratory—wells, and my work commute went from an hour boat ride to a six-hour hassle involving an international flight, a van trip, and a three-hour crew boat ride to the oil rig. The first leg of this bi-weekly trip by twenty of us was in a chartered Air Afrique DC-3, and the trip began, of course, at the tiny Cotonou airport bar well ahead of the evening flight.

After takeoff at 10 p.m. there was not a light to be seen below. Whatever isolated villages existed down there were unlit, and there was certainly no place to land in an emergency, which made our ensuing antics even harder to understand. Perhaps a subliminal death wish took hold of us: once the plane had leveled off a few thousand feet up, we whispered among ourselves like children planning a prank, then lined up single file in the DC-3's narrow center aisle. At the shout "Go!" twenty men jumped to the left side of the plane, thereby shifting three or four thousand pounds of humanity and causing the DC-3 to bank sharply left, like a World War II dive bomber arcing over in attack. After plunging awhile, the pilot straightened out the plane, at which point we lined up again in the aisle and on command jumped to the *right* side, forcing the plane to arc out of control in that direction. A short while after the plane was righted again, the French pilot came lunging from the cockpit, screaming curses at us for trying to kill him. We grabbed him and with much good-natured joshing forced him to drink a bottle of beer before we released him back into the cockpit. In retrospect, this was group insanity; we already had hazardous jobs on an offshore drilling platform in Africa and now we were flying over a remote jungle with a beer-soaked pilot.

While this was going on, an Austrian roustabout named Rolf wandered down the aisle to play a unique, private game. Attached to the overhead pipe racks for luggage storage were small, unshielded ventilation fans, their whirring blades the only source of relief from the stifling tropical heat. Rolf, not a stable man even sober, now amused himself by stopping the whirring fan blades with his nose. It is not clear what he got out of this game, but each set of blades slashed a deep cut in his nose and by the time he progressed halfway to the tail he looked like someone who had staggered out of an emergency room, blood splattered all over his face and shirt, but he always smiled in perverse enjoyment. Nobody paid Rolf much attention after the first flight, yet he never tired of his personal bloodletting.

After an hour-and-a-half of flying and downing beers, the droning engines were putting us to sleep as we approached Accra, the capital of Ghana. Perhaps because of the beer we had forced down his gullet, the French pilot sometimes bounced the DC-3 during landings, making one or two long hops while we weakly cheered. We then had a half-hour van ride to the harbor, where we boarded our German crew boat for a three-hour ride out to the *G.L. Temple* some 53 miles offshore. Mountainous seas were the norm once we cleared the harbor breakwater, but we were reasonably comfortable ensconced in airline-style seats within the snug cabin. However, the combination of drink and rough seas was deadly, and soon several men were seasick, the sounds of their feeding the fish on the aft deck mercifully drowned out by the roaring diesel engines.

We would all have gotten seasick if not for one of the Brits who diverted us with his repertoire of rugby songs and recitations. These smutty lyrics are said to be recited in pubs after rugby games in the U.K., but they never had a more intent performing audience than us inmates on the corkscrewing crew boat. Trying hard to ignore our heaving guts and verdant gills, we focused on recitations with leading lines such as:

"The harems of Egypt are fine to behold, the harlots the fairest of fair..."

or:

"When a man grows old and his balls go cold, and the tip of his prick goes blue..."

To this day I recall the words to, respectively, "Ivan Skavinsky Skavar" and "Eskimo Nell"—the latter with fifty-six stanzas and said to have been first performed by Noël Coward in a Paris nightclub in 1919.

One of my enduring visualizations of that hideous if colorful year in West Africa is seeing the crew boat as if from 100 feet in the air. The little speedboat approaches through the mist from land, wallowing and plunging through the ocean swells while the side windows reveal men seated in the bright interior, their mouths opening and closing in song. As the boat approaches my elevated vantage point, I faintly pick up the sound of men singing, which swells in volume as the gyrating boat approaches: "*The harems of Egypt are fine to behold...*" The ragged male voices reach a crescendo as they draw abeam of me, "*the harlots the fairest of fair...,*" then fade away as the laboring craft vanishes in waves and weather toward the distant platform lights, "*and the fairest of all were owned by the sheik named Abdul Abulbul Amir.*" It is one of the few pleasant remembrances of my year in West Africa, the closest thing to camaraderie in life that I had long sought but rarely found.

The rough seas at the oil rig made it hazardous to board the *G.L. Temple.* The German captain had to keep his crew boat a few feet away from the much larger tender or risk being crushed. Our first job was to throw our luggage across several feet of turbulent water into the arms of waiting roustabouts on the tender. We could not toss people across in the same way, though some of the bigger guys would have been willing to try, so we transferred by swinging Tarzan-style on a knotted inch-thick rope tied off to the tender. This was not the best way to end a day that had begun by over-imbibing at the Cotonou airport six hours earlier, continued in a Third World DC-3 filled with death-wishers, and ended with a gyrating three-hour boat ride in the West African midnight. On the bright side, the tender did not move as much as the crew boat, so once aboard our gills quickly faded from green to pink.

Industrial accidents are common on oil rigs and the *G.L. Temple* was no exception. A classic example was when the Union Oil K-12 teacher wanted to spice up his life during a break from teaching in Cotonou. He wangled a job on the oil rig as a beginning roustabout, learning valuable life skills such as chipping paint, tightening bolts, hosing down the deck and carrying heavy things. He and I were bullshitting in a group one day, surrounded by a tangle of pipes and loud machinery, and when the hardhatted sewing circle broke up, he turned around and took just a single step before knocking out his front teeth on a large pipe that ran at head height above the deck. He walked into the pipe full force and we all heard the crunch as his teeth gave way; so much for "How I spent my summer break." We platform regulars knew enough to instinctively look before taking a step in any direction. In a sense, working in Oil Patch had made me acutely aware of surrounding danger, a trait that was to serve me well when I later worked in the wilderness.

My own industrial accident on the *G.L. Temple* was nearly fatal. I was stepping down the widowmaker in the 3:00 a.m. darkness, peering down to make sure my boots landed on the grillwork steps and not in the voids between them. A stiff wind was blowing and a glaring work light high on the derrick cast deep shadows across the widowmaker, making footing problematic. I suddenly had a strong precognition of danger and tightened my grip on the railings, pulled my hardhatted head into my shoulders and shut my eyes just as hundreds of gallons of drilling mud slammed into me with tremendous force from the left. Hot liquid mud the color and consistency of chocolate milk is continuously pumped from the mudroom on the tender up to the platform in an eighteen-inch-diameter rubber Kelly hose, sped along by 2,000-horsepower pumps. The mud is hot from circulating deep in the earth and from being forced along by the large pumps, and at a pH of 10 it is exceedingly caustic. The heaving of the tender up and down in the storm had ripped apart the Kelly hose while I was on the widowmaker, and the stream of corrosive chemical stew was blown over me by the stiff wind. The impact was terrific; had I been standing up straight instead of crouching and holding onto the widowmaker railings, I would have been flung into the shark-infested Gulf of Guinea and disappeared without a trace.

I yelled for help but nobody was around to hear me. Knowing that the caustic mud would seep into my eyes before long, I still had to take slow and deliberate steps down the widowmaker, because drilling mud is designed to be super slick and the footing on the open-grillwork stairway was now treacherous. My leading foot felt around in empty air when I finally reached the end of the widowmaker. I now faced the daunting problem of getting from the widowmaker onto the tender, which normally floats right below the end of the widowmaker. However, during a storm such as the one now lashing us, the wind and waves can move the tender far off to one side, leaving the widowmaker hanging over empty ocean. In my blinded condition I had no idea if the widowmaker hung over the tender or over the shark-infested sea.

I had no time to think about it. I backed deliberately off the end of the widowmaker, holding first to the railing then to the bottom step as I lowered my body farther and farther down, hoping to feel the tender's deck with my boots. I clung desperately to the widowmaker's bottom step, terrified of falling into the sea, but the slick mud steadily weakened my grip, so my fate was going to be sealed very soon. I thrashed my legs in desperation, feeling for the tender. Had I kicked anything solid, even machinery, I would have let go and gladly crumpled onto the deck. My flailing legs encountered nothing, and I listened with utter concentration, but the howling storm overrode the usual sound of waves slapping against the tender. I momentarily saw myself from afar, a lonely figure struggling for life on a steel island in the predawn darkness on the remote edge of a boundless sea. My grip weakened as I was overcome with desolation; it was time to do or die. I took three deep breaths and said, "Please, God, let me live," and fell into eternity.

I hit the tender's deck after falling a foot or two and instinctively lunged backward onto some anchor winches, desperate to avoid rolling over the edge of the heaving tender's bow. The rush of relief at being saved from death by drowning or shark attack was intense but brief; I would not be safe until the alkaline mud had been washed away from my eyes. Feeling around, I recognized where I was in the maze of walkways and machinery on the tender's weather deck and shakily made my way down a level and through corridors to a shower room. I sprayed my face and hands for a long time before opening my eyes, then, grateful to be alive, leaned on my knees and panted. A Norwegian roustabout, Big Rudy, an unusually tall and muscular blonde-headed giant whose head was too big for his hardhat, walked by and appraised me. "Why in fuck are you taking a fucking shower in your fucking clothes?" he asked. I could not answer just then, being in shock and shaking like a leaf. A scenario like this had not been part of my boyhood wish for an adventuresome life filled with strong emotions, although it fit the bill in a technical sense. It seemed like a hell of a way to make money for grad school.

Serious injuries often resulted from endemic violence on the rig, and the worst brutality I witnessed was when Peter Devaca, a crane driver, used his ever-present homemade Bowie knife to slash a Ghanaian roustabout. The Ghanaian, a welder's assistant, was making his way across deck, lugging his welder's face shield and gas hoses. Peter was absorbed in touching up the base of his crane with thick, yellow paint. As the African passed close by, he said, "Hey, Devaca, got a cigarette?" I had a ringside seat for the unfolding vignette while idly leaning against a rack of welding bottles nearby and sucking on a wood splinter. Upon hearing the Ghanaian's request, Peter dropped his paintbrush, grabbed the poor guy by the throat, and smashed his head against the steel crane. Peter then unsheathed his knife and cut the Ghanaian's throat. As the knife flashed, Peter calmly said, "You know I like people to call me Peter, not Devaca." He smiled coldly at his victim as blood welled from the poor bastard's throat, then unclenched his fist from the guys now-mangled throat.

The stunned African slumped to the deck, felt his throat and observed the blood on his hands, then crawled off on all fours to the toolpusher's office for medical help, leaving a wide trail of blood. Peter took up his paintbrush and got back to touching up the crane, whistling quietly to the tune of "I've got a lovely bunch of coconuts" while he worked. I had often seen random violence on the rig and in town, but this callous display sent a shudder of fright through me. Peter looked at me and winked, as if he had just pulled off a clever stunt. I rethought my friendship with Devaca, I mean *Peter*. Previously I had spent time with him alone, smoking Tusker cigarettes and bullshitting by the stern winches in the predawn hours, but now decided to skip that potentially fatal pastime. I was learning that some people in life are to be avoided at all costs.

Peter was the most dangerous man on the *G.L. Temple*, but the most hated was a mild-mannered, pudgy and bland fellow named Cyril Lakis, who was in charge of the living arrangements and food service and oversaw a Dahomeyan staff of cooks, stewards, janitors and room boys. The problem with Cyril was that he was dishonest, shortchanging our food budget and keeping the difference for himself. Feeding substandard food to hardworking men did not win him any friends and we regularly cursed him to his face, but he did not care because he was getting rich.

Sweet vengeance unfolded when the mud engineer, Benoit Lafitte, wondered why we never saw Cyril naked. Benoit hailed from Cajun country in southern Louisiana and had a boisterous sense of humor and a suspicious caste of mind. He was pleasant on the surface, but he was a pugnacious man who was not to be messed with. Benoit began wondering why it was that Cyril never appeared in the communal shower room, even though everyone else showered at least once a day in that tropical clime. Cyril evidently was secretive about personal hygiene and Benoit had an inquiring mind; he started paying attention to Cyril's routine.

Benoit's bunkroom was just down the hall from Cyril's, and Benoit kept watch through his cracked-open door until his victim departed his room one late evening wrapped in a towel and headed toward the shower room. Benoit tiptoed down the hall into Cyril's room, where he saw that three of the four bunk beds were piled high with sheets, towels and cigarette cartons. He climbed into a top bunk and rearranged the towels so he was hidden from view but still able to peek out. Cyril returned from his shower, locked the door, dropped the towel from around his pudgy waist, and turned on a cassette player; a caterwauling screech of unidentifiable origin filled the compartment. He twirled in circles while snapping his fingers overhead and whistling tunelessly. It was almost impossible for Benoit not to burst out laughing, but he reached deep and stifled himself. After giving the matter some thought, he summoned up reserves of intestinal fortitude and produced a sharp, loud fart. Cyril froze in mid-twirl, silent lips puckered, arms above his head, eyes casting about. "Who is that?" asked Cyril. "Who is there?" Benoit was now in a paroxysm of stifled laughter and farts behind his towel wall, straining to muffle sounds from both ends of his body. The background creaks and groans of the drilling tender rolling in the Gulf of Guinea reassured Cyril that he had imagined someone's presence.

Cyril resumed his slow gyrations, his face canted up and lips pursed, hands clapping high, fingers snapping above his head on swaying arms. Unable to contain himself in any sense of the word, Benoit now unleashed a chain of long, loud and wet farts. Cyril froze in shock and confusion, sure that he had company but not knowing what the hell was happening exactly. At that moment, Benoit burst from behind his fortification of towels and pillows, scattering cartons of cigarettes before him, as he hit the deck running and yelled, "Gotcha, asshole!" Benoit, wearing only boxer shorts himself, scooped up a deer-frozen-in-the-headlights Cyril Lakis and ran upstairs with his naked, stunned prey to the galley where many of us were eating a midnight meal. Surprised to see a nearly naked Benoit carrying a completely naked Cyril, we clapped and cheered. Cyril began screaming, "Put me down! Goddam Yankee! I kill you!" The muscular Benoit had both arms under Cyril's squirming, naked body, displaying him around the galley to appraising looks.

"My granddaughter's got a bigger pecker than that," opined one roughneck.

"Yeah, but look at the set of tits on him," I added.

"He's so fat we don't need to drill for oil, we'll just boil him up," suggested a roustabout.

"Shee-it, he doesn't even have any hair on his body; I gotta get me some of that," declared Ralph, the Union Oil toolpusher.

Cyril squealed and squirmed as he cursed us roundly but could not escape his muscular tormenter. Benoit strode out of the galley with Cyril screaming bloody murder, headed toward a doorway leading onto the deck.

"I'm gonna throw this bastard to the sharks," announced Benoit, "he's offended mud engineers everywhere."

"Don't! I wanna pork him first, I've already got a hard-on," insisted Ralph the toolpusher. Benoit made two circuits of the tender's living spaces before releasing Cyril to return to his room, which he never again left unlocked.

Cyril's misfortune continued weeks later when I observed him tentatively making his way across the machinery-cluttered deck of the tender toward the platform, stopping often to look up at the derrick as if it were a novel attraction. I was witnessing Cyril's first visit to the platform in a year of living with it daily as the most prominent feature in his life, and awakened by this momentary break in ennui, I quickly hatched a plan to take advantage of his mistake. Unreeling a high-pressure fire hose, I alerted one of the French roughnecks, Gilles, to Cyril's hesitant progress up the widowmaker, and once Cyril was well up onto the platform, Gilles turned the hose on full blast.

Cyril was forty feet away and twenty feet below me when the powerful stream of sea water bowled him off his feet. The entire drill crew laughed uproariously as he rolled toward the edge of the platform, arms flailing and legs kicking, while uttering wild screams of surprise and horror. My plan was to roll him over the edge of the platform and have him drop sixty feet into the choppy waters of the Gulf of Guinea. The splash of this corpulent turd would surely attract one of the sharks that constantly circled the rig, which would improve food service for them as well as for us on the *G.L. Temple.*

Cyril prevented his plunge into the sea by grabbing an exhaust stack near the edge of the platform and swinging his pudgy body behind a ten-foot-high spool of drilling cable. He was safe from being knocked overboard, but could not show himself for the next hour, until I tired of the game. A minute or so after Gilles turned the hose off, Cyril dashed for the widowmaker like an escaped zoo animal, never again to leave the tender.

Cyril's dousing was a welcome break in tedium from my monotonous and hazardous job, but at a deeper level I was profoundly disturbed to have fallen so low on the morality scale that I had made a joke of trying to wash someone overboard into a shark-filled sea. The surges of violence and cruelty that shaded my whole year in Dahomey may have been attempts at stimulation, but they were clear signs of a corrupted morality desensitized by seeing endless suffering ashore and experiencing routine cruelty and danger offshore. Unfortunately for my soul, my slide toward the moral abyss was not over yet.

A blessed intellectual diversion presented itself when the rig was towed back to Dahomey. In Ghana the platform had been sitting in 200 feet of water, so its supporting legs had been fully extended downward to the seafloor. During our three months in Ghana, algae, sponges, corals, barnacles and other small epibionts had grown thickly on the grillwork legs, and snails had homed in on this natural smorgasbord, while small clams snuggled amid the tangle of epibionts, safe from predators. The legs of the platform were in effect an artificial reef sheathed in a rich tropical biota, all of which was exposed when the legs were raised to drill in just 100 feet of water in Dahomey. The top half of the grillwork legs were now exposed to the air and the marine plants and animals had dried in place. I thrilled at the chance to collect seashells, which had been my passion since high school tidepooling field trips with Uncle George in Southern California. Nobody else on the rig understood any interest in dead things on the platform legs, but I was thrilled at the chance to exercise my scientific brain and add to the body of knowledge about West Africa mollusks.

I had tried collecting shells ashore, but Dahomey's sandy shoreline lacked the rocky beaches where most shells live. The exception was the Cotonou harbor breakwater, which was constructed of giant cement versions of the pickup jacks that children play with. The one time I did adroitly wiggle my body into the cement breakwater openings, I discovered that the few seashells were guarded by an army of extraordinarily large rats, so I paid a local kid to collect for me. I cautioned him about the rodents, but he ignored them while gladly earning a penny per shell. My collection from the breakwater and the platform legs, like my collection from Chile five years before, ended up at the Los Angeles County Museum of Natural History.

It would have been nice if collecting seashells had formed a final, pleasant memory of Dahomey, but it did not. Instead, I turned fully murderous for a moment in my life, because a guy had stolen from me.

This event took place near the end of my interminable year overseas, when my body was exhausted from continual wawas, my brain was baked from a year in the equatorial tropics, I was sick of heat rash tormenting me at every joint, sick of bugs and cockroaches, sick of Africa, sick of the criminal class that peopled the rig, sick of trying to speak French to the second-tier colonials who lived in that hellhole of a former French empire.

My search for activities to fill up the empty hours hit pay dirt when I borrowed a heavy-duty fishing rig from Rob Wencome, an English ichthyologist with whom I played mahjong when onshore. The fishing outfit had a reel as big as a pie tin that clamped to the tender's handrail and was wound with several hundred yards of 700-pound-test monofilament line tipped with a chain leader and a large hook. Using a chunk of goat meat from the galley as bait, I went after the sharks that constantly circled the rig. Catching a hammerhead was a major event, but I knew from growing up a fisherman's son that even a dead-looking shark can bite a man's arm off, so getting a hooked hammerhead aboard was a challenge until I thought of Peter Devaca and his industrial crane. Once the shark was beside the tender, Peter swung his crane over and I looped the chain leader around the crane hook so Peter could hoist the animal onto the deck. Someone radioed ashore and before long a large canoe with several paddlers arrived alongside. Peter lowered the shark into the canoe and the Dahomeyans thanked me profusely for the free food. It felt good to be doing something rewarding for a change.

I was surprised one day to see some of my distinctive fishing line tied off roughly to a railing on the platform. Pulling my gear out of the water, I was dumbfounded to see that someone had cut my line shorter by 200 feet. Seeing this, the accumulated trials and frustrations of a year in Dahomeyan Oil Patch hell welled up into boiling rage and I went looking for the thief with a black heart. Anyone who has grown up repressed builds up a head of steam, and mine was ready to explode. Big Rudy remembered an Aussie roustabout tying my line off to the platform railing and I began stalking the bastard, searching the drilling tender compartment by compartment with grim determination. As I exited one of the heads, I heard the crew boat pulling up for a crew change and at the doorway I suddenly bumped into the thief.

It seems that *he* had been looking for *me*, once he had discovered that I had "stolen" *his* shark line.

"Hey, asshole," he said, "someone ripped off my shark line and I heard it was you."

"You dumb shit," I said, "you stole *my* stuff and now *you're* mad? I tossed the stolen gear overboard."

We stood an arm's length apart, glowering hate, when I slowly reached up with both hands and grabbed my hardhat firmly by the rim, then swung it down viciously, breaking his nose with a sickening crunch. He staggered backward as I replaced my hardhat and lunged forward, clutched his shoulders and smashed the back of his bare head again and again into the steel bulkhead. The back of his head left a bloody streak down the gray steel wall as he slumped semiconscious to the deck. Mad beyond reason, I kicked and stomped him with my steel-toed work boots, then grabbed his feet and pulled his limp body out of the compartment, hearing with satisfaction as his head slammed wetly against the raised steel jamb. I was going to toss him overboard so he could do a little personal shark fishing; it would not have taken the hammerheads long to sniff out the rich outpouring of blood. I was one doorway away from getting him outside when Big Rudy happened by, sized up the situation, and pulled me off the Aussie. Big Rudy was twice my size and had no trouble pinning me against a bulkhead while he checked that the Aussie was still alive. A couple of other roustabouts dragged me away as I raved about killing the thief in the future, then they tossed the victim into the crew boat to get doctored up in Cotonou. It was satisfying to think he would be treated by the alcoholic Dr. Strake.

In retrospect my volcanic anger was rage at myself, for subjecting myself to an entire year in that shithole of a country, on the worst oil rig I had ever worked on, with the worst men I had ever met. It is easier to explain beating up a thief than to understand how I could have done such things to myself. Even with the perspective of hindsight, I cannot imagine why I subjected myself to those terrible conditions for a year of my young life. I went to that tropical purgatory to earn money for my

PhD and earned $14,400 in 1970 dollars, which was around twice the American family's income back then, plus an additional $2,000 bonus for staying a full year.

I left Dahomey after 375 days, 10 hours and 18 minutes, touchdown to takeoff, by boarding an Air Afrique flight to Dakar, Senegal. One of the roustabouts I was terminally sick of from the *G.L Temple* boarded the almost-empty flight and sat down next to me.

"May as well sit together to kill time," he declared in greeting.

"Fuck off, Bubba," I snarled.

Bubba took the hint. In Dakar I was stuck in a waiting area overnight; the guards would not allow me into the main terminal, and I had no food or water. I had given my last CFA francs to my houseboy, Sam, as a parting gift, along with all my clothing, so I had no bribe for the airport guards. A sleepless night on a hard bench, bitten to pieces by voracious mosquitoes, was West Africa's final indignity. Boarding the Lufthansa flight to Chile the next morning was like entering the kingdom of heaven.

For a year I had acted like a dog that had been chained and muzzled all its life, then suddenly set free of all restraint. Perhaps I had needed to get some—make that *a lot of*—wildness out of my system before settling down to the last surge of school and a life of scholarship. Within the limitations of Dahomey, I had howled up a storm and pushed my moral limits to the brink of depravity. I was a man and not a boy now, I had tested my limits, but pulled back at the perishing edge, and I was now confident of myself as I had never been.

A year in Dahomey had almost put me into an early grave, and not one day of it was enjoyable, fun, pleasant or healthful. I was beset with illness, learned nothing, and ultimately earned nothing. Within a year of returning home I was broke again, most of my earnings in the pockets of doctors. Years after I returned home, my 6'1" frame weighed just 135 pounds and I underwent major abdominal surgery, but still I suffered twenty-five years of the wawas, to control which I carried around a dropper bottle of tincture of opium. Mercifully, after a quarter-century of suffering, it turned out that you could take Africa out of the boy as well as the boy out of Africa. People may or may not leave their hearts in San Francisco, but they definitely leave great bleeding gouts of their colon in West Africa. Goodbye, Dahomey, and up yours.

In my first few minutes back in the USC Paleo Lab one of the new grad students, a heavyset, boisterous guy gave me a hard shove in a youthful display of attempted male dominance. He mistakenly thought that I was another schoolboy, like him. I roughly grabbed his throat, rocked him back on his heels and drew back my right fist to break his nose, knowing that the best way to win a fight is to start it. Suddenly realizing where I was, I froze my cocked fist and lowered it when I saw that his eyes were the size of saucers and his mouth sagged open. I unclutched his throat, half smiled and apologized, but my eyes were not smiling. It was not the best way to meet a fellow grad student and I felt embarrassed for myself and sorry for him. It would take a while for the African poisons to leach away.

Another thing I could not abide any more was classwork, and my doctoral advisor, Bill Easton, recognized I had advanced beyond classroom instruction. Even though PhD work in the sciences is notoriously difficult, I gloried in it as the final step on my long educational road. I burned the candles at both ends my last three years at USC by focusing on the Cenozoic evolution of a marine gastropod, or snail, lineage for my dissertation. I soon discovered to my relief that my mind still worked at a research level after a year of stewing in alcohol and pot.

I had stopped drinking when I left West Africa, but the wawas and other ailments followed me home and within a year I was once again broke. Recognizing my desperation as well as my drive to finish my education, Dr. Easton found a year's private scholarship money to keep me going.

In addition to my dissertation study, I worked overtime to describe the modern mollusks I had collected in Chile six years earlier while visiting my father. My doctoral work and Chilean mollusk study reached a fever pitch in my final year, when I spent eighteen hours a day in the Paleo Lab; bringing my lunch, dinner and midnight snack to USC, I stayed chained to my specimen collection and portable manual typewriter. My booklet on Chilean mollusks was published in the winter of 1973, so I could focus exclusively on finishing my doctoral work that June. I was finally a professional paleontologist, my goal since age ten, and I even had a publication record.

▲ ▲ ▲

"My goodness you have a big one!" exclaimed one of the pretty young Chilean whores.

"Is that all you?" inquired another.

"Where do you normally hide that thing?" asked another inquiring mind.

"You are too young to have such a big fish!" commented an older prostitute.

"Come by and see me any time!" shouted the youngest member of the troupe.

I laughed and called out in Spanish that I did not have time just then to visit. I was struggling by the La Gaviota motel, which had been reborn as a whore house, with a four-foot-long, foot-wide baby giant squid in my arms. The girls lounging in the morning sun could not resist commenting on my hilarious juggling act. Carrying the rubbery mollusk was like lugging a seabag full of Jello: if I supported the ends, the middle drooped, and if I propped up the middle, one end or the other poured toward the ground. I knew this was the biggest mollusk I would ever find, so I had to collect it from a tidepool where I had spied it rolling around that morning and get it to my father's house a half-mile away in Iquique (ee-KEY-kay), Chile. Whenever I passed by the La Gaviota in later days the girls invariably made reference to my "*calamar gigante.*"

The photo I sent to my boss in California for Christmas 1969, to thank him for sending me to Dahomey.

Finding the giant squid was the high point of the summer spent with my father's second family in Iquique. We had barely been in touch since he had abandoned my family seven years earlier and I had few memories of him. He was hosting me in the hope that he and I would become more comfortable with each other, but he had a lot to make up for in the previous nineteen years and one summer was not long enough for the task. Collecting seashells daily was my joy and escape, just as an oak tree had been a regular haven from my boyhood family in San Pedro.

For hours each day I swung along the coast in high-top leather boots with lug soles, wearing a flannel shirt, with a geologist's hammer on my belt and cloth collecting bags stuffed in my pockets, exactly as I had imagined doing as a child after reading *All About Dinosaurs*. I spent hours each day diligently poking around tidepools, overturning rocks, looking under seaweed patches and digging holes until I had collected thousands of clams and snails that I happily shipped to the museum in L.A. My labor of love had an unexpected payoff, because no scientist had intensively collected shells in northern Chile since the 1840s. I was collecting specimens in virgin territory, just like my hero Roy Chapman Andrews had been doing in the Gobi Desert in the 1920s. It was my first crack at a scientifically pristine molluscan fauna, and it turned out that several of the species were new to science, and many others had been seen only rarely. My detailed observations about the various species' habitats, which Uncle George had taught me to record, were unknown for most of the species and would become a valuable addition to the scientific literature. My father and I had not become any closer, which was never realistically in the cards, but my scientific experience took a major leap forward in Chile. ▲

DRIFTWOOD,
ALASKA

"This is fucking scary," shouted Jim "Moley" Molnar, a fellow Texaco geologist and USC alum, with a note of rising panic in his voice, as the twin-engine Piper Apache plunged toward the ground yet again. "We've almost screwed into the ground two or three times."

"No shit," I replied between gritted teeth, equally agitated, as the craft reversed its fall and surged giddily upward on another demonic air current. We both clutched barf bags but were trying hard not to puke as the small plane corkscrewed and yawed through ragged clouds, batted every which way by swirling winds.

Through jagged tears in the gray clouds we glimpsed snaggle-toothed 9,000-foot peaks of the northern Alaskan Brooks Range that reached their stony fingers up toward us. We were on the final leg of a trip from Los Angeles to the North Slope as part of a month-long Texaco geological field party, and both Moley and I doubted we were going to arrive in one piece. Some of our friends already had not.

On the tundra at Driftwood, on the North Slope of Alaska, with an eagle feather in my hat.

Jobs were thin on the ground for paleontologists when I got my doctorate in June of 1973, and I was fortunate to land a job with Texaco in L.A. The $19,000 salary got me searching for another 1963-67 Corvette to replace the 1967 coupe my advisor Bill Easton had made me sell when he thought it did not look right for an impoverished student to be driving a fancy sports car. Unfortunately, after the intensity and scope of doctoral work, my job assignments at Texaco were not challenging and I did not care about petroleum geology. I had already learned all I needed to know about crude oil in Cook Inlet and Dahomey.

My job's saving grace was being picked for the June 1974 North Slope field party. At last I would collect fossils in the wilderness, which I had longed to do since I was a child. However, fate intervened when a scientific society asked me to organize and chair a technical meeting in L.A. on fossil mollusks at the same time, and Texaco kindly—and as it turned out, fatefully—assigned another geologist to the June field party and moved me to the July field team.

A month later, our boss gathered the five geologists of the July field party and announced that the June group had perished in a fatal helicopter crash. The pilot and five geologists, including the new hire who replaced me, died in a tangle of wreckage one morning when their helicopter had a problem and plunged onto the barren tundra. Our July group was pushed back to August and changed from mandatory to voluntary participation.

"I'll go," I said as I raised my hand to be the first to volunteer for the August field party.

"Thanks," replied our boss, "but I'll give everyone overnight to decide, since the married guys need to talk with their wives."

"I'm single and I've already thought about it and I'm good to go," I said quietly, anxious that the others might resent my eagerness. The wilderness had been calling me for decades and I was not going to miss a chance to see it, no matter what. In the end, all the men chose to go.

The whole office attended the two funerals that were in Southern California, and I wept unashamedly as the caskets were lowered into the ground. I pondered the role of fate in my life, since I had escaped death on the oil rig in Africa, and now again in Alaska.

Moley and I were big-eyed, cringed passengers as the pilot of our Piper Apache bounced to a frightening landing on the bumpy gravel airstrip at the Itkillik (it-KILL-ik) pipeline construction camp, our North Slope destination. His round face relaxed into its normal mustache-topped seriousness as he slumped in his front passenger seat while we enjoyed a moment of stillness on the ground. With his sports car cap and ever-present shades, he was once again the only guy I knew who looked "cool."

"Hey, you two, time to come out and join the fun," quipped Alex Feucht, our party chief. We referred to Alex as "Little Leader" because of his stature, but his always well-combed blonde hair and Van Dyke beard gave him a purposeful air.

"No problem there," I replied, "I can't get out of this crate fast enough."

"After this flight I never want to get in a plane again," added Moley.

I shook hands with the other geologists, Don "Oltzie" Oltz, a solid-looking pipe smoker with an intellectual air, and Mike Simmons, the youngest of the group and as short as Alex but more obviously a gym rat. The group had dubbed me "Doctor Clam." I looked around at the motley crew of construction workers who had met the plane, including a middle-aged Eskimo man with a grotesquely mutilated face.

I leaned close to Alex and asked quietly, "What's the deal with the Eskimo guy?"

"He's a mechanic and walked into an airplane propeller a few years ago in the winter. He was working on the plane in a hangar and forgot about the prop for a moment. It pretty much took his face off, but the prop got damaged so they had to wait a couple of days for a storm to blow out until another plane could evacuate him to Fairbanks," replied Alex sotto voce. "Watch out for your own head," he added, "there's a lot of whirling blades around here." The Eskimo guy's misfortune reminded me that, like on oil rigs, I was again working well beyond the pale limits of normal life, in a place where life-altering accidents happen all too often.

We stopped talking when the Piper Apache revved its engines loudly to turn around for Fairbanks, having refueled and taken aboard a passenger.

"That's gonna be one bumpy-assed ride over the mountains," commented Moley.

"Yeah, don't I know it. There's one plane and pilot I don't need to see again," I added.

We cheered feebly and waved as the plane roared down the gravel strip in a cloud of gray dust and lifted from the earth. But not for long. As I gaped in shock, a gust of wind lifted the plane's right wing and the machine flipped left and plowed hard into the tundra. Flames sprouted from one engine as its prop ripped off and bounced along the ground.

"Holy shit!" said Alex. "Let's get down there!"

The Eskimo guy handed me a fire extinguisher and he lugged a second one as we all ran toward the crash. "Put out whatever's burning," he added.

The pilot and passenger leaped out, banged up but unharmed, as we ran up. "Are you guys okay?" shouted Alex, but the passenger looked too disgusted and the pilot too embarrassed to answer as they stalked by. I doused the burning starboard engine in CO_2 while the Eskimo guy billowed a white cloud into the port engine.

Coming on the heels of the summer's fatal helicopter crash, and our scary landing just minutes earlier, this new disaster continued my eye-opening introduction to the world of Alaska bush planes, especially since Moley and I had just spent two hours in that very same plane flying over the storm-lashed tundra and mountains of remotest Alaska with an underskilled pilot. Our scary flight, the smoldering crash, and the Eskimo's ruined face impressed on me that the Arctic is a place where serious accidents are a heartbeat away.

Despite all, however, I was standing for the first time on the North Slope, the broad east-west coastal plain of northern Alaska upon which some of my life's greatest personal and professional events would play out.

"Damn, Moley, this is the flattest place I've ever been," I remarked as I swept my arm from the brooding Brooks Range in the south to the Arctic Ocean over the horizon northward.

"No kidding, but it's not exactly the Garden of Eden, what with no trees and all," he commented as he pointed to some scraggly bushes. "On the other hand, there *is* a lot of grass." We both smiled at the lumpy tussocks of low grayish-green grass that marched to the horizon all around and were the very definition of "tundra."

We were beguiled that is was 10:00 p.m. but the sun was at its *10:00 a.m.* height for Los Angeles. No matter how many times we glanced at it during those first few days, the sun stayed at the same height while it circled around the entire horizon. I was smitten with the stark beauty and strangeness of the surreal and disorienting landscape, feeling like an ancient sailor might have as he approached the imagined edge of a flat earth. We were a long way from anyplace familiar.

We flew out the next morning in a Bell 206B Jet Ranger helicopter to the northern foothills of the Brooks Range and dropped off in pairs to explore the geology and collect lithology samples of the Jurassic-age rocks some 175,000,000 years old. Texaco would perform so-called porosity and permeability, or P&P, analysis on the rock samples to determine if they were suitable as petroleum reservoirs. As Texaco's only molluscan paleontologist, I would identify any fossils we found to hopefully add some age control to our studies. My partner Moley and I had to constantly refocus on the geology while being besotted with the lavish, encompassing beauty of intimate valleys, pristine creeks, and hill-sides carpeted with purple lupine in full bloom. The added possibility of meeting a grizzly bear around the next bend added a frisson to the moment, especially since we had never practiced with or even fired our Remington rifle. Feeling blessed to be alive in such untouched country on a sunny and warm day, we refreshed ourselves from the crystalline waters of Lupine and Cobblestone creeks. I had hiked in the Sierra Nevada Mountains but never viewed countryside as crisp and alive as the Brooks Range foothills, and the profound beauty of the remote Alaskan bush drew me back for the next thirty-three years.

After a few days of geologizing out of Itkillik, we packed up our gear to work the rest of our month at Driftwood, an unpopulated campsite on the Utukok (YOU-to-kok) River some hundreds of miles to the west. Most of the group went in our two helicopters while I rode in a twin-engine transport plane that had seen better days. Once the plane was packed full of gear and supplies, the pilot and I could not enter or exit the machine except through a small side window on his side, which would not have been great in an emergency situation. We made an unplanned landing at the tiny settlement of Umiat (UU-me-at), population four, because the plane's engines were leaking oil at a horrendous rate and the oil tanks needed topping off. It was beginning to look like flying in the Alaskan bush was more dicey than I had imagined, and the upcoming month would cement that impression forevermore.

The remainder of the flight to Driftwood was a grand tour of the North Slope. Flying west, the craggy Brooks Range of dark, sawtooth mountains was a spectacular site to the south, with the highest peaks at 9,000 feet still bearing snow patches. The Arctic Ocean was a sometimes-glimpsed splash of blue and white out the right-side window. The North Slope is essentially as flat as a billiard table and about the same color, with an occasional rumple of hills here and there; many medium-size rivers flowed across the Slope—as everyone refers to it—from the Brooks

Range north toward the Arctic Ocean. We paralleled the meandering, chocolate brown Colville River while I had no inkling of how large a part it would play in my future: I would nearly die in it, I would make one of my most important scientific discoveries along its banks, and I would have a transcendent spiritual experience beside it. I was fascinated by the ever-changing nature of the green and brown tundra—tundra being basically low, lumpy grass and dwarf plants—the relative sparseness of bushes, and the complete absence of trees. The ground is frozen solid to more than a thousand feet deep, which is called permafrost, but the summer sun melts the top foot or two and creates millions of small "thaw lakes." These small lakes are shaped by the wind, because waves that erode their banks over time slowly elongate the lakes in the direction of wind flow. One side of each thaw lake has a straight margin, where small waves constantly eat at the tundra; this has the beneficial effect of letting a bush pilot know wind direction if he suddenly has to land.

Camp at Driftwood on the Utukok River.

Eventually the Utukok River hove into view, its clear waters burbling past the patch of ground called Driftwood, a mere swath of bare earth flat enough to land a plane on, where I would spend the next month of my life. We quickly unloaded the cargo plane and set up our ten-foot by ten-foot sleeping tents along the river, then made a fuel dump for the helicopters, a small mountain of crated fuel tins, well off to the side. Our field party of five geologists was expanded to include a cook and camp tender, Dorothy Lecke, plus two pilots and a helicopter mechanic. Driftwood lacked permanent structures, and the only evidence of past occupation was four fifty-five-gallon oil drums marking the four corners of the primitive, unimproved landing strip. It was my first sight of a bush airstrip, which was simply a flat spot where a plane could land and, more importantly, take off. The Utukok River, a crystal clear braided stream around fifty yards wide, flowed beside camp and was fordable in places. Arising from melting glaciers in the Brooks Range twenty miles to the south, its water was cold enough to make my teeth hurt when brushing each morning, a recollection that still makes me smile.

We spent our days collecting P&P samples while wading along shallow rivers in thickly insulated shoepacs in the western foothills of the Brooks Range, while I also kept my eye out for marine mollusks or other fossils. It was not intellectually challenging work, but simply being in the remote wilderness fed some core pleasure center of my brain. The gurgle of the clear, rippling creeks, the streambed cobbles shifting and clonking together under my boots, hiking over lumpy tundra while hearing the creak of the leather rock hammer holster and Brunton compass case on my belt, the thunk of my rock hammer chipping samples from the rock walls, the sight of tundra grasses and flowers, the frisson of keeping an eye out for grizzlies, and pleasant back and forth banter with Moley amounted to being in a Garden of Earthly Delights.

"What in hell's that?" I said, pointing back the way we had just hiked. I had just turned around for a routine grizzly check, which one of us did every few minutes, while slopping our way across a patch of wet tundra. The circling sun was at just the right angle to glint off of what looked like silver ground fog.

"Beats me," said Moley, "maybe some kind of marsh gas."

After a moment we realized that the "ground fog" was in constant motion and made up of mosquitoes, billions and billions of tiny bodies forming a diaphanous cloud about a foot thick. Bug-eyed—pun intended— for a few moments, we walked to higher ground and added a new layer of bug dope, especially around our sleeves and pant cuffs.

I had not seen insects in such numbers even in Africa. All of the Arctic, however, is the grand breeding ground for mosquitoes as well as other blood suckers such as no-see-ems, black flies and deer flies. They were so numerous, and so aggressive, that every morning we slathered our skin in layers of Cutter's lotion, sprayed our thermal underwear, then our outer shirt and pants, then our hands and face. Finally, I closed my eyes tightly and tucked in my lips, then sprayed my face directly from the can. These precautions kept the predatory skeeters a couple of feet away to start with, but as we sweated during the day the bug dope wore off, and the flying pests flew closer and closer. Eventually the bravest among them would do a kamikaze dive at our skin, pulling up at the very last millimeter as the Cutter fumes overcame them, which told us it was time to reapply the bug dope. We had to be careful with the bug dope, because it melted plastic, including my cheap watch, and we were especially careful around the helicopter, since we could leave a permanent hand impression in the expensive plastic bubble by simply leaning on it. There were costs to being in a Garden of Earthly Delights.

We had beginners' luck with the month's weather of occasional overcast skies and passing rain squalls, which was fortunate, because I needed heavy-duty parkas and rainsuits in later years to survive the perishing weather that often occurs on the North Slope. Our worst weather at Driftwood was a siege of 40-50 mile-an-hour winds that grounded both choppers for nine tedious, enervating days, until we had read all our own books and everyone else's during the 24-hour sunlit days and nights. Luckily, I had brought along several Jack London novels, which I loaned out to anyone else, but held tight to my poetry anthology that I read at bedtime. The percussive flapping of the tent walls banished solid sleep and in any case we had to get up every few hours all night long to check that the tent stakes were not pulling out—they always were—and hammer them back into the tundra.

The windstorm also grounded our weekly food flight from Fairbanks, but we were well stocked for just such an emergency. A more serious problem was that our limited supply of beer had run out and after several alcohol-free days, the nine of us were sulking in the pilots' tent one evening, the shrieking wind and flapping canvas getting on all our nerves. I got up and left as if to take a leak, then hurried over to my tent and retrieved two bottles of Bacardi and Jack Daniels I had been hiding. I do not recall why I had so much booze with me, since I had pretty much given up drinking after Dahomey—maybe because I had read too many Jack London stories about the Far North—or why I kept it hidden in my footlocker so long. I then walked back to the pilots' tent where my eight disconsolate partners sulked, unzipped the entrance fly, conspicuously flaunted a bottle in each hand with a cheery and theatrical, "Anyone want a drink?" then quickly zipped the flaps closed. A huge bulge distended the tent wall outward as seven men and one woman stormed the closed up entrance like an indoor rugby scrum. The mingled shouts of excitement and exasperation were something to hear as each tried to untangle from the others but not give away any advantage in fighting to the exit. Being a woman benefited Dorothy not at all, but she was bigger than Alex or Mike and muscled out ahead of them.

Eventually my eight thirst-crazed companions sorted themselves out, by which time I was sitting in the cook tent, contentedly glug-a-lugging rum and Coke from a can. We had transformed from sullen campers to merry adventurers, and I supplied the evening's entertainment by reciting all fifty-six stanzas of Noël Coward's rugby recitation "Eskimo Nell," learned in faraway Dahomey, which begins:

"When a man grows old and his balls go cold,
and the tip of his prick turns blue,
and it bends in the middle like a one-string fiddle,
he can tell you a tale or two."

After that it gets smutty, and as a follow-up I recited Robert Service's classic poem "The Shooting of Dan McGrew." The camaraderie in that Driftwood cook tent in August 1974, in the remote wilderness on the Arctic rim of North America, resides in memory as one of the warmest high points of my life. Perhaps because of our closeness that night, the vision of the tall, dark-haired woman appeared to me as I was falling asleep. Still in the same room cozily decorated with curios and artifacts that somehow related to me as well as to her, I knew she was smiling even though her face was again backlit. I still had no idea who she was—or if she was a real person—but she was clearly accompanying me through life.

There is nothing like a good fire to make the wilderness cozier, and luckily we had a shit-barrel for that purpose. Evenings found us gathering the day's refuse from camp and privy to burn in a fifty-five-gallon drum on which I had painted "Fuck Texaco" in rude, bright-orange letters. The flames got brighter one evening when someone observed that we had a lot of Jet A chopper fuel left over as a result of not flying during the nine-day windstorm, and that we would have to haul full fuel cans back home at the end of the season if we did not burn the fuel beforehand. No sense doing that, so to use up the fuel we soaked the nightly trash barrel lavishly in Jet A before torching it. In an additional fit of creation that could only take place in a remote tent camp with an oversupply of testosterone-marinated young males, someone came up with a more spectacular use for the excess fuel. With the shit-barrel already tossing up flames several feet high, one of us poured a half-gallon or so of Jet A into a black plastic trash bag, then swung it arm-over-arm in a forward circle as he ran at the burning barrel. The trick was to time the overhand swing so that the fuel-filled bag was on the downswing into the inferno as you ran by the shit-barrel. The ensuing WHOOMP and flaming mushroom cloud of the rising fireball showered burning embers and red-hot tin cans upon us to the accompaniment of raucous laughter. At times the burning bits were worrisome, but not on the evenings when Moley generously shared hits on his joint, at which times the fire balls were *amazing*. Had we stayed at Driftwood much longer we might have invented a new religion, given the combination of wilderness setting and personal visions.

Left to right: Jim Molnar, Mike Simmons, me, Alex Feucht, Don Oltz, behind the barrel in which we burned refuse each evening.

One of the pleasures of the wilderness is encountering animals unaffected by humans, and the first wild animal I ever saw up close was a wolf around dinnertime when someone spotted it loping toward us from the direction of Meat Mountain to the east. It headed right toward us until it stopped to inspect our camp from across the Utukok, a full-grown animal in the prime of life, magnificent in snow-white fur from head to tail. We were mesmerized by its primal beauty, its aura of command over the land, its perfection. It assessed us for a full minute, holding its head high, beautiful beyond imagining, and seemed to know that it was the very embodiment of the wilderness, then slowly trotted upstream along the Utukok and vanished from sight before anyone spoke.

We sometimes saw grizzly bears from the air, and if they were within a mile of camp we chased them away with one of the choppers, a defensive measure that is frowned upon today but seemed smart to us at the time. I went along as passenger a couple of times and observed grizzlies running twenty-five miles an hour for fifteen minutes straight, which disabused me of my previous impression that grizzlies could only sprint short distances—useful information for future years when I worked alone in the Alaska wilderness.

As thrilling as grizzly bears and wolves were, the most engaging wild animals showed up after dinner every evening in the cook tent. A couple of siksiks, or Arctic prairie dogs, which we had named Fat Ass and Skinny, popped into the tent to grab crumbs before scurrying away to store them in their burrows before returning. During one of their forays, while I was sipping vodka in Tang, I noticed that the chopper mechanic was doing some mechanical maintenance using a hypodermic needle, and my mind put two and two together. I filled a borrowed spare syringe with Smirnoff, then infused it into several of the green grapes that the siksiks loved.

When Fat Ass and Skinny next ventured into the cook tent, I rolled over some high-octane fruit, which they cautiously sniffed before they stuffed them into their cheek pouches. They made three or four trips out to stash their new treasure underground, each time reappearing just a little less steady on their four feet. Their final trip that night was memorable, because after filling their mouths with loaded grapes, right after munching a few in front of us, they were too woozy to stagger even on four feet. They crawled slowly across the tent floor toward the entrance;

formerly they had leaped over the four-inch canvas door sill without a moment's hesitation, but now they could only stare up at it like tourists at the Empire State building. Head resting on the canvas floor, neck craning upward, mouth open, Fat Ass put one wilted paw on the tent sill and collapsed, unconscious. Skinny had passed out closer to the grape supply. I gently picked up their limp little carcasses—after putting on some heavy leather gloves in case the possibly rabid little bastards tried to bite me—and set them outside beneath staked ropes along the tent wall, so nobody would step on the rodents while they slumbered. I never gave them a second chance to imbibe, because our vodka supply was running low.

Moley and I learned a valuable lesson in sanitation when we spotted some buildings from the air near the coast of the Chukchi Sea, an arm of the Arctic Ocean. The large trailers on skids turned out to be a geophysical camp, which in the winter were pulled by tractors around the North Slope while crews set off underground explosive charges to learn about subsurface rock layers from the reflected sound waves, but which were in storage during summer. The sole occupant was a caretaker, who was delighted to have company drop in and he plied us with coffee while talking nonstop; we were his first visitors all summer and it was late August.

In the next instant the old fellow casually voiced magical words while pointing to the trailer next door: "There's a hot shower here. Would you guys like to use it?" Moley, Hank the pilot and I launched ourselves at the exit door as one man, grabbing for the handle. By the creative use of elbows, knees and guttural threats I won the tussle and sprinted into the shower trailer. My god, it was luxurious to feel hot water pour over my head and body and get clean for the first time in three weeks. We were three happy and clean campers when we lifted off and winged back to camp, and for the entire hour ride home we joked about how we would lord it over our smelly campmates who, like us, had been reluctant to bathe in the Utukok's ice waters.

My life has been rich in irony, which displayed itself all too well when we landed at Driftwood. Moley, Hank and I strutted our cleansed bodies before our begrimed tent mates and bragged about our cleanliness, proudly displaying our clean white hands and faces for all to see. Then the stench of their rotted bodies hit us, and the effect was like being downwind from a decomposing goat. Enveloped in the ghastly effluence of humanity at its worst, we three well-scrubbed human beings gagged and sidled to the upwind side of these filthy wretches. They repaid us for our conceit by forming a circle around us and flapping their arms up and down with vigor while yelling vengeful catcalls. Fortunately, the caretaker at the geophysical camp had said that the rest of our group was welcome to fly in for showers too, and we enthusiastically encouraged our stinky campmates to pile into both choppers. Lesson learned: I never again made the mistake of getting clean in a tent camp of unwashed bodies.

The worlds of Corvettes and helicopters do not usually collide, but they did one afternoon a few thousand feet over the North Slope while returning to Driftwood after a long day of collecting rocks and fossils. I was up front in the Hughes 500 with pilot Hank while Moley was in the back seat. Moley and I were trying to stay awake but the constant drone of the engine and rotor blades was beckoning us to sleep. Falling asleep was the last thing we wanted to do, since Hank would then perform one of his patented "death dives," during which he plunged the machine earthward while loudly bellowing "AAAAA!" until we bolted awake in stark terror while he laughed out loud like God playing the trickster. Not cute after the second or third time.

Sitting up front in the four-place bird, I saw from the gauges that we were chugging along at a mere 100 miles an hour, and from our altitude it seemed like we were barely making headway; the same lake or hill seemed to hang motionless below the bubble for long minutes. At this point I jokingly commented over the radio something to the effect of,

"Heck, my '63 Corvette back home goes a lot faster than this, and girls like it better too." I looked over at Hank and smiled; he looked back at me and did not smile. Moley, with finely tuned instincts for survival, chimed in with, "Don't do anything crazy, Hank! Lou didn't mean anything by that! Your whirlypig is way faster than his Vette!"

I am not sure Moley helped our cause by blurting out "whirlypig," since Hank was not fond of that nickname for his flying machine. Still, based on Moley's psychological reading of the pilot, he knew Hank a lot better than I did. Hank the God of Flying was silent for a few moments in deep thought, then calmly asked, "Can your Corvette do this?"

From 1,000 feet up, Hank gave the bird full throttle, pulled up hard on the collective and we surged six-tenths of a mile straight up to 4,000 feet. We hung there for a few long moments, during which I was smugly congratulating myself that our upward surge had not been all *that* scary, and I was dealing with it just fine—until Hank turned the engine off! Holy shit! I had never been in a silent helicopter! Or one plunging straight down! 3,500—3,000—2,500—2,000—this was getting serious. We hurtled to earth like a stone, one thrown by a vengeful god. All of a sudden those lakes and hills that had been creeping by molasses-like were expanding upward with astonishing speed to fill the clear bubble below my boots.

"Okay," I blurted out in a shaky voice, "your chopper's faster than my Vette! You're right, I take it back, girls *hate* my car. Turn the goddam engine on!"

Our sicko pilot was slouched down in his seat like a rag doll, his helmeted head nodding forward in feigned sleep, his hands slack on the controls. I peered out the bubble between my boots; the ground was twice as big as before. The rotor blades were slowing down. We had fallen at least two thousand feet and were mere seconds away from becoming a dusty mushroom cloud on the tundra. Hank had gone insane and we were going to die! Moley started screaming something about my ancestry and personal habits while hitting my helmeted head with his pointy rock hammer, making a hollow "thwack" sound, but I ignored him in the developing emergency. He was normally a pretty relaxed person, but now he was agitated and blamed the whole thing on me, even though my hands were not on the chopper controls, and began raving that he was "gonna kill" me. Not the most soothing words to hear from someone with whom I shared a sleeping tent.

I was silently staring wide-eyed at the slumped pilot, trying to think of anything to say, and finally blurted out,

"You can *have* my Vette, just start the fucking engine." Hank perked right up, suddenly bright and alert.

"Really? I can have your Sting Ray?" he said.

"Uh, yeah, sure," I replied, "just start the goddam engine."

A quick downward glance revealed an enormous Earth rushing up at us like we were an inbound meteorite. With immense relief I heard the whiney starter motor crank over as Hank spun the turbine engine up to speed. We kept falling, but at a slower rate and finally leveled out at 500 feet.

It seemed to be all over and we were alive, so I began to breathe easier, even though Moley was still loudly striking my helmet with his steel rock pick. He did not think I was sorry enough, even though I kept saying I was. Unfortunately, Hank was not done yet with his bizarre flying demo and chimed in with, "I'll bet your goddam Vette can't do this either!" and began to fly in a sort of vertical sine wave the last few miles to camp, like some demented mechanical kangaroo. We zoomed up to 1,000 feet, plunged to 500, lunged back to 1,000, plummeted again to 500 *ad nauseum*, literally, because Moley and I were both on the verge of losing our cookies. The thirty-minute ride back to camp brought forth a long and sometimes admirable string of swearing from Moley, the likes of which one is privileged to hear but once or twice in a lifetime, even if it was directed at me. Partway home, Moley became weak enough from nausea to stop whacking my helmet.

The normal procedure when landing was for the passengers to wait until the machine had settled onto the ground, then look for the pilot to give a nod that it was OK to exit the doors, carefully closing—not slamming—and latching the doors behind us. However, before the chopper skids even touched the ground, while still a couple of feet high, I bolted out the front door and was off like a scalded dog, while an enraged Moley lunged from the rear door swinging his pointy rock hammer at my now helmetless head while cursing a blue streak. We had been friends from USC days, but now he had turned mean. His bellowed oaths sounded serious enough that I did not slow down until I had run the full length of our tundra airstrip, then cut behind the shithouse tent, and over past the 55-gallon drum I had painted "Fuck Texaco" on, at which point even he was too tired to carry out his vivid death threats. I cowered and abjectly apologized, promising never again to taunt a whirlypig pilot to the point of insanity. We were friends again. But I did not sit near him at dinner, or stand close to him at the ritual post-dinner shit-burning. Live and learn, as they say. Compared to a Hughes 500, there really are some (scary) things that a 1963 Corvette Sting Ray cannot do. But, I still know which one girls like better.

I learned a lifelong lesson about the kind of clothing to wear in the wilderness when Moley and I were sitting on the tundra beside a small river at the end of the day waiting for the chopper at an agreed-upon pickup spot. We heard the chopper approaching but waited for it to land and have the pilot nod that it was safe to approach. Instead of landing, the machine flew along slowly past us, a mere 100 feet away, while we waved vigorously but unseen. It returned and passed us by again before it dawned on us that we were wearing tan clothing and the guys in the chopper could not pick us out from the background dirt. We stood up and waved, but they still did not see us until I used my Brunton geological compass to flash the sun in their eyes. The pilot and Oltzie accused us of hiding from them for fun, and I learned the lesson to always wear bright clothing in the wilderness.

On every future trip to the Arctic I wore brighter clothes than anyone else, to the point of being kidded about it, and I always carried a square yard of DayGlo orange nylon to wave for extra visibility. For much of my career in the remote wilderness I would work alone, and it was a revelation to learn early on how difficult it is to spot someone on the ground from an aircraft. A seemingly small detail like clothing color can turn a routine pickup into a possible survival situation.

The only exit from an overloaded bush plane was this small window.

I made a major scientific discovery one morning while brushing my teeth in the Utukok River. Squatting on the riverbank at the usual place, while scooping icy water into my mouth I noticed fossil mollusks on rock chips in the river gravel. Spreading them in my hand, I recognized species that were about five million years old and found only in southern Alaska, a thousand miles south of Driftwood and a lot younger than the 100,000,000-year-old Mesozoic rocks we were collecting for Texaco. These mollusks, when alive, could only have migrated to northern Alaska, where we were camped, if Bering Strait—the seaway that connects the Arctic Ocean with the Pacific and separates Alaska from Russia—was open. The age of Bering Strait's opening was one of the greatest of geological mysteries and I was holding the answer in my hand! The few shell scraps I clutched meant that a major "Bering Strait" outcrop loaded with fossil shells must lie upstream along the Utukok.

I was already writing the scientific paper in my head as I dashed over to Alex Feucht, our party chief, and excitedly told him the news; then we returned to the discovery site and picked more shells from the riverbed. We showed them to the other guys, who were suiting up for the day. I then proudly announced that we would make scientific history by hopping in the choppers and scouting up the Utukok until we found the outcrop of young "Bering Strait" rocks.

I assumed my buddies would be as enthusiastic as I was to track down this paleontological mystery. However, Alex declared that Texaco had sent us here at great expense, we had only a few days to go in the field season, and he did not think we should be wasting precious time and fuel chasing after something of no petroleum-specific interest.

"But this is *Bering Strait*," I said. "Geologists have scoured Alaska for 100 years for evidence of when that seaway opened."

"Yeah," replied Alex, "but we're short on time for getting our own work done."

"We could make history!" I declared. "Bering Strait is the last seaway on the planet whose age is unknown."

"Right," Alex said listlessly, "but Texaco doesn't sell history, it sells oil."

"But, this is science. Texaco would get credit for making a big scientific breakthrough instead of just being a money-grubbing oil company. Our bosses would get their names in the paper, us too." I pleaded.

"I think Doctor Clam has a point," added Oltzie, the other educated member of our field party. "Making a big scientific discovery would be great for the company's image." Things were looking up. Oltzie had a PhD in paleontology too, even if he only studied fossil pollen grains under a microscope.

"I don't know," said Mike, "it's late in the month, the weather's turning cold, and we have to be out of here in a week. If we spend a day at this Bering Strait place, then a storm kicks up for the next week, Texaco's gonna be mad."

"Who knows when anyone will be here again," I pleaded, starting to worry at the change in momentum. "We're the field party to make the big discovery. You need a shell specialist like me to trace the specimens to their source in the mountains; nobody with my knowledge of Cenozoic mollusks will ever again be at Driftwood."

Alex was staring at storm clouds gathering in the east and declared in a voice filled with doom for my plans, "I think we better do Texaco's work for now. If we have a day left at the end, Lou can go look upstream for the Bering Strait shells."

I could hear the door shutting on the most important scientific discovery I would ever make. Or not make, as it was turning out. Alex's simple-minded devotion to the work objectives of a grease company was torpedoing my plan to solve one of the great scientific mysteries in Pacific-Arctic oceanography and paleogeography. Science was being sacrificed on the altar of Big Oil.

"Besides," said Moley, "the chopper would use a whole tank of fuel farting around in the mountains. That's seventy-five gallons we might need ourselves."

"We have enough fuel to burn shit every night!" I protested. "We have plenty!" I said in a rising, agitated voice.

"OK," said Alex, "I'll take a vote. Who wants to go look for the Bering Strait shells tomorrow morning?" Oltzie and I held up our hands. "Now who wants to work for Texaco tomorrow?" Moley, Mike and Alex held up their hands.

"That's it," said Alex looking straight at me, "you're voted down. We won't go on a scientific side trip."

I was stunned. They were kissing off a major scientific discovery just to save seventy-five gallons of kerosene and some flying time. What kind of retards was I working with? I begged, I pleaded, I threatened—about what, I do not remember—I pouted; nothing worked. Science had lost out to Big Oil on a 3-2 vote.

I was tormented, but helpless. We were a good twenty miles from the foothills of the Brooks Range to the south, where the Bering Strait fossil shells must crop out. I could not walk that far—and back—with a full backpack and loaded rifle and get any kind of work done. All that day in the field I decried the injustice of it all to Moley as we collected rocks and took notes.

"I can't believe those idiots voted against making a huge scientific discovery," I nearly shouted, forgetting for the moment that Moley was on the other side of the issue.

"Thanks," said Moley, "it's always good to have one's opinion respected."

"Not you, it's those other idiots," I fibbed. "They can't conceive of anything more important than grubbing for oil. Like science doesn't matter."

"Well, Uncle Tex paid a hell of a lot to put our asses on the North Slope, so we have to think of doing a good job for the company first."

"Yeah, sure," I grumbled, my enthusiasm for the discussion having evaporated.

I was in a black mood back in camp and did not say a word during dinner. Later, during our after-dinner ritual of standing around the flaming shit-barrel watching our day's waste turn into heat and flames, Alex brought up the Bering Strait fossils. I was sulky and murmured about it not being *that* important, but when I looked up from staring at my boots I noticed that Little Leader, as we called Alex, was smiling. Smiling? At my discomfiture? How cruel he was; had I misjudged him for the past year? Then I noticed that *everybody* was smiling. At me. Was my fly open? Was I on fire from the shit-barrel? I checked my clothing for smoldering spots. I could not puzzle it out.

Then Alex said, "The young fossil shells were left in the chopper when it came from its last job in southern Alaska, a thousand miles away."

"Yeah," said Hank the pilot, "I was sweeping out the chopper and Alex noticed the shells on the floor. I told him I'd been working along the south coast with some other geologists just before joining you guys, and Alex knew the shells from there were relatively young compared to North Slope fossils."

"So we put our heads together and decided the best use of the fossils was to salt the Utukok River right where you brush your teeth at the same spot every day," declared a grinning Moley.

"It worked like a charm," smiled Oltzie. "You fell for it hook, line and sinker, Dr. Clam."

"We were all watching you brush your teeth when you found the shells. It was hard as hell not to laugh out loud," declared Mike.

Everyone was in on the gag. They had salted the river bed with fossils just where I was sure to see them during my morning ablutions. I suppose I had a blank look on my face as the truth sunk in, but I had been the butt of a clever practical joke and could not help but laugh too. I did not know it then, but later in my career I would get a legitimate crack at resolving the age of Bering Strait.

If events had gone just a bit differently the next morning, it would have been my last one on earth. My final photo would have been with Oltzie and Hank looking happy and relaxed beside the egg-shaped Hughes 500. Once the picture-taking was over, Hank and Oltzie got in the front seats and I buckled myself into the inertial-reel shoulder harness in the left rear. Hank fired up the turbine engine, checked the gauges, made sure that no one outside was too close, spun up the blades, then lifted off and crossed over the Utukok. I once again enjoyed the panoramic overview of our tent camp strewn along the river's right bank and settled in for the hour-long commute as we rose through 300 feet.

At that instant there was a tremendous BANG just above my head, where the engine and transmission were located, and an acrid burning smell filled the cabin. Three things happened in the next split second: Hank flicked the chopper into autorotation mode by tilting the nose of the machine upward; he twisted the rotor blades to their minimum pitch to lessen their air drag; and the three of us simultaneously shouted, "Oh, shit!" into our headsets. Then we fell 300 feet and had hardly finished our shout when we thumped hard onto the tundra. A quick calculation shows that falling at a rate of 32 feet/second/second made our earthward fall last a bit over four seconds, but our surprised and muddled brains skipped over a couple of those.

Tents lighted during a nine-day wind storm at Driftwood.

My eyes were firmly shut when we hit the ground, in anticipation of The End. I peeked out of slitted lids when the crashing and banging stopped, my fists clenched tight against my body, jaws locked tight, my head pulled into my shoulders, not knowing if I was dead or alive. It took me a couple of long seconds to comprehend that I was still alive, while trying to decide whether or not heaven looked like the inside of a helicopter cabin. I had to remind myself to start breathing.

I had unbuckled my inertial-reel shoulder harness and cracked open my door, assuming deep inside that we were going to explode or at least burn when we hit the ground. Fortunately, neither one of those nasty things happened. Our intrepid pilot shouted for me to shut the door—which I did not do—as he jockeyed the controls around and gingerly lifted the machine from the ground. I had assumed we would walk back to camp—why *not*, since the whirlypig has just crapped out and we were only a quarter mile from our tents?—and here was Hank bravely offering up Oltzie's and my lives to his personal experiment in nursing a ruptured helicopter home. Gee, will we make it or not? I wanted out of that goddam machine more than I had ever wanted anything in my life. The memory of five of our comrades dying in a helicopter crash in this same part of Alaska just two months earlier flashed through my mind, and I wondered if they had felt the same things I experienced as they tumbled to earth.

The transmission overhead was making a loud grinding sound and emitting billows of acrid smoke as we skimmed across the tundra at walking speed. My heart was in my throat as I watched the ground creep by through the door opening; I was primed to leap for my life if the machine crapped out again, although the rotor blades slashing overhead and the maniacally spinning tail rotor a few feet behind left me with limited leaping options.

Crossing the Utukok was slow-motion agony, because the machine would certainly pitch over sideways and potentially drown us if the skids touched the rapidly flowing ice water just two feet below. I saw the people in camp, just across the river but an eternity away, rooted in place as they watched us crawl toward them. Dorothy, the camp cook, had actually seen us fall and had flashed back to Texaco's fatal June crash when she had been in camp.

When we touched ground by the fuel cache, I could not get away from that devil machine fast enough, although Oltzie was a few feet ahead and showing me a clean pair of heels. He later asked why I was so slow to leave the crippled machine, but he had the bigger front door to jump out of. Hank stayed at the controls to shut down the machine, but he knew more than we did about its mechanical safety and did not have to deal with our overheated imaginations. Our mechanic discovered that a transmission bearing had disintegrated just over my head and had a replacement flown in from Fairbanks the next day. The Hughes 500 performed flawlessly the rest of the summer, but the sensation of falling in it was permanently seared into my brain. Oltzie and I acted as if we took the accident in stride when we talked with the others, but I knew that inside he was shaking too.

By early September it was time to pack up camp and head home, before we ran into "termination dust," the year's first snowfall that curtails many activities on the Slope. We broke camp about midday and everyone but Dorothy, Mike and I lifted off in the two choppers, one headed south to Fairbanks and the other north to Barrow.

The plan was for Alex to guide a twin-engine de Havilland Twin Otter bush plane from Barrow back to Driftwood to evacuate us. Driftwood was too insignificant to appear even on USGS topo maps and none but the most experienced bush pilots would know where the place was. We hoped the plane would arrive about six o'clock in the evening, although bush planes have no schedules, and we had plenty of work to do bundling up tents, boxes of rocks, surplus food, and camp gear. Thanks to our nightly tossing of fuel into the shit-barrel, we did not have to worry about hauling many fuel tins home; we simply flattened a few hundred two-gallon cans and bundled them up.

It began to rain hard in the midafternoon while we perched on our mounds of gear and waited for the inbound Twin Otter. This was in the days before we knew about the necessity of wearing rainsuits in the Arctic, so Mike, Dorothy and I got thoroughly soaked.

"Looks like the river's overflowing," said Dorothy as she pointed over to where our tents had been staked. A tongue of turbid brown water had overflowed the Utukok's right bank and was eating its way across our runway.

"Crap," said Mike, "there's barely enough airstrip to land on now."

"Yeah, it's excavating a channel straight across our strip," I exclaimed as we watched the water progress. "Now there's a third less length to land or take off from."

The rain pounded down heavily for hours and we began to wonder if we had been forgotten, or maybe that the plane from Barrow with Alex in it had gotten into trouble. The heavy downpour tapered off around 9:00 p.m. and an hour later we heard a plane and anxiously looked to the *north*west toward Barrow for the Twin Otter, which is a boxy high-winged plane. To our surprise, an unidentified low-wing plane approached from the *south*west. As it buzzed low over us, we saw that it was a well-used Piper Twin Beech with numerous dents and faded markings; once landed, the pilot introduced himself as Buck Masters, who turned out to be a well-known bush pilot. We were glad to see him but wondered why he had come from the wrong direction in the wrong plane.

Buck informed us that Alex, our party chief, had gotten to Barrow in our Hughes 500 chopper and located the Twin Otter that Texaco had hired. They took off after he pointed out to the pilot on a topographic map exactly where in the middle of nowhere Driftwood was situated. Alex intently focused on the terrain features to keep track of their location, because there were no roads, trails, buildings or other cultural artifacts on the North Slope's nearly featureless tundra. While counting rivers and marking distinctively shaped lakes to mark their progress, he also noticed that the pilot looked uncomfortable and was sweating.

"What are those, like, squares all over the ground?" asked the pilot.

"That's patterned ground," explained Alex, "ice polygons formed by freezing and thawing." Patterned ground covered thousands of square miles of the North Slope and Alex began wondering why the so-called bush pilot did not know about it.

"Why are the lakes all lined up like that, with one straight side?" continued the pilot.

"They're thaw lakes," said Alex, "they're only liquid in the summer and the constant wind from one direction erodes the downwind shore into a straight line."

It was highly unusual for a bush pilot to exclaim in wonder at common North Slope landscape features, as if he had never seen them before.

"Haven't you flown on the Slope before?" inquired Alex.

"Uh, no, not at all. This is my first job" admitted the pilot.

"Your first job on the Slope?"

"Well, no, this is my first job as a bush pilot."

Alex was flabbergasted. "You've never flown in Alaska in the bush before?"

"No. I've been flying Boeing 707 airliners up til now. Today's my first day bush flying. I came to Alaska to find out what it's all about and I don't like it. I thought it would be fun, but it's just scary."

Halfway from Barrow to Driftwood the tyro bush pilot admitted that he was frightened out of his wits, said he did not want to be a bush pilot after all, did not want to continue the flight and did not want to make his first tundra landing in the middle of nowhere. He carefully banked the Twin Otter and pointed it back toward Barrow as Alex threw a fit in vain. If he had thought to bring a gun, it would have been a no-brainer to force the pilot to continue ahead and pick us up. Another lesson that I filed away for the future, except I never ran into another chicken-hearted bush pilot.

Bush planes in Alaska are booked weeks and months ahead of time, and pilots can legally fly only so many hours per day, so Alex could not find a plane in Barrow. Fortunately, the dispatcher at the airport took pity on him, called around the North Slope and found Buck Masters in the Eskimo village of Kotzebue, in the Bering Strait region some hundreds of miles to the south. Negotiating by radio, Buck agreed to pick us up since he was returning in the direction of our camp from another flying job, which is why his Piper Twin Beech, instead of a de Havilland Twin Otter, rolled to a stop at Driftwood. It took an hour to load our bulky, heavy gear into the smaller Twin Beech, then Dorothy, Mike and I crawled on top of the pile, there being no passenger seats.

Takeoff was going to be a problem. Not only was our smaller plane overloaded, but the overflowing Utukok River had dug a deep ditch across our landing strip two-thirds of the way along its length. To make matters worse, hours of torrential rain had turned the muddy tundra airstrip into sticky gumbo that clung to the tires. Buck backed the Twin Beach as far onto the lumpy tundra as he dared, not wanting the tail wheel to sink into the muck, then revved up the engines for a long time, while standing on the brakes, until the whole plane shook violently.

Dorothy and Mike had drawn, pale faces, as I undoubtedly did. Dorothy made the sign of the cross as Buck let off the brakes and we began to roll forward slowly and reluctantly picked up speed. My mind fixated on the moat partway down the muddy strip and I wondered if it would be our final destination. The engines roared, the plane shuddered and bumped down the primitive airstrip, then I felt the fuselage go horizontal as the tail wheel lifted off. Unfortunately, the main wheels were still making grooves in the tundra as the sucking mud clung to them. We were almost in the moat by that time, but Buck magically made the plane hop up just long enough to clear the rain-cut ditch, then set it down again as we splashed toward the end of the strip. Huge plumes of dirty water spumed back from the wheels and clots of mud flying off the wheels thudded a loud tattoo against the fuselage. We had almost reached the oil drums I had painted bright orange to mark the end of the strip when Buck lifted the plane off the ground and retracted the wheels as we labored skyward.

The takeoff had been hair-raising and I started to breathe again once we left the ground. Buck slowly gained altitude as the engines strained toward Fairbanks, 300 miles south. A month's worth of rock samples, plus eight heavy ten-foot by ten-foot canvas tents, fuel tins, and camping gear with three passengers was more than the little plane was designed to haul, especially over the 9,000-foot Brooks Range. Still, we were safe now, and while belly-flopped onto a rolled-up tent, I gazed in a reverie at the natural wonders going by below and thanked my lucky stars that I was fortunate enough to experience such wild and rugged country. I was living the adventurous, emotional life I had dreamed of long ago as a boy in San Pedro.

It is truly shocking how fortune can so quickly flip to misfortune in the wilderness. Our luck slipped away amid a gush of oil from the starboard engine as the prop slowed then stopped. We all turned toward the pilot, who was furiously flipping switches and, as evidenced by his moving lips amid the roar of the one remaining engine, cursing up a storm. Holy shit, we were going down! We had been cruising serenely above the scenery and now we were headed down toward it. The needle-sharp peaks of the uninhabited and desolate Brooks Range were now reaching their stony fingers closer and closer to our fragile aluminum coffin.

My mouth felt like cotton and I broke out in a cold sweat as I stared out the porthole. I turned toward Dorothy and Mike, and they looked frightened too; then we all turned toward Buck Masters, the only person in the world who could extend our lives for more than an hour, who shouted over the roar of the one straining engine,

"We can't make it to Fairbanks. It's too far away and the mountains are too high. Our only chance is to land at Kotzebue on the coast, where I live."

I yelled back, "We can toss out any of our stuff. The boxes of rocks and the tents would be easy to push out the hatch." We five geologists had spent a month collecting thousands of pounds of rocks that were of great interest to Texaco, but were just ballast in our coffins to us. All three of us agreed, "Toss out the heavy stuff!"

Buck replied, "Let's save that for a last resort. If we can't get over the last ridge before the coast, we'll toss the rocks and tents. And don't open the hatch without my okay, you might get sucked out if you're not roped to the plane." Sounded reasonable to us, except for tossing the heavy stuff as a "last resort." Why not do that as a "first resort" to increase our chance of survival?

There was nothing to do but silently ponder our fate while spread-eagled awkwardly atop rolled-up tents, crates of rocks, industrial-size propane tanks for tent heaters, Dorothy's kitchen gear, and bundles of flattened fuel tins. Never before or since has time crawled by so slowly. I have been as focused as anyone else at times in life but never both focused and heart-stoppingly *terrified* at the same time. The hands of my watch seemed frozen in place.

The mountains got higher and higher, as our overloaded plane with its broken engine steadily lost altitude, until we were flying *between* the jagged snow-sheathed peaks instead of *above* them. There were no settle-ments, no villages, no flat place to land such a large plane; there were only potential crash sites passing beneath our fragile wings. A couple of times we spotted a dirt strip laboriously hacked out of a narrow valley by hand, where prospectors or hunters had once landed a tiny Piper Cub on soft, cartoonishly plump "tundra tires." Our Twin Beech could not land on any of those strips even if we ran out of fuel; we were either going to land on one engine at Kotzebue, wherever that was, or we were going to disintegrate on some nameless Brooks Range mountainside, our remains, picked over by the wildlife, and found the following summer by a search party.

I must have been in a kind of stupor or shock, because I cannot remember almost two hours of time. I have flash images of the mountain peaks getting farther apart and the valleys getting wider and the rugged ground closer, but not a coherent memory of flying along. I snapped awake when Buck shouted,

"There's only one more ridge left before the coast."

Dorothy, Mike and I crowded together behind the cockpit, straining to see the last barrier to our salvation. All I saw was an ominous, dark ridge looming ahead. Dead ahead.

I asked Buck, "Is that ridge straight ahead of us the last one? Is it really lower than we are?"

Buck shot back, "That's it! I think we're high enough to make it over."

I could not believe we were talking about the same topographic feature. The "ridge" I saw was a dark massif that looked to be higher than we were. Even on one engine and overloaded, our Twin Beech barreled along at a tremendous rate, pointed straight at the side of a mountain, so we were not going to have long to think about our fate.

Buck was the only one breathing as we cleared the ridge at phone-pole height. To make things worse, this ridge seemed to be one of the few in the surrounding mountains that had trees growing on it. The tips of tall trees rooted on top of the ridge flashed by at wing level in front of my bugged-out eyes. For one heart-stopping moment I was sure we were going to disintegrate against the trees and rocks. Later, Dorothy said she saw a fox running away from the spot where we zoomed over the ridge. We were that close.

A whole new world—in this case, the rest of our lives—opened up as we zoomed high above the flat Arctic Ocean coastal plain. Flat ground never looked so good; we were saved! Buck made a beeline to the Eskimo village of Kotzebue and our troubles seemed to be over, until he reminded us, "Hold on to something big, I still have to land this thing on one engine. We're pretty heavy and she isn't responding to the controls too well."

Damn, we still might die in the next few minutes. Buck had radioed ahead to assemble an emergency crew, which consisted of some locals in a pickup holding fire extinguishers and shovels. They would use the extinguishers if we were only a little unlucky, the shovels if we were a lot unlucky.

The entire population turned out to watch Buck set us down gently on the paved runway, and there my memory pretty much ends. I do recall leaving the plane and walking over to a wooden building where we spent the night, but I have zero recollection of dinner, sleeping, breakfast. Nothing. The next thing I recall is getting into that damned Twin Beech the following morning to continue our aborted flight to Fairbanks. Buck explained that an engine oil line had parted and that it was an easy overnight fix. Dorothy, Mike and I had a different take on the matter, namely that the plane was cursed and we should not even think about getting on it again. Buck laughed at our worries, herded us aboard, and we flew to Fairbanks, Dorothy's home, in maybe three hours, every moment of which we were staring at the engines and praying silently.

Left to right: Alex Feucht, me, Don Oltz, Jim Molnar; enjoying a lunch stop on a North Slope ridge.

Our reassembled field party celebrated that night at the Malamute Saloon in Cripple Creek, outside of Fairbanks, everyone in an upbeat mood after our month on the Slope. Enjoying the safety of civilization after the perils of 30 days in the bush, we all drank too much and that night I saw the only aurora borealis I would ever witness, while lying inebriated in the bed of a pickup truck on the way back to our motel. A band of luminous green arced across the heavens from horizon to horizon, like the handle on an Earth-size Easter basket. It was not a moving curtain of light like I had seen in pictures, but still it was too perfect for this world and lured my thoughts into a larger realm. While fully enraptured, my inner eye fixed upon the woman in the cozy room, whom I almost felt was gazing upward beside me, her head resting upon her hands, and my last experience in Alaska that summer seemed to be more of a beckoning onward than a departure.

My longing for an adventuresome scientific life had been sparked by reading about Roy Chapman Andrews's paleontological exploits, and I had wished with my whole heart to have adventures and perilous confrontations with primal Nature and to be challenged and tested to the ultimate. My first field summer in Alaska had been a cautionary tale about being careful what one wished for. Being tested was one thing, but the prospect of an early grave was another. Until that August I had not realized that the flip side of adventure in the wilds of Alaska was disaster and possibly death. Still, by the end of it all, deep inside I knew that I could not get enough of the wilderness, that my life was to be intimately bound to this visceral, remote and surreal part of the planet.

My inchoate longing for wilderness science and adventure *somewhere* now had a lodestone—Alaska. After a disaster-fraught summer like mine, most people would not think of returning to the Far North, but I could not wait to get back. I had seen the northern wilderness and just as clearly glimpsed my destiny, and even though danger was a big part of the attraction, I had learned many lessons about survival. My doctoral studies had touched upon Alaskan Cenozoic molluscan faunas, so I knew that there were extensive unstudied rock formations with marine mollusks in a state two-and-a-half times the size of Texas. The scientific possibilities seemed irresistible, as did the smorgasbord of adventure and danger that the scientific pursuit entailed. Deeper down was a yet-unrealized desire to make up for my especially dull growing-up years and to burst forth in the full-blooded pursuit of my boyhood dreams.

Left to right: Don Oltz, pilot Hank, and me, ten minutes before we fell from an altitude of 300 feet when a helicopter part failed. Our fuel dump is in the background.

Leaving Texaco was easy when I won a competitive post-doctoral fellowship, then a job, at the U.S. Geological Survey (USGS or simply "Survey") in Menlo Park, California, which was then perhaps the greatest concentration of top-notch geologists the world has ever seen. By some galactic synchronicity, the Survey needed someone to conduct research on Alaskan Cenozoic marine mollusks at the same time I was falling in love with the Alaskan wilderness. That was *exactly* how I wanted to spend my life, as a research paleontologist at a first-class facility, with wilderness adventures added to the mix. My life would transcend the normal quiescent path of a scholar, which is something I had instinctively wished for as a boy. I would enjoy all the satisfaction of labwork, writing scientific papers and speaking at conferences, but these would be underlain by a solid foundation of wilderness paleontology and adventure. I had miraculously hit the bullseye that I had drawn a bead on 22 years earlier, when I had first read *All About Dinosaurs.* ▲

LITUYA BAY, ALASKA

The end of the day found us hiking north on the bleak beach into blustery cold rain, endeavoring to warm up by hiking in the direction from which our pickup helicopter was coming, when my partner suddenly yelled out "Bear!" and roughly ripped the rifle from my shoulder. He chambered a .30-caliber round like he knew what he was doing and leveled the gun at a huge grizzly that was just coming up onto its hind legs from a patch of brush that had concealed it. I definitely *did not* know what to do; being the son of a commercial fisherman, I knew little about firearms.

"Holy shit, that thing's ten feet tall!" I exclaimed. The gigantic predator was only fifty feet from us and making a low throaty growl. It had been scrounging for food in stunted willows that fronted the coastal hardwoods and my more experienced partner had detected its presence from the way it disturbed branches as it rooted along.

"Don't move," he commanded. "It's close and we have to see what it'll do."

My first USGS field day, in front of La Pérouse glacier near Lituya Bay, Alaska, 1975.

The bear's chestnut brown fur dripped rainwater as it appraised us with its clawed paws hanging loose from its lifted arms and its snout sniffing high for our scent. The sheer fright of being so close to a full-grown grizzly, as powerful a predator as exists on earth, while it was making up its mind to turn us into food or not, was close to overwhelming. I froze and waited, not knowing what to do. The grizzly abruptly got down on all fours with a loud "Whuf!" and went back to rooting around in the brush. My partner and I stepped backwards for the next 100 yards, going in our original direction, he holding the rifle at the ready. Even after we put the bear behind us, we swiveled our heads backward like two inquisitive owls every few seconds for the next mile or so. The thunder of big rollers crashing in from the Gulf of Alaska onto the rocky shoreline beside us injected additional drama into the scenario and increased our anxiety by muffling any sounds the bear might make charging us. This was the first of my many close grizzly encounters over the next three decades, and far from the most dramatic.

It had been an exciting first day collecting fossil shells in the mountainous rainforests around Lituya Bay, a fiord in southeastern Alaska, on my initial USGS scientific expedition into the wilderness. The trip marked a solid advancement in my career over my collecting work for Texaco the previous summer at Driftwood. Instead of the results of my summer's efforts being secreted in company files, I was *supposed to* publish the results of my Lituya Bay investigations and add to human knowledge of the Far North.

The previous day I had watched Juneau, with its quaint wood-framed buildings, nestled among vertiginous mountains falling to the sea at the head of a fiord, fall behind from the fantail of the USGS research vessel *Don Miller*.

"I'm living out my boyhood dream of heading into the wilderness to do science," I said to my fellow geologist, Vince, a burly but baby-faced guy my age who had worked in southeastern Alaska previously.

"We're definitely lucky dogs," he replied. "Just remember we're going into as wild a place as there is on earth. First you have to come back, then you can publish whatever you find."

"Yeah, there's that," I said almost inaudibly, thinking back to last summer's helicopter and plane catastrophes and lost companions.

"The rainforest jungle we'll be in makes it hard to even find rocks and fossils, and you can hardly see the grizzlies through the foliage even when they're close, so you have to stay alert all the time," he continued. "Plus, we'll be taking off and landing in wind and rain from a ship's helipad that's smaller than a driveway. That'll be a first for me too."

"That wouldn't make a very good Chamber of Commerce talk," I commented dryly, and we both snorted in amusement. Despite his warning speech, I felt vast satisfaction at being a member of a geological research team setting off into the unstudied wilderness for a month. I could not have felt more excited or, to be honest, more proud of myself for persevering through the vicissitudes of life to achieve my boyhood dream of hunting fossils in the wilderness.

We hove to in front of Lituya Bay after a 100-mile overnight run, and I saw that unlike the spacious fiords in Scandinavian postcards, this one had an entrance only about 100 feet wide, or only about three times the beam of our 105-foot vessel. As our captain scoped out the currents and wind before making his run at the bay entrance, I remembered that the bay's discoverer in 1786, the Frenchman Jean-Francois de La Pérouse, had lost twenty-one men right here when he misjudged the currents and tide and two small boats overturned. Our own captain made a better job of it and we anchored in the middle of the nine-mile by two-mile fiord. Strangely, he did not appear again for the next four weeks, taking meals alone in his tiny wheelhouse where he stayed continuously drunk. About halfway through our month, a single-engine float plane landed in the bay to deliver mail for us and a case of scotch for the captain.

Lituya Bay is famous among Arctic geologists for a landslide-induced surge of water in 1958 that produced the highest wave in world history when forty million cubic yards of mountain plunged into the head of the bay and kicked up a wave 1,720 feet high. It was easy for us to see how tall the wave had been, because it splintered millions of huge trees high up the mountainsides and the denuded slopes were clearly visible, and a cause for worry, as we sailed into the bay only seventeen years later.

Research Vessel Don J. Miller, *on which we lived for a month moored in Lituya Bay.*

The geology around Lituya Bay was virtually unknown and no paleontologist had ever been there, so my assignment was to decipher the ages of the rock strata using marine mollusks and to infer the paleoenvironments—especially the paleoclimate—represented by the shell species. The R/V *Don Miller* had a tiny helipad built into its upper works, upon which sat a helicopter surrounded by fifty-five-gallon fuel drums, an arrangement that made for anxious takeoffs and landings, especially when the boat was rocking in a storm. Not exactly LAX, but good enough for our purposes. Much of the time I worked with the party chief, Joseph, a tall, rangy, fleshy-faced geologist approaching retirement age. The chopper typically dropped us a few miles inland each morning at a spot from which we would make our way several miles down a narrow valley to the coast for our evening pickup. Once on the ground we double-checked our scientific gear, tested our walkie-talkies with the pilot, loaded our .30-caliber rifle, waved goodbye to the pilot and vanished into the rainforest jungle. We were in a different world once we headed into the impossibly dense old-growth stands of spruce, fir, hemlock and cedar. The close-set trees choked out the sunlight, and centuries of dead-fall rotted by 300 inches of rain a year blocked our every line of advance. The contrast in countryside could not have been greater with the treeless tundra where I had worked the previous summer on the North Slope. The daily weather was in the high thirties and low forties with rain, but within minutes of the chopper's departure we were bathed in sweat from toiling through the dense undergrowth while swaddled in parkas and rainsuits.

We informally named one valley Deadfall Creek, because it was choked with a Brobdingnagian set of children's Pick-Up Stix, the "stix" being thousands of huge trees and their attached branches that had been knocked down by time and storms. The tangle was impenetrable in most places, so we had to clamber over, under or between the slippery, moss-sheathed logs, my pack and rifle getting caught regularly on the vegetation. At times I was suspended in a cat's cradle of vegetation well off the ground, after I had toiled through the latest jumble of timber, panting and gasping for air in the claustrophobic valley while I planned my next move. The other geologist, well-experienced in Alaska, was having as much trouble as I, so my self-esteem was not suffering. It was difficult to find decent fossil shells under these conditions, as predicted, but slowly I accumulated a nice selection of species.

At one point we had to cross Deadfall Creek on a rotted log that wore a lush mantle of moss that was made even slicker by the constant drizzle. Its side branches had long since rotted off to short stubs that were obstacles to crossing. The stream below was too deep and turbulent to ford, so teetering slowly along the log was the only way to get across. It did not help that we were near the end of the day, so my backpack was filled with weighty fossil specimens. I took a short, tentative step onto the spongy moss, feeling the slippery footing and seeing that I had twenty feet of log to cross. After a couple more steps, taking care to not trip over the broken branch stubs, my partner chimed in with a story.

"This reminds me of the time I was with a Shell Oil geologist on Kodiak," said party chief Joseph. "I'd already crossed the log, which was really slippery, like the one you're on now."

"Later, Joseph. I'm trying to focus. This is dangerous shit," I said as I baby-stepped along in my clumsy insulated rubber boots.

"No, this is important," he continued with a note of malice in his voice. "The Shell guy slipped and fell and got bung-holed on a stubby branch."

"Oh," I said, focusing on my boots.

"They heard him yelling back at camp a mile away," continued Joseph the Tormenter. "It took two of us to lift his asshole off the stub. The whole log was covered in blood and we had to fly him to town to see a doctor. What a mess. I hope that doesn't happen to you."

"Don't worry about me," I said, "I'm almost across."

"I'm not worried about you," opined Joseph, "I just don't want to waste the chopper time getting your asshole to town." Then he broke into seemingly uncontrollable, exaggerated laughter. That summer I had had no choice of field partners, but I learned that choosing them was fundamental to the enjoyment as well as success of my projects.

We had Korean War-vintage combat rations for lunch, and I took to smoking the three ancient Lucky Strike cigarettes that came in each box simply to warm my fingers, my hands tightly cupped around the glowing ciggie butt. We burned the C-ration packaging and buried the ashes, then carried the empty food cans out with us. Even though nobody would ever come across our lunch site, we respected the pristine forest.

One hazard I first came across at Lituya Bay was glacier-fed streams. A narrow stream that we easily stepped across during an overcast morning became a raging yards-wide icy torrent in a matter of hours if the sun came out and melted the source glacier a few miles away. Once the water got knee-deep we cut an alder branch to steady ourselves while crossing the forceful stream. I learned the rule that only one man at a time crossed, while the other watched from shore, ready to rush in if help was needed. Dying was more than a theoretical possibility, because our ship, the R/V *Don Miller*, had been named for a veteran Survey field geologist who had drowned in an Alaska river along with his field partner. One of them probably got into trouble in the icy stream and the other went out to help and drowned also.

Our daily takeoffs and landings were made from a tiny helipad beside danger-ously close barrels of aviation fuel.

One of my more challenging assignments was a two-day project to measure the thickness of rock strata and collect fossil mollusks at a stratigraphic section called Fairweather Glacier, twenty miles north of Lituya Bay, with a field assistant, Lee. It was the first time I had landed on top of a glacier, a treacherous experience because our lug-soled geological boots could not grip the slippery glacial surface, but at least it was summer and there was no snow to conceal the crevasses. The pilot had landed as close as possible to the edge of the glacier, but we still had over 100 yards of glare ice to negotiate by taking baby steps while zigzagging among bottomless crevasses until we reached firm ground.

The "firm ground" was actually a gigantic talus slope, talus being the word for the rock detritus that accumulates at the base of any bluff. Talus is the dirt that dribbles back into the hole when you are digging in your backyard, but at Fairweather Glacier the talus consisted of boulders the size of cars jumbled together with every other size and shape of rock particle, down to sand grains. It made for a laborious 100-foot climb up a 40° slope from the glacier's edge to the rock outcrops that formed an impressive cliff some 200 feet high. The cliff was especially attention-getting because its top jutted out over its base, which meant that it also jutted over our heads. Working the Fairweather Glacier section that summer was the first and last time I needed to wear a hardhat in the field as protection from the constant rain of rocks falling from the cliff. Fist-size rocks hit both Lee and me several times and would have badly injured us if not for the hard hats and the parkas and rainsuits we wore, more for impact protection than for the cold.

The Fairweather Glacier section was the first place in the Arctic when my instincts saved me from injury or worse. The party chief had told us to begin measuring the thickness of the stratigraphic section at its northern end, right where the stupendously large glacier made a sharp U-turn to the left. Unfortunately, stacks of fractured ice the size of office buildings loomed high over our start point, and as I gazed at that spot it looked strangely darker than the rest of the rocky landscape, as if it were shadowed by clouds that were not present on that bright day. I decided to skip the icy U-turn for now.

Later, during our C-ration lunch we heard a deep-throated, cascading BOOM coming from the U-turn area and were shocked to discover that several of the huge ice towers along the margin of the glacier had collapsed into the gullies where we would have been at that very moment, and had filled them to the brim with chunks of ice the size of cars. If I had not paid attention to my intuition about the darkened landscape, no trace of us would have ever been found, our bodies entombed for centuries or millennia until the ice melted or the glacier carried our frozen carcasses to the coast. This experience had a profound effect on me; at some level I understood that survival in the Arctic was not solely a matter of experience and attention, but partly a matter of intuition or perhaps precognition.

At Lituya Bay I was exercising my scientific research muscles on my own for the very first time, and I was likely the only professional who would ever collect the molluscan fauna in this remote wilderness. Fortunately, I had been trained well for that very task.

▲ ▲ ▲

"Please answer me why it is that 'Louie' sounds so much like 'phooey,'" asked my mentor, George Kanakoff, universally known and beloved as "Uncle George."

"Well, Uncle George, it only sounds like that if you have a thick Russian accent," I laughed back.

Uncle George was an unusually colorful character who had been raised among the privileged class in Imperial Russia, attended artillery school in the Crimea—which accounted for his deaf left ear—fought for Czar Nicholas II during the Russian Revolution and afterward escaped to America. In some unrecorded and unlikely turn of events, when the world of science was less structured than today, and despite having a college degree in philology, he became the curator of invertebrate paleontology at the Los Angeles County Museum of Natural History. He was exactly the sort of worldly, adventuresome and accomplished man I needed guidance from after my sequestered childhood. A high school science teacher introduced me to the Museum's many wonders, especially the behind-the-scenes activities of its departments.

Uncle George, my mentor and father figure, collecting Pliocene shells south of San Diego, California, 1961.

Once I had completed Uncle George's semester-long Saturday invertebrate paleo course, I volunteered nearly all my Saturdays in his lab for many years. Along with other volunteers, I patiently plucked shells from an endless supply of fossiliferous sediment he had collected in the field and sorted them into orderly ranks of specimen vials. In a matter of weeks I could identify hundreds of shell species and dozens of genera;

names like *Dentalium neohexagonum* and *Polinices reclusiana* tripped off my tongue effortlessly. I was so enthused that I took the work home and happily sorted through sediments on my mom's kitchen table, which befuddled her because nobody in the family had ever shown an interest in such an arcane pursuit. I was finally doing paleontology and my mind absorbed it like a sponge. Uncle George identified species for us students while he bantered, joked and passed on bits of life's wisdom as he made us feel like a team that was accomplishing important work, a feeling of companionship that was new and delicious to me.

After a year of learning to recognize taxa (i.e., genera and species) Uncle George rewarded me with collecting trips to my hometown of San Pedro and other fossil sites around Southern California. In my boyhood wanderings among empty lots in my neighborhood I had unknowingly collected shells over 100,000 years old, an early taste of what fate had in mind for me. Our biggest trips were weeklong summer expeditions to collect Pliocene mollusks some two to three million years old in San Diego. It was the thrilling realization of my young dreams to actually be in the field at age fifteen, wearing combat boots and a flannel shirt, digging for fossils and uncovering species new to science. Uncle George truly set me on my path to becoming a professional paleontologist, and in the absence of a father he became my role model. Sheltered under Uncle George's wing, I found the safe haven and guidance I had longed for in the world.

If my parents had not divorced, and we had not moved from San Pedro to Hollywood when I was thirteen, I would not have met Uncle George. Not only did I thrive under his paleo tutelage, I began to think that I could make something of myself in life despite the lack of encouragement at home. With an adult taking an interest in me for the first time, I opened myself up to larger dreams.

No matter how exhausting the day had been, after dinner at Lituya Bay I spent a couple of hours doing standard paleontological "preparation" in a space I had cleared above the R/V *Don Miller's* engine room: drying, cleaning, gluing together, numbering and wrapping fossil specimens, and meticulously recording collecting localities in my field notebooks and on topographic maps. I was being especially attentive about keeping records because I was collecting unique specimens from a place in Alaska that no other paleontologist would likely ever visit. Just as Uncle George had taught me.

One night the party chief happened to be peeing over the side of the R/V *Don Miller* at 10:30 p.m. when he saw rock outcrops of the rarely seen Topsy Formation in clear sunlight thousands of feet high on a mountain that was normally hidden by dense overcast. He rousted three of us out of our bunks, shoved our sleepy asses into the chopper and we were up on the mountain by 11:00 p.m. The fossil pickings were few, but the overlapping age ranges of two bivalves, or clams, *Lucinoma acutilineata* and *Macoma brota*, and two gastropods, or snails, *Neptunea plafkeri* and *Natica oregonensis*, told me that the Topsy rocks were twelve to sixteen million years old, or quite a bit more precise than prior estimates of ten to thirty million years. I was thrilled to be the first to collect age-specific fossils from these rocks and solve one small Arctic age mystery. Not bad for a hurried after-dinner excursion. We were back aboard ship at 2:00 a.m. and we never again saw those rocks peek out of the overcast. Neither has anyone else, and this incident taught me to take advantage of any weather break to get the job done in a part of the world where weather controls all.

Cenotaph Island, in the middle of Lituya Bay, which got its funerary name from the monument placed there by the French explorer La Pérouse in 1786 after some of his men drowned in the bay, became my main collecting site once I discovered its excellent exposures of fossil-rich sandstone. The deckhand who transported me the mile from ship to island in an aluminum skiff had a wild side and ran the outboard engine at top speed as he maneuvered among ice floes and sheets. Inevitably, with our eyes narrowed to slits by the icy wind as we peered toward our destination, we sometimes smacked into an invisible sheet of clear ice at speed. This launched the skiff into the air, the engine suddenly revved like crazy when the propeller left the water, and we got a second or two of "hang time" before smacking down into the water again. We laughed like a cowboy riding a bull, while not dwelling on the consequences of getting tossed into the freezing water, although our laughter stopped the one time we broke the propeller's shear pin and had to haul the motor out of the water to replace it. It felt wonderful to do wild things in the wilds of Alaska, even if it was risky.

I never anticipated the animal encounter I had one day while picking my way along a ledge on Cenotaph Island in the search for new fossil beds. The foot-wide ledge was perched five feet above the ocean to my right, with a smooth 100-foot cliff looming above to my left, and the ledge had been getting narrower until it finally pinched out and stopped my progress. However, by hugging the cliff and craning my neck around a corner made by a vertical rock rib, I saw that the ledge continued on the other side. If I could twist and bend my right leg around the rib, I thought I could push off and land on the ledge on the far side. It seems like an utterly foolish maneuver in retrospect, considering that I could not swim and was wearing heavy boots and gear, but I was thirty-one years old and still had an eternity to live.

Bending my right leg around the rocky corner, I put some weight on my boot and felt something soft underfoot, which I supposed was a pile of seaweed. The moment I added more weight, however, my right leg was shockingly flung upward, followed by a large splash in the ocean just beside me, and a large and indignant sea otter promptly started hissing loudly at me. I was too busy to pay attention, because I was precariously tottering on my left leg and clutching the vertical cliff in a death grip with my left hand, while my right leg and right hand with rock hammer were wildly flailing in thin air. If I did not regain my balance I was going to be in icy Lituya Bay with a very ticked-off sea otter. My rock hammer had been poised to strike and I jammed its point into a crevice to steady myself while I replanted my right foot on the ledge and retreated slowly backward, to the accompaniment of the otter's angry hiss. It took a while for my heart to stop pounding while I caught my breath. The whole episode had been needlessly hazardous, and was a lesson in how not to take chances when working alone.

I spotted the large gray wolf a hundred yards away just after the chopper had dropped me off alone at Icy Point, a coastal headland some twenty-five miles south of Lituya Bay. The locale was already forbidding enough, being a group of sandstone monoliths as large as buses that I scoured for fossils while wearing hip waders as the cold sea surged around my legs and I kept an eye out for rogue waves that could sweep me away. I did not need a wolf to divert my attention.

I waved my arms to spook it, but to my surprise, instead of slinking off into the adjacent forest it bounded toward me like Rover coming in for an affectionate hug. More-experienced Arctic field geologists had told me that *rabid* wolves sometimes acted like friendly dogs, so when it came within fifty yards I fired a rifle round in its direction and the blast sent it ducking behind a boulder, where it later appeared as a nose and eyeballs keeping tabs on me.

I could not ignore a possibly rabid wolf and it distracted me from collecting fossils. I considered shooting it to reduce my anxiety and danger, but decided I could not kill an animal that was not doing me any harm. I eventually took to throwing rocks in its direction, so as not to use up my few rounds of ammunition.

Lunch was nerve-wracking as I dug into my U.S. Army C-ration with the wolf lying down and staring at me from 100 feet away. I suppressed my instinct to toss it a few morsels, but late in the day with the chopper approaching I emptied my spare food onto the ground for the animal to feast on once I was gone. As an extra treat, since it was my last day in the field, I added an emergency ration, a greasy brick-like concoction, likely composed of sweepings from the Armour & Company loading dock, that contained thousands of calories but was virtually inedible. Perhaps the wolf was not rabid, just underfed, and the ration would give him a boost. In any case, better for him than me to eat it.

On a weeklong trip in 1961 with Uncle George near San Diego, living my boyhood dream of collecting fossils in the field.

Previous reconnaissance paleo collecting at Icy Point had implied an age of about thirty million years for the sandstone crops there, but I found the same mollusk species I had collected from the Topsy Formation that one night high above Lituya Bay and inferred the same age of twelve to sixteen million years. Fossil mollusks from the Fairweather

Glacier section, where the ice stacks had fallen near us, and from Ceno-taph Island were five to ten million years old, a bit younger than expected.

I was delighted to make small steps in deciphering the geology and paleontology of Alaska, but at a more fundamental level I was ecstatic to be part of a formal scientific research team for the first time in my life, working in as wild a place as exists on earth, contributing my special knowledge to the success of the expedition. It was everything I had hoped for as a boy and more, because beyond the science I had encoun-tered wild predators, survived challenging natural hazards and carried my full weight in rough and rugged conditions. Lituya Bay will always be a special place to me because I had taken the final steps there in my appointed journey from schoolboy to wilderness research paleontologist. One other heartening aspect of the expedition was that, unlike the year before on the North Slope, there were no aircraft accidents and nobody got killed. ▲

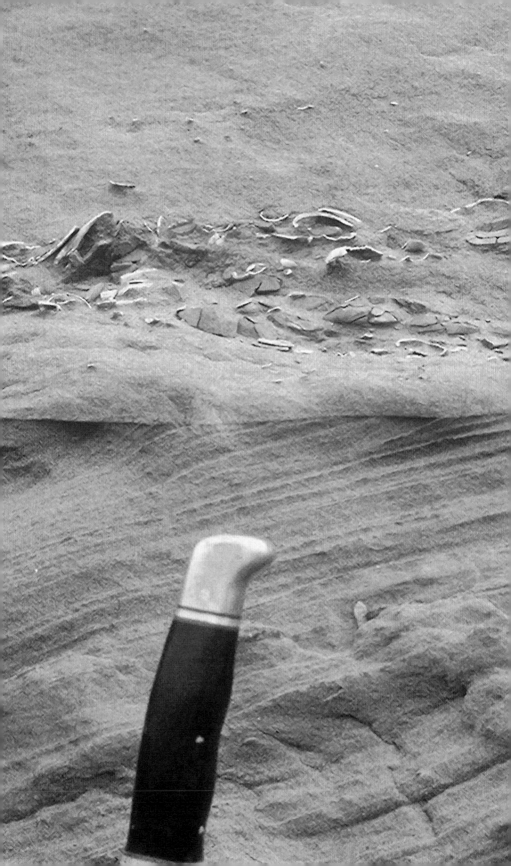

BEYOND NORTH,
ALASKA

"You look as excited as a kid on the night before Christmas," remarked the helicopter pilot as we lifted off from beside our World War II quonset hut at the tiny North Slope settlement of Umiat.

"That's how I feel," I replied into my helmet mic as we rose above the tundra. "We're going to a place where nobody has *ever* collected fossil shells. This is going to be way better than any Christmas I remember."

"The same place I took you and Travis yesterday, that cliff on the Colville River?" he asked.

"Right. The place is called Ocean Point for some reason, even though it's thirty miles inland from the Arctic Ocean."

"What's so special about the fossils there?" he wondered.

"When I looked over the shell beds yesterday I recognized about half the molluscan genera in the rocks. They're the same ones I've seen everywhere else in Alaska and they're at most 65 million years old. The strange thing is, though, that I didn't recognize any of the species. Plus, the other half of the mollusk genera were new to me, and I think they're more typical of a geological era more than sixty-five million years old—when the last of the dinosaurs were still around," I explained.

Layer of 60-million-year-old shells at Ocean Point; sheath knife handle for scale.

"So, what does that mean in English?" he asked with a smile.

"The older shells aren't found with the younger shells anywhere in the world—they're supposed to be mutually exclusive in time—so if they were living together here it means that something really unusual was going on in the environment and I want to find out what that was. Maybe whatever killed off the dinos wasn't as fatal for marine mollusks here in the Far North."

Our conversation was interrupted when we spooked a grizzly from an alder patch and we watched it haul ass across the tundra.

"Hope you brought your gun," said the pilot.

"No problem there," I replied. I hadn't been raised around firearms, but I became proficient with a 12-gauge shotgun loaded with Magnum lead slugs after another Survey geologist had lost both arms in a bear attack while working alone, as I would be doing today.

The pilot could not stay with me at Ocean Point, because the three other Survey geologists back in Umiat needed the Jet Ranger all day for their own studies. The party chief had generously agreed to have me dropped off early at Ocean Point, then the chopper would return to pick me up at the end of the day. I could not have asked for more: a solid ten-hour day collecting fossils, which would give me an excellent idea of the faunal composition and be the basis of a future, more extensive collecting trip. However, this was the very first time I was going to be dropped off alone in the wilds of Alaska, and I was going to spend the day sixty miles from the nearest human being, so besides my excitement about the fossils I was also anxious for my safety.

In the early morning hours I had nervously packed and repacked my full-frame backpack to the brim with fossil-collecting and survival supplies, hoping to bring everything I might need for a day alone at a remote fossil locality:

- High-top leather boots with lug soles
- Wool socks with silk liners

- Goose down parka
- Goose down vest
- Bright orange rainsuit
- Two pairs of insulated leather gloves
- Paper towels, TP and cotton rolls to wrap delicate fossils
- A quart of Glyptal lacquer, Krylon clear spray lacquer and model airplane glue to repair
- Cracked specimens
- Pick mattock and folding army shovel
- Four-pound maul and set of chisels
- Topographic maps in a clear waterproof cover
- Roll of orange plastic flagging and orange spray paint to mark fossil localities
- Dozens of cloth collecting bags
- Masking tape to wrap specimens
- Folded mirror-finish sleeping bag-like Mylar tube for survival in a storm
- Brick-size walkie-talkie
- Spare parts for repairing my pack
- Square yard of DayGlo orange nylon for signaling a helicopter
- C-ration lunch, lots of candy bars and emergency survival ration
- Water bottle and can of soda
- Small spotting scope for checking out animals
- Bright orange multi-pocket Filson work vest
- Yellow plastic three-ring notebook with Rite in the Rain waterproof pages
- Mechanical pencils
- Marks-A-Lot black markers for labeling fossils and bags
- Small brushes and dental picks for excavating fossils
- Ten rounds of 12-gauge Magnum rifled slugs
- Remington 870 shotgun in a padded cloth shoulder case

- U.S. Army web belt
- Estwing rock hammer in a leather holster
- Sheath knife
- Pen knife
- Brunton geological compass in a leather case
- 10X Hastings Triplet loupe and U.S. Army P-38 can opener on a cord around my neck

I was already sweating in my thermal underwear in the confines of the cockpit as we buzzed along in the kind of warm, clear weather bush pilots refer to as CAVU, ceiling and visibility unlimited. It was simpler to sweat a little on the flight than to go through the hassle of stripping off my lace-up boondockers, pants and shirt to slip on my thermals in the field when a blustery rain squall sprang out of nowhere, as often happened. All in all, I felt like the Compleat Paleontologist, with my pack weighing in at thirty-five pounds before collecting a single fossil, the loaded shotgun adding ten more pounds.

We flew along the chocolate milk-colored Colville River, the 100-foot river bluff on our left weathered into broad folds of brown drapery, the cliff face itself incised by V-shaped gullies cut by summer-melt water draining from the permafrost. As we neared Ocean Point after an hour's flight, the miles-broad S-shaped curve known as the Big Bend of the Colville came into view, and on the far side of the S-bend the cliff rocks changed color from monotonous medium brown to gold, gray and light brown, signaling the change from non-marine to marine sediments. The pilot circled Ocean Point for a minute to check for grizzlies, then landed on a beach at the base of the river bluffs.

"I didn't see any bears, so you might live another day," he joked.

"I'd call it a lucky day for the bears," I boasted. "Word's gotten out about all the target practice I've done, and now I think the grizzlies fear me."

"I think we're all afraid of you holding a loaded gun," he chuckled. "Time for me to fly off to safety."

I made absolutely sure that I had all of my collecting and survival gear before he took off, and did a brief radio check. The Motorola walkie-talkie transmitted only a few miles, but was a lifesaver for guiding the pilot back to me at pickup time. I loaded my Remington with Magnum slugs as the machine arced into the sky.

I knew at once that I had hit the Mother Lode as I hiked along the cliff and scanned the sediment layers chock-a-block full of well-preserved clams and snails. I was awestruck at the richness and spectacular preservation of the shells and fascinated by the mix of familiar and unfamiliar genera. The ancient deposit was so rich that the fossil mollusks were touching one another, and many of the clams were in life positions, oriented just as they had been in life, with their minutely delicate filigreed sculpture perfectly preserved. Not only were they preserved as well as shells on a modern beach, but the sediments enclosing them were soft enough to excavate with a pocketknife blade or even a fingernail. The Ocean Point shells were the find of a lifetime, the fauna every paleontologist dreams of but rarely finds: an untouched bonanza of perfectly preserved, abundant and diverse fossils of mysterious provenance that were easy to collect.

Reverently, I ran a finger along some of the bigger shells, gently blowing drifted sand off specimens to reveal their minute sculpture. *You've waited here for tens of millions of years, and I'm the lucky devil who found you. I'll see that you get a good home in a collection drawer instead of weathering to dust here in the wilds. You're in good hands now.*

I recognized many of the clam and snail genera as characteristic of the Cenozoic Era (0-65 million years old), which was my main professional focus, but others looked to be more typical of the Mesozoic Era (65-145 mya) which I knew less well. The two eras were separated by the well-known extinction event that killed off the last of the dinosaurs 65,000,000 years ago. However, both ages of shells from Ocean Point were equally well preserved—instead of the "older" ones being more worn and broken—so there was at least a chance that they had lived together, instead of being taxa from different ages that had been mixed together by subsequent geological processes. If the "younger" and "older" species *had* lived together, they would provide unmatched insight into marine conditions in the virtually unknown Arctic Ocean realm of sixty-five million years ago. Whatever the precise age of this fauna, it was right at the frontier of what I or anyone else knew about Arctic Cenozoic mollusks, and studying it was going to be one heck of an important research project.

I worked through lunch, digging out specimens from the soft sand and wrapping them for storage in my pack, in case the chopper came back early and curtailed my collecting work. I needed to get a representative sample of the fauna to learn its significance and to justify coming back for a major collecting trip next year.

Even mesmerized as I was by the fauna, I observed the first rule of Alaskan fieldwork, to look around every few minutes for grizzlies. I spotted no bears, but after gleefully collecting shells for hours, exulting in one find after another, during one of my grizzly scans in the afternoon I noticed dark clouds moving in from the north, where the Arctic Ocean lay thirty miles away. The bright blue sky was slowly and ominously disappearing. A storm was on its way, and if it rained heavily the Colville River might rise quickly and sweep me away, judging from the cliffside floodwater marks high above my head made by previous storms. I stuffed my gear and fossils into my now-bulging pack, which was now too heavy to sling on like usual, so I sat below it on the sloping river bank, put my arms through the straps and stood upright to shoulder the load.

I needed to get to the top of the 100-foot river bluff fast, and scanning upstream I saw no place where I could climb up while lugging a large pack and gun bag. I headed downstream, where I thought I remembered seeing a gully when the chopper had circled for grizzlies, and was relieved to find the gully after a short hike and waddle up it. From the clifftop I saw boiling dark clouds filling the northern horizon and coming on at a startling clip. This storm was going to be a real mother. I zipped on my goose down vest, parka and orange rainsuit, laced my boondockers extra tight, and pulled on my insulated leather gloves, then kept my pack from blowing away by tightly wedging it into the tundra in a muddy trench left by a melted wintertime ice wedge. *Thank goodness I had put on my thermals before leaving camp.* After pulling tight the seals at my ankles, wrists and hood I hugged the cased Remington 870 to my chest and waited.

View upstream on the Colville River at Ocean Point, North Slope, Alaska. The immediate foreground is where I was standing when I had my out-of-body experience.

But not for long. The rain, wind and fog came on like a moving wall, hurtling toward me at the speed of suburban automobile traffic, kicking up dirt from the tundra like debris at the base of a tornado and whipping the surface of the river into a frenzied, pearly froth. The sight was frightening; it looked more like an onrushing, churning cloud wall in a Dust Bowl documentary than anything I had imagined in Alaska. It was the

worst weather I had ever seen by an order of magnitude and fear tightened my chest when I realized that the only possible help was the Survey
field party sixty miles away in Umiat.

The storm burst over me like a bomb as I instinctively dropped to my
knees and curled protectively forward over my shotgun to take the brunt
of the onslaught; I was instantly enveloped in a maelstrom of hurricane-
force wind, drenching rain, and near-zero-visibility fog. The deafening
sound of large rain drops pounding against my rubberized rainsuit was
raised to a higher crescendo when the wind picked up sand and gravel
from the river bank and flung them up the 100-foot cliff and straight at
me on the open tundra. The savagery of the wind and rain was shocking
enough, but I had never even *heard* of hurricane-force fog. No "creeping
in on cats' feet" for North Slope weather.

My mind raced through the litany of possible dangers, from hypo-
thermia to starvation, remembering that I had once been in a nine-day
windstorm at Driftwood, where I had had shelter and food. Inevitably, I
focused on one particular hazard—grizzlies. The fog limited my visibility
to a mere twenty feet, the length of a suburban driveway, and my mind
fixated on the image of a grizzly that might even now be stalking me,
swinging its massive head and salivating jaws left and right as it followed
my scent upwind. If a grizzly head suddenly poked through the fog wall, I
would have no chance to unlimber my Remington, rack the action, assume
a shooting stance and aim to kill. I began shaking like a leaf, my mind
close to paralysis from fear and I wondered if I might perish that very day.

The storm continued unabated for hours while the demonic
shrieking of the icy wind and the thought-destroying din of pounding
rain and gravel overpowered my senses and sapped my energy. Sometime in the late afternoon the Arctic hurricane backed off a little, the rain
tapered away, and the fog lifted enough for me to scan the horizon and
see to my immense relief that no grizzly was in sight. The fog rose slowly
to coalesce into a heavy cloud layer 200 hundred feet over my head, but

the clouds were otherworldly, pitch black and dark gray, fiercely churning, blossoming and boiling like nothing I had ever seen. I scanned agog left to right from my cliff-top vantage point as quilted black and gray cells of enraged clouds streaked overhead at sixty miles an hour from horizon to horizon. I had a flash image of myself as a speck of protoplasm, an orange-suited dot lost in the immensity of the green tundra, awestruck, mouth agape, clutching the shotgun to my chest, completely at the mercy of the storm. The buffeting wind rocked my body, but I could still feel my heart trying to pound free of my chest. Terrorized by the dark clouds above, I forced my gaze down toward the flat ground across the river, looking for something familiar and comforting, but where I expected to see a tundra-clad plain there was only blackness. It was like staring into the mouth of a mile-wide cave.

That was the last straw. Something happened in that moment that forever changed my view of life: my spirit departed my body in a seamless transition from the everyday aspect of reality to another, previously unsuspected realm of consciousness. In the blink of an eye, my spirit or consciousness was hanging at the base of the clouds—which had somehow dispersed into bright skies—high over the center of the Colville River and 200 feet above my body that was clearly standing below me on the cliff-top tundra. From my vantage point above the river, I looked down on my body shaking in terror while clutching the shotgun to its chest.

I was at peace, enveloped in a profound sense of love, serenity, oneness and *knowing*. I was at the edge of some unimaginable immensity that was ever-present but just out of my ordinary everyday grasp, and somehow I knew I had been part of it my whole life. I definitely was not *having* a waking dream, but knew without question that I had just *awakened* from one. Unlike the muddle of images in a hallucination or dream, while detached from my body I clearly remembered my entire day up to that point—the flight from Umiat and collecting fossils in the cliffside fossil beds—and my thinking ability and scientific mindset were fully intact. The ineffable experience was clearly a glimpse into a reality well beyond the everyday kind.

I somehow *knew* with certainty that nothing bad would happen to me—to my body—that day. I tried to mentally communicate to my body below that everything was going to be okay, that no harm would come to it, but my corporeal self could not tune in to my conscious thoughts. My body remained a secondary object that was separate and somehow a lesser thing than my detached consciousness.

I had no sense of time while out of my body, but I later estimated that the out-of-body experience, or OBE, lasted several hours, because the hurricane-force wind of sixty to seventy miles an hour had to drop to 35 mph or less for our small helicopter to safely come and rescue me. Based on my Alaska experience up to that time, and decades of experience afterward, it takes at least several hours, even days or a week, for such high winds to subside on the North Slope. Toward the end of the OBE I heard the faint but swelling sound of helicopter blades from my left, and as I turned my attention upriver to catch a glimpse of the machine, I was instantly back in my body standing on the clifftop. There was no transition, and I was once again a terrified man alone in the middle of nowhere.

Peering intently upriver from atop the cliff, I saw the speck of a machine being batted around the sky over the Colville by the still-dangerous winds. The pilot was taking an awful chance with the weather, but I was grateful for his daring. The dark clouds were gone, as they had been when I was up in the air. I suddenly realized I had broken a cardinal rule of working in the wilderness: I was not waiting for the chopper at our agreed-upon location. The pilot had let me off beside the river, but now I was on top of the cliff and a quarter mile away from my drop-off spot, so he did not know where I was. I broke out a square yard of DayGlo orange nylon and waved it furiously to catch his attention, and once he was within a mile I clicked on my rain-soaked Motorola walkie-talkie and was surprised that it worked.

"Bill, it's Lou. I'm not where you dropped me off. I'm on top of the cliff at your one o'clock, just beyond a big gully, waving a DayGlo flag!"

I felt immense relief as the chopper banked toward me and the pilot chimed in, "I got you. What's the ground like?"

"It's firm tundra, you can land anywhere," I almost shouted in relief.

I hurriedly retrieved my pack and unloaded the shotgun as the chopper approached, then assumed the standard position of back to the wind, arms held straight out in front of me to show the pilot the wind direction at ground level and pointed to a landing place I thought was safe.

Once the pilot nodded his okay for me to safely approach, I ran to the ship, packed my gear in the luggage compartment and strapped myself into the front seat, frantic to be gone.

"Thanks a million for flying in this crap. I really appreciate it," I said.

"We were all worried about you being alone out there, but I had to wait a few hours for the storm to calm down before I could come get you," he explained.

We did not talk much more as the pilot focused on fighting the controls in the brisk winds that kept us corkscrewing through the sky. Silence was fine by me, as I tried to make sense of what had happened at Ocean Point. Leaving my body had been as natural as breathing, but who was going to believe me? Not the older, hard-core geologists back at camp. I was early in my career, and describing an out-of-body experience to my fellow PhDs in 1977 likely would have ended my career. I could imagine the grizzled party chief saying, "As long as you left your body, why don't you keep on going and leave the Survey? We don't need someone around who hallucinates in the middle of his first big storm."

At the time I had this experience, and for at least a decade afterward, I knew nothing of OBEs, had never read about such a thing, and could not relate it to the rest of my life, so I suppressed it. Looking back from the present, at Ocean Point my mind was clearly in a higher natural realm of consciousness than everyday reality, but a realm in which I could reason, observe the material world and form memories. The experience was so lucid, and so much more real than everyday life, that to this day I recall every detail exactly. In contrast, everything else from that summer falls into the ordinary realm of jumbled, faded memories, and I must read my own field notebooks to recall what else I did in Alaska in 1977.

My discovery of a remarkable fossil fauna accompanied by a transcendent glimpse into a larger realm of consciousness transformed the barren tundra and rock outcrops at Ocean Point into a touchstone of my professional and spiritual life. ▲

BEAR LAKE, ALASKA

"There's a big bear coming our way," said my field assistant, Jim, pointing upstream.

"He probably hasn't seen us yet. They don't usually bother two or more people." I stood up and waved my arms high and shouted, "Hya! Hya!" then turned and said, "That should do it."

"Hope so," he replied. He was a summer hire and this was his first grizzly encounter. We had been dropped off near the headwaters of the Bear River on the Alaska Peninsula of southwestern Alaska and had searched all morning for fossil shells without much success.

Once I had shouted, the bear stopped and seemed to take a real interest in us for the first time; it picked up its pace. Maybe it had not seen us earlier, but now it had heard us thanks to my shout.

"He's getting too interested," I said. "Hand me the gun."

Showing off by hanging over a thousand-foot dropoff during a windstorm at Sandy Ridge, with a shotgun, maul and handful of chisels for added weight. At the time I did not know that the williwaw wind could suddenly stop.

I quickly unzipped and tossed aside the padded cloth shoulder carrying case from the Remington Model 700 .375 H&H Magnum rifle, which we had been passing back and forth all morning because it was such a heavy lump to carry. Jim was a newbie to Alaska from some place that did not have bears, whereas I had been doing wilderness fieldwork for five years, often alone, and had taken USGS shooting classes and was a regular at target ranges.

The grizzly increased its pace to a lope, then broke into a run straight at us from 150 yards away. Confident in my shooting skills, I drew back the well-oiled rifle bolt to chamber a round from the four-shot magazine. My jaw dropped when I stared down in shock at the empty magazine. There were not any bullets in the gun.

"Where are the fucking bullets?" I screamed.

"In my pack," said Jim, adding a meek, "Sorry."

I violently upended his backpack and out tumbled clothes, chisels, glue, collecting bags and finally a box of 270-grain Winchester Silvertip bullets that I grabbed and ripped apart in one motion as brass cartridges flew in every direction. I glanced up and saw the grizzly a mere 100 yards away—five or six seconds—hurtling toward us at twenty-plus miles an hour, an onrushing fur ball with teeth and claws leading the way. I barely had time to insert a single round into the firing chamber—it is possible to jam the bullet askew and render the gun useless if you get that part wrong, so I had to be deliberate while my brain was screaming at me to rush—no thought given to loading the four-round magazine. Slamming the bolt home, I automatically assumed a shooter's stance: left leg forward and bent at the knee, body leaning forward, right leg braced back. Thank God I had practiced endlessly at home and on the range for just such a surprise encounter. Jim screamed, "Shoot! Shoot!" right next to my ear and the grizzly was so close I could not miss unless I screwed up big time. Which was possible. My shooting instructors had recommended crippling a charging grizzly with a leg shot, then finishing it off with a second bullet.

My problem was that I could not see any legs in the tall grass the monster was running through. The bear was eating up the ground between us at a ferocious rate and I could see its teeth in its open jaws. I centered the Remington's iron sights on the middle of the onrushing fur ball, adjusting my aim as it zigzagged left and right over the rough ground, and squeezed the trigger at fifteen yards, as my mind fixated on the mantra, "Center mass! Center mass!" The mammoth boom of the .375 sounded like a distant popgun to my brain soaked in raw adrenaline.

I hated firing that particular weapon in practice, because of its monstrous recoil, twice that of a .30-caliber rifle, but this time I gave it no thought. At point-blank range the .375 Magnum round and its 4,300 pound-feet of energy did the job. After making a finger-size entry wound, the lead-tipped, partially copper-bound, hollow-point projectile mushroomed as intended, which created an internal pressure wave in the grizzly's body that probably exploded its heart and other internal organs. If the bullet hit bone it likely fragmented, spraying a lethal cone of semi-molten lead throughout the bear's chest cavity before punching out its back. The oncoming corpse thudded heavily onto the stream bank a mere twenty-five feet away—the length of my driveway at home—while Jim and I stood frozen in a tableau of flinched terror and disbelief. There was no second bullet in the rifle. Blood leaked into the sand from the grizzly's jaws and trickled down its fur from the large, ragged exit wound where its spine had been. The big, mottled brown bear had a prominent grizzled hump but looked gaunt, its hide draped in loose folds; maybe it was old and came after us because it could not catch caribou or moose anymore. I shakily loaded a round into the rifle and shot the monster by its ear hole, then loaded the magazine.

Jim had inadvertently broadcast our life-or-death encounter to the world when he held down the "transmit" button as he clutched our walkie-talkie in a death grip. The chopper pilot a few miles away heard our shouted conversation followed by a big Boom!, and once Jim let go of the transmit button, the pilot learned where we were and landed while we were still recovering from the ordeal. I had never really thought that I would shoot a bear and I had been cool and collected when it counted, but now my body betrayed me: I felt numb and cold and could hardly breathe as I kneeled down on one leg and rested my shaking hands on the rifle for support.

"The body should be eaten by its friends in a few days," said the lodge owner, a professional hunter who had guided hundreds of customers to shoot trophy grizzlies.

"So I don't have to file a report with the state or feds?" I asked.

"The law says you do, and you're supposed to skin it and give the pelt to Fish and Game along with the head and claws," he replied.

"I don't want to see that place again, and I've never skinned anything," I said. Screw the rules, I thought. We were alive and nothing else mattered.

"The bear sounds like it was pretty moth-eaten, and if you don't tell anyone I won't either," he said with a wink. Like any good Alaskan, he had a strong independent streak and thoroughgoing disdain for government regulations.

I smiled back in appreciation, but was disappointed when nobody complimented me on keeping my head and taking down the first charging grizzly of my life with a single shot under extreme duress. No pat on the shoulder and hearty, "That was a hell of a shot!" Lack of appreciation was a family trait that kept following me around.

I would never again carry an unloaded weapon in Alaska, and never trust anyone to load a gun for me. Only a couple of years earlier, a Survey geologist had lost both arms to a bear, and after my own bear encounter I became obsessive about firearm skills because I worked alone so often and had to be confident that I could protect myself. I worked up to being the second-best shot in competitions among USGS Menlo Park geologists who worked in Alaska. Another wilderness lesson learned the hard way.

Heading into the field through an Anchorage tourist shop, 1998.

We had almost been ripped to shreds and consumed by a monster grizzly bear because of global warming. Not today's piffling phenomenon, but a more profound global episode about fifteen million years ago that had allowed tropical seashells to migrate to southern Alaska on ocean currents from Japan that had been invigorated by the warming ocean.

These ancient warm-water shells were now preserved in sediment layers that cropped out on the mountainous Alaska Peninsula of southwestern Alaska. During the late 1960s and early 1970s USGS and oil company geologists had brought back a few tantalizing mollusk specimens from a place called Bear Lake, but information on exactly where they had come from geographically and geologically and the full extent of the fauna were unknowns.

I was enthralled by the breathtaking beauty of the land during my first bush plane flight along the Alaska Peninsula. The choppy gray-green Bering Sea lay just to our left, still roiled from a days-long storm, the narrow and rocky coastal plain with black-sand beaches passed below, and black volcanic rocks formed vertiginous cliffs just to our right. The steep slopes were covered in a variegated green carpet of willows and alders, while occasional patches of fireweed flamed across hillsides.

Like much of Alaska, the Peninsula is free of human activity save for an isolated hunting lodge, cannery or village connected only by bush planes, at least when the weather cooperated. There were thousands of mountains, ridges, valleys and other geographic features that would have been named generations ago in the Lower 48 but were nameless and lost in Alaska's towering vastness. I loved the Alaska Peninsula the first time I saw it.

Our destination, the Bear Lake Lodge, was set amid snow-capped volcanic peaks zigzagging toward the sky, glacial valleys filled with deep blue ice, and placid braided rivers whose interwoven channels were lined with gray shingle and fringed with vividly green tall grass. The lodge is accessible only by plane or helicopter, the nearest roads being 100 miles south at the village of Cold Bay. Landing at Bear Lake for the first time is unsettling, because the published description of the runway reads: "loose gravel in poor condition; soft, undulating surface with swales up to eighteen inches and rocks to eight inches." Bouncing to a safe landing at Bear Lake was always a relief, perhaps due to a few muttered Hail Marys.

"That's some gun collection," I remarked while craning my neck up at the lodge's raftered ceiling.

"Yeah, there's around 100 rifles here and we have more in a back room," said the lodge owner.

"Why are they lined up in the rafters?" I asked.

"Because lots of hunters come here from countries where owning firearms is forbidden, so they buy a rifle in Anchorage to hunt moose, caribou and bear, then just abandon it when they go home with their trophies."

The great room had a long wooden bar and a pool table, and a menagerie of stuffed wild animals. Mounted heads and walrus tusks lined the walls, as did numerous, basketball-size green-glass fishing floats and slabs of fossil shells. Picture windows overlooked Bear Lake and the snow-capped Aleutian Range beyond. The lodge owed its existence to the abundance of trophy-size grizzlies that we saw every day from the lodge or in the field—monsters standing nine or ten feet tall—which was catnip for hunters but a hazard for geologists, one of the reasons that this part of Alaska was relatively unstudied. The country outside the picture windows was devoid of trails, except those made by grizzlies, moose or caribou; the land was sheathed in tall emerald-green grass and dense stands of dark green alder bushes up to twenty feet high intergrown with smaller pale green willows, but it lacked true trees owing to the Peninsula's severe weather.

A more serious hazard than large bears on the Alaska Peninsula was the atrociously violent weather when high winds, fog and heavy rain made flying, or even being outdoors dangerous. I was used to losing a third of

my time to bad weather in other parts of Alaska, but on the Peninsula I
normally lost *half* my field days to storms, mainly because flying in our
small helicopters was simply too hazardous.

Enjoying a hillside of lupines during a break in hiking.

Fortunately, my first working day at the Bear Lake Lodge held only
light rain and fog as the helicopter lifted off for an hour's haul to Yellow
Bluff Creek, where a few fifteen-million-year-old warm-climate shells had
been found a decade earlier by an oil company geologist. I was accompanied by Alexei, a visiting Soviet paleontologist on his first visit to the U.S.
A strongly built man of average height, his sandy hair and beard framed
a hangdog face that had gotten him far in the Soviet system by revealing
nothing. Prying him out of the Soviet Union at the height of the Cold War had
taken me a tedious year of negotiations with U.S. and Soviet bureaucrats,

but he had the same special interest in Cenozoic mollusks as I did and I wanted to learn from his experiences with Siberian faunas. Alexei was not supposed to travel more than half an hour from my Menlo Park USGS office without FBI permission, yet here we were 2,500 miles from California without permission.

Alexei had recently been in Iceland and seen the movie *Doctor Zhivago* for the first time; now he could not get the movie's tune, "Lara's Theme," out of his head and he also would not stop humming and whistling it. He had become a pest, which was somewhat tolerable in California, but in the close confines of an Alaskan lodge he was increasingly enervating. I was learning yet gain about one of the less obvious hazards of Arctic fieldwork, which is putting up with your colleagues' personalities in an isolated situation.

By the end of the day we had done a thorough job of being the first people, and probably the last, to scientifically collect fossils at Yellow Bluff Creek, and many of our specimens were the extinct scallop *Fortipecten mollerensis* that are the size of dinner plates. Resplendent with their raised radial rays that looked like a Shell Oil logo, each lithified scallop weighed three or four pounds and made our large-frame Kelty backpacks ludicrously heavy. However, I had to assume that no paleontologist would ever again visit Yellow Bluff Creek, so we hauled out as many specimens as possible. It was impossible to pick up our weighty backpacks and sling them on like usual. We had to sit below them on the steeply angled slope and cinch the shoulder and waist belts before rising up on wobbly legs, using the shotgun as a crutch while the other guy pushed from behind. Alexei and I felt every ounce of weight as we labored slowly down from the outcrop in blustery rain while bundled in parkas and rainsuits. Our main concern was twisting an ankle or falling and breaking a leg or arm, since the footing was treacherous on the steep talus slope made up of loose cobbles and boulders that dislodged at every footfall. One step at a time, then a moment's wait for the rocks to stop moving, then another step. At times our feet became trapped under tumbled boulders and we needed the other guy to free us up. After laboring along painfully for a minute or so, I had the uncharitable idea that maybe someone other than myself should be lugging ten pounds of shotgun. I handed the gun to my partner, saying,

"Alexei, you are my special guest in America, so I give you the honor of protecting us from grizzly bears."

He grudgingly accepted the additional weight, but a couple of minutes later said,

"But, Lou, you are the leader of our expedition; you should have the honor of carrying this weapon," then handed the hated object back to me. In a short while I handed it back, stating,

"You have shot three bears in Siberia during fieldwork, but I've killed only one, so I think we will be safer if you have the shotgun."

He brooded over this for a while, then retorted, "In my opinion, to be a good Arctic paleontologist you must shoot at least two bears, and for this you must have the gun."

By this time we were at the bottom of the talus slope and searching for openings in the looming alder thicket, so it was not worth the effort to hand the shotgun back to Alexei. Bulked up like the Michelin Man in our parkas and rainsuits, stooped over beneath heavy packs, and already approaching exhaustion from our day's work in a cold, steady rain and our talus slope descent, we picked our way through the abattis of alders guided by the sound of the landing helicopter. My backpack had begun the morning at 35 pounds but at the end of the day it weighed 125 pounds on the lodge's freight scale, meaning my overburdened 6'-1" frame was carrying more than 300 pounds. It rained hard the next few days and we never got back to Yellow Bluff Creek, nor has anyone else in the last thirty-nine years, so stuffing our packs with fossils has been the right thing to do. Anyone interested in those fossil shells will find them in a museum drawer, thanks to our suffering that day. Unfortunately,

Alexei had fallen victim to a professional hazard for geologists in the Arctic and wrecked his back, a victim of the cold weather, weighty pack, rugged terrain, and squatting down all day chiseling fossils out of rock with a sledge hammer—looking like "a monkey humping a football," as an insensitive colleague put it—and after a few days of intense pain returned to California.

▲ ▲ ▲

"Here's where the chopper will drop me off this morning," I said to the lodge owner as I stuck a red pushpin into the topo map taped to the wall, "and here's the farthest I'm likely to hike today," I continued as I inserted a blue pushpin a mile to the west on the nameless ridge on the other side of Bear Lake. Everyone at the lodge, not only the pilot, would know where I was, in case the helicopter had an accident *after* dropping me off alone for the day. In addition, one channel of my Motorola radio was programmed to the helicopter's radio frequency and the second channel tuned to a U.S. Coast Guard emergency channel for that region of Alaska. Even with a range of only about five miles, the walkie-talkie was powerful enough to talk to any chopper or plane searching for me as long as they knew my general locale.

The pilot nodded toward me just before he lifted the Bell 206B Jet Ranger from the steep, bare brown-sandstone hillside a couple of thousand feet above the Bear River Valley, to alert me to hold onto my pack and hat before the rotor wash blew them away. I took my usual minute to gaze appreciatively through the crystalline air at the surrounding scenery of rugged, snow-capped hills rising above a fringe of dark green alders. Once again I was the lucky dog who was the first to collect rich fossil beds in a remote wilderness site that was lavishly beautiful, fully aware that I was traveling along a lifetime arc of scientific adventure drawn in boyhood.

Snapping our of my reverie, I scouted along the ridge for a promising sandstone layer and came across a foot-thick bed containing packed thousands of the extinct mussel *Mytilus gratecapi*, which told me that the fossil bed was about fifteen million years old and was once a rocky shoreline. The day looked promising as I shucked off my pack and settled in to collect as many prime specimens as possible, hoping to find a continuous series from juveniles to mature adults. I was soon engrossed in collecting with rock hammer, four-pound maul and chisels, penknife, dental picks and glue, while keeping one eye out for bears and weather changes. As usual on the Alaska Peninsula, I did not have to wait long for the wind to increase and sweep low, gray clouds and heavy rain in from the Bering Sea. Before long it was blowing at gale force, too fierce to work in, so I wrapped up work and stuffed the fossil shells into my pack before they blew away.

Self-portrait in a 1982 120-mph hurricane near Bear Lake, with pack and shotgun close at hand.

I was exposed on a bare hillside with no obvious place to duck out of the storm, which steadily increased to hurricane force of seventy-five miles an hour. The rain stayed heavy while the wind rose to a punishing, then dangerous, then incredible speed. I had been in plenty of Alaskan storms, but this was blowing at another level and I stood a fair chance of being plucked from the ridge and blown through the air, tumbling hundreds of feet down to the valley floor. Crouching low, I dragged my pack and gun bag along the ground as I scrambled and slid 100 feet downslope to duck behind a compact car-size boulder, the only shelter on the hillside. Even there, simply holding on to Mother Earth took all my strength, with boots wedged against boulders and gloved hands clutching at crevices, my hooded head pressed to the ground. The satanic howling of the wind was unnerving, unlike anything I had experienced, as was the sight of sturdy six-foot willows with long, tangled roots that had been ripped from the valley floor and flung hundreds of feet into the air. The previous year's North Slope storm when I had had an out-of-body experience was gentler than this one, but at least this time there was no enveloping fog to possibly conceal grizzly bears.

I had wedged my backpack into a crack and piled rocks atop it on the other side of the car-size boulder so I would not have to hold on to my gear. I learned later that the anemometer at the Bear Lake Lodge, a dozen miles away on the coastal flats, had been ripped from its mounting pole at 100 miles an hour, and the lodge owner estimated from long experience that the winds in the mountains where I was had reached 120 miles an hour. My only option was to wait out the storm, and even if it had kept blowing all night I was glad to be alone. I knew that I had the inner resources to hike to the lodge through a storm in country thick with the largest bears on earth, and I would not have to worry about anyone else. However, the storm blew itself out through the afternoon, the winds gradually tapering below hurricane force. Now and then I half stood up to look around for grizzlies, but mostly I was content to hunker down on the lee side of the boulder and wait for a chopper pickup once the winds dropped below thirty-five.

My senses snapped alive in an instant when I heard something move on the other side of the boulder. Maybe it was the wind. Then I heard the *distinct* sound of movement. Damn! I focused intently, every nerve strung tight, my eyes big and mouth slightly agape. Whatever it was moved again. It had to be a grizzly; no time to think. Act! I quickly unzipped my shotgun case and cycled a 12-gauge Magnum slug into the firing chamber, then instinctively pulled a replacement slug from my rainsuit pocket and clicked it into the Remington's magazine. Four rounds in the magazine and one up the spout. I felt my heart thumping hard over the wind howl as my ears picked up a semi-rhythmic scraping sound, as if a grizzly was advancing while sniffing and swinging its huge head back and forth.

"I may as well get this over with," I thought as I took three calming breaths, rose to a crouch with my boots solidly under me and lunged around the boulder, barrel first. My ungloved finger was on the trigger, the gun hard against my shoulder, my jaw clenched shut as I focused on the advancing object, within a heartbeat of firing. Eyes wide, determined to do or die, I perceived in disbelief that the moving object was my bright red backpack. The gusting wind had been buffeting the pack uphill as it lay on loose sand grains, then the pack slid back downhill a fraction as the gust slacked off. I had retrieved a snack earlier and neglected to weigh the pack down again with boulders. The whole episode was my imagination in overdrive and I was eternally grateful that I had not pulled the trigger; the one-ounce Magnum slug would have blown a large hole completely through my backpack. Explaining away a large, ragged hole with singed edges in my pack to a bunch of smiling, macho geologists and hunting lodge denizens would have been a low point in my career.

Once the storm's violence died away, the still air behind it felt like a dimensionless liquid, so clean and crystalline I felt like I could extend my arm and touch the snow-capped hills three miles away. I moved upslope to a new fossil bed at the top edge of the ridge, where the ground flattened out to a narrow plateau, and soon afterward a fog bank crept in from the Bering Sea and wrapped me away from the rest of the world as I quietly pried fossil snails and clams out of the crumbly sandstone with my pocketknife and slowly filled my backpack with wrapped specimens. I was penciling my finds in my waterproof notebook when the fog bank slowly lifted, revealing to my delighted eyes a small herd of caribou munching on the tundra fifty yards away. They were silently browsing for grass while I was silently browsing for fossils. We appraised each other for a minute and continued on with our activities, but not long afterward our tranquility was shattered by approaching helicopter blades pounding the air. The 'boos hauled ass to escape the fast-approaching sky monster while I packed up my gear. It had been an unforgettable day in more ways than one.

▲ ▲ ▲

I was almost certainly standing where no human being ever had, on a rocky shelf that took a near-vertical climb to reach and was perched high above the headwaters of the Bear River.

"There's no way I can land there, it's too narrow," the chopper pilot had explained as we hovered above a mile-long, thousand-foot-thick jumble of buff sandstone tilted up at a 45° angle.

"Damn. From eyeballing the geometry of the rock layers, they should have fossil shells in them just like the rocks a couple of miles away where we were yesterday. There's gotta be a place to set down," I pleaded.

There was, a quarter mile away, but the grassy knoll was so narrow that I could not retrieve my gear from the outside luggage compartment of the Jet Ranger, so first we flew to the valley floor and I transferred my pack and gun to my lap, then flew back to the grassy knoll. Once we landed, I hunkered down in a whirlwind of flying gravel as the chopper lifted off right beside me, and an hour's uphill hike put me at the base of a precipitous wall of dark conglomerate split by a vertical crack as wide as my body. The rocky shelf I had seen from the chopper was at the top of the twenty-foot-high bluff. Fortunately, the Peninsula was experiencing one of its rare sunny days, so I cached my pack of bulky clothing, stuffed my bright orange Filson work vest with collecting supplies, slung my uncased Remington across my back, then worked my way up the fissure.

Dropped off alone on a narrow ridge with my backpack and shotgun. The Spirit River, which I later officially named, flows behind.

Awaiting me was a pirate's treasure chest of paleontological gems, hundreds of undisturbed fossil clams and snails that had gently weathered from the enclosing sandstone over the past century or so. They would not have been there if a geologist had visited this spot in living memory; there were no marks from a rock hammer, chisel or maul. I even looked in vain for arrow heads, but the bare, rocky perch was too far from game trails to be a useful lookout, so Aleut hunters had bypassed the site too.

The first paleontologists arrived along the fringes of the Alaska Peninsula in 1899 aboard ship, but the rocks I stood on probably were first glimpsed by a geologist in the 1960s as helicopters became reliable enough to use in such remote terrain. The few geologists who worked this area in the 1970s mostly mapped the rocks from helicopters, since it was too time-consuming to land and "field check" the rocks and fossils on every unnamed ridge of the New England-size Alaska Peninsula.

Pausing to savor the idea of being the first person in the history of North American exploration to stand on that patch of earth, I soon fell to wrapping up the shells lying in the open, then settled down to pry apart a particularly fine bed of well-preserved specimens and beheld the first fossils of the marine gastropod *Crepipatella* ever found in the Arctic. A beautiful cap-shaped snail with delicate sculpture on its outer surface, and an exquisite mini-cup within the shell where the animal had once been attached, it was a delight to the eye. With measured blows of my rock hammer and small chisels, in the manner of a gem cutter, I trimmed the rough rock down to a foot-diameter circular slab some four inches thick, then padded it thickly in paper towels that I bound up in windings of bright orange plastic flagging. Once back in California I would patiently free the specimens from the rock matrix, and later describe them as a new species in a scientific journal. The *Crepipatella* slab weighed twenty pounds and was too awkward and heavy to carry in my work vest, but it was an easy toss down the bluff into my backpack, which would cushion its fall.

Standing at the edge of the dropoff, I hefted the slab a few times as I aimed for my pack twenty feet below; with a little luck it would stay horizontal and land flat. After a final heft, I arced it gently over the ledge and let go. As if guided by an unseen hand, the slab rotated 90° left as smoothly as an Olympic ice dancer, hit hard on the bare rock just downslope from my pack, then rebounded high into the air and rocketed into the Bear River Valley as if possessed of the Spirit of Flight. The tissue-swaddled round slab, festooned in orange flagging, made several bounces above the alder bushes as it accelerated down the steep slope, rebounding into occasional visibility like Br'er Rabbit hopping above the Briar Patch. As it lost height, I followed its journey by observing the downslope shudder of alder branches long after the slab disappeared from view. I was stunned. Silence returned to the Bear River Valley when the only *Crepipatella* specimens that would ever be found in the Arctic settled into their final resting place. I stared after them a long time, mourning the loss. I had been privileged as probably the first in human history to stand on that ridge, and the first to find a fossil *Crepipatella* in the Arctic, even if I could not prove it, so I felt fortunate rather than angry. I gave no thought to scrambling hundreds of feet down through dense alder thickets to search for the priceless specimens because the largest grizzlies on earth roamed that part of Alaska. There were limits to my devotion to the cause.

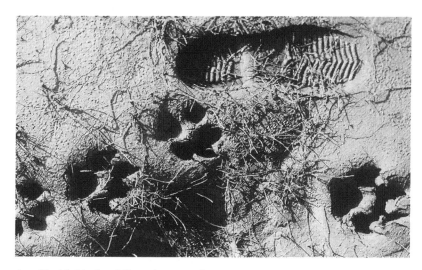

A wolf with big feet followed me one day.

As I plopped beside my pack to munch on a grilled caribou sand-wich, my eye caught a movement in the alders twenty feet away and I reflexively lunged for my shotgun, but stopped in mid-motion when I found myself looking at a mink, not a grizzly. I continued chewing while the motionless furball stared at me. I wondered if the escaping *Crepipatella* had spooked it, then thought it might be more interested in grilled caribou than in me, so I flicked a piece of 'boo over to the little critter, who eagerly pounced on the meat and tore it to shreds in seconds, then resumed its staring. Bit by bit the two-pound predator ate a half pound of caribou and left me with the bread, then darted off.

I was alone again, absent both *Crepipatella* and lunch, but it was worth giving up my entrée to interact with a wild creature. I opened my poetry anthology and it fell open to Longfellow's "Loss and Gain":

When I compare
What I have lost with what I have gained,
What I have missed with what attained,
Little room do I find for pride.

I am aware
How many days have been idly spent;
How like an arrow the good intent
Has fallen short or been turned aside.

But who shall dare
To measure loss and gain in this wise?
Defeat may be victory in disguise;
The lowest ebb is the turn of the tide. ▲

BERING STRAIT, ALASKA

"Eu-re-ka," I said as I lovingly turned the clam specimen over in my hand—savoring the moment, the luck of the thing—as I examined it from every side, "I've got Bering Strait's age nailed."

"What do you mean?" asked the curatorial assistant in the collection room at the California Academy of Sciences in San Francisco, my new home base after I left the USGS. "What's so special about an ordinary-looking clam?"

"It's the genus *Astarte*, which evolved in the Arctic Ocean and dwelled only there and in the North Atlantic for over 100,000,000 years. It never migrated into the North Pacific until Bering Strait opened as a seaway connection with the Arctic Ocean. This specimen was collected in southern Alaska, almost a thousand miles from the Arctic Ocean, so it's an unambiguous signal that Bering Strait was open when this shell lived," I enthusiastically explained.

Clambering around the steep Sandy Ridge stratigraphic section was always hazardous. Photo by Anton Oleinik, 1998.

I knew immediately that the little clam in my hand was the key to unlocking the Bering Strait age puzzle. Scientists of all stripes had labored for more than a century to discover when the strait had first opened, because it was the last seaway on earth whose age was unknown and one of the biggest unsolved mysteries in geology and especially in paleontology. Straits between continents or major islands control the flow of seawater in the same manner that open or closed doors control airflow between rooms in a house. When Bering Strait opened, it allowed cold-water taxa such as *Astarte* to migrate into the North Pacific for the first time in a million centuries, and likewise let warmer-water Pacific species flood northward into the Arctic Ocean and ultimately to migrate into the North Atlantic. An open strait drastically reorganized the ocean circulation of the entire Northern Hemisphere and strongly influenced its marine and terrestrial climate. The strait was important not only to paleontologists interested in north-south marine migrations, but to oceanographers and climate modelers interested in the global flow of ocean currents, as well as to vertebrate paleontologists interested in east-west mammal migrations between North America and Asia.

Conventional wisdom cited the age of Bering Strait at 3.5-4.0 Ma (Mega-annum, or millions of years ago) based on indirect evidence. The lack of hard evidence was maddening until my moment of discovery in the Cal Academy collection room. Feverishly looking up locality information for the *Astarte* in dusty, oversized record books, my heart leapt when I discovered that the clam had come from the Sandy Ridge stratigraphic section near Bear Lake on the Alaska Peninsula, where I had done fieldwork years before. I felt my career pivot in a new direction, because I knew from seeing them in the field that Sandy Ridge mollusks were five to ten million years old, far greater than Bering Strait putative age of 3.5 to 4.0 Ma. I knew I was going to be the one who figured out Bering Strait's age.

In the California Academy of Sciences, holding the specimen of the bivalve Astarte *that was the key to unlocking Bering Strait's age.*

▲ ▲ ▲

"Snap the picture!" I shouted over the roar of the stiff wind as I leaned far out over the edge of the precipice at Sandy Ridge, my left hand wrapped around a four-pound maul, my right grasping a bundle of chisels, and my trusty Remington strapped across my back.

"Just a second," replied my field assistant as he fumbled with the unfamiliar controls of my camera.

I was counting on the "williwaw" wind, blowing at thirty miles an hour, to hold me up, because the cliff I was leaning over is identical to the vertical dropoff atop the nameless 4,000-foot peak across the valley in the background. I hung there longer than I wanted to, but it is my favorite photo of myself in the Arctic, taken atop Sandy Ridge with the wind ballooning out my rainsuit coat but pressing my pants tightly to me, with my hooded face staring straight down into oblivion.

It was invigorating but foolish, and had I known more about williwaws I would not have trusted my life to one blowing steady for long, as I learned the next week when four of us were scouting the mountains west of Bear Lake. The wind had been blowing steadily from the left for at least an hour as we hiked down a narrow ridge of bare rock and we had to lean into it to proceed in a straight line. The wind abruptly stopped, as if someone had switched off a blower, and all four of us staggered left a step or two and instinctively squatted down to avoid tumbling down the steep flank of the ridge. We stood up after a few moments and commented on the surprising turn of events, at which point the wind instantly began again and smacked us just as hard from the *right* side and we struggled again to keep from being blown off the ridge. The wind direction had switched 180° in seconds with undiminished force, which I learned that day was the signature characteristic of an Alaska Peninsula williwaw. Had the wind switched direction like that at Sandy Ridge the week before, I would have had a long fall before smacking into the valley floor.

"What in hell was that?" I asked.

"I forgot to tell you about the wind changing direction like that," said our party chief, Buck, a grizzled and wizened older geologist who had spent thirty years studying Alaska. "It happens all the time around Bear Lake," he said as he fiddled with his pipe.

"When were you going to tell us?" I asked.

"This morning," he answered, "but I forgot."

"I was leaning over a cliff at Sandy Ridge last week and counting on the wind to hold me up," I said.

"I wouldn't have done that," commented our droll leader.

"Anything else we should know?" I asked.

"Well," said Buck, "I'd watch out for bears."

"Thanks," I replied, "you're a real walking survival manual."

"I do what I can," he said as he relit the pipe.

So much for the grand tradition of passing hard-won wilderness lore from generation to generation, the older hands keeping the younger ones safe from harm.

I learned about the hazards of flying in a williwaw along with a Russian paleontologist, Sasha Golikov, a sincere looking Muscovite with squared off brown hair who looked more like a wrestler than a geologist, when our Bell 206B Jet Ranger was descending toward a ridge in the mountains east of Bear Lake. The wind had picked up to forty miles an hour and the pilot said he would have to call it a day, thirty-five being the safe limit for his craft, but we asked to examine just one more locality. The winds had blown steadily from the east all day, so the pilot was crabbing the chopper through the sky with the machine's nose canted far left into the wind, each new gust sending a shudder through the craft. I was grateful for my crash helmet, which not every helicopter has, and which I had bought just for this expedition, because it softened the blows of banging into the ship's ceiling.

As the pilot set up our landing on a narrow ridge, the ship hanging fifty feet above the jagged rocks, we flew through an invisible wind-shear curtain and had the biggest fright of our lives. The wind that had been howling from the east instantly reversed direction, and the Jet Ranger snapped left into a full 360° counterclockwise spin. The craggy ridge spun full circle beneath us before the pilot regained control, and it took a moment for me to comprehend what had happened.

"Did you do that?" I asked in a shaky voice as I mechanically turned toward the pilot.

"No," he replied in an eerily calm voice. "The wind snapped 180° and just spun us around."

I craned my head around to look at Sasha in the back seat and he was robotically shaking his head left and right with a blank look on his face. He was never a particularly calm flyer in American helicopters, since they were so much smaller than the Russian ones he was used to in Siberia. We did land and did not find the fossil beds we had hoped for, but it was hard to focus on fossil collecting after our Tilt-A-Whirl landing and we were grateful to head back to the warm, dry, stationary lodge.

The severity of Peninsula weather was further impressed on me at the end of a July day that had been an unrelieved parade of blustery rain, sleet, fog, hail and snow. As the light was failing, we were perched on a naked rocky hillside overlooking a nameless glacier. I peered intently west at another freezing squall rumbling in from the Bering Sea that would soon envelop us, wondering if we should pack it in for the day or stay out longer. As I stood swaddled in parka, rainsuit and insulated rubber boots, my colleague Sasha took a long look at the weather then stated,

"Lou, even for a Russian, this is shitsky."

"'Shitsky?'" I repeated. "What's that?"

"It means summer in Siberia is nicer than this. This weather is shit to work in, so I say 'shitsky,'" explained Sasha. This new word in the English lexicon grabbed my attention.

"You're right," I agreed, "this really is shitsky. Let's go home."

Unfortunately, our pilot said he was low on fuel and could not make it to the lodge in one load with me, Sasha and Anton, a tall, sandy-haired molluscan paleontologist whose sharp features and intelligent eyes radiated competence and who always seemed to be more neatly dressed than the rest of us, like a model out of a North Face catalog. In addition, a fourth geologist, Brian, who looked and sounded a lot like the George Costanza character on the *Seinfeld* TV program, had been let off earlier a few miles away at Sandy Ridge and needed a ride home too. As party chief, I was responsible for getting everyone home safely, so I sent Sasha and Anton back first. After refueling at the lodge, a tedious matter of turning a hand pump to transfer Jet A from 55-gallon drums into the chopper, the pilot would return for me, scoop up Brian next, then head for home. If the weather held I would be picked up before the incoming squall hit; if not, there was a chance I would spend the night alone and exposed on a storm-lashed hillside, so the pilot had tossed out a duffel of survival gear and food before he left. Once they lifted off I tried to radio Brian, five miles away on Sandy Ridge, to pack up his gear and get set for a pickup, but got no response.

I would savor the hour until the chopper returned, even though I was alone in the remote wilderness, perched on a bare rocky slope where possibly no one had ever stood, subject to being eliminated by several forces of nature—from bears and bad weather to landslides and exposure. Yet I felt free, light in spirit, in control of my own fate. I would stay in this state for as long as the solitude lasted, caught up in the storm in my own way. Gazing through tumbling mist toward the weather-beset Bering Sea coast I profoundly sensed that the Earth was a sphere, that all people and life were connected, and experienced a vivid feeling of oneness with all of creation, knowing that the very rocks I stood on partook of the same energy as I did in some immeasurable way. My experience did not make lab-scientific sense, but I could not deny what I was feeling. The modern concept of science has become bogged down in laboratory studies, which cannot adequately assess many natural processes, and the full extent of nature is undoubtedly greater than the world of everyday experience. My feet felt like they had roots growing through my Danner boots directly into the ground, intimately connecting me with Earth. The savage mountains, the full-blooded rage of the elements beating against my manly body, the lavish diorama of a nameless mountain falling away into a nameless valley split by a river with no name, and my own effort to intellectually conceptualize and emotionally grasp it all, was the apotheosis of being alive. I had had such feelings before in the wilds of the Arctic, but not of such intensity, save for my out-of-body experience on the North Slope years before and a full thousand miles away from where I stood. For a long moment I had a clear feeling that the slender artist of my visions was standing beside me, but when I turned my head slightly there was only the rocky hillside.

My reverie was cut short by throbbing helicopter blades, their rhythmic sound rising and falling through the gusting wind. I scrambled downslope to point out a good landing place for the pilot, my back to the wind and arms extended straight out to a flat spot I had chosen earlier. Once aboard I appreciated the warmth and stillness. Time to pick up Brian at Sandy Ridge on our way to the lodge, but I again failed to raise him on the walkie-talkie, nor could the pilot on his big radio, so it was time to start worrying. A fog bank rolled in from the Bering Sea just as we arrived over Sandy Ridge, concealing most of its 2,000-foot height. We circled above the ridge, hoping for a break in the fog, and occasionally spotted a hole, but not one big enough to land through. At last, the pilot spotted Brian and I wagged my walkie-talkie at the figure on the ground. He put one thumb down while holding his radio. The dumb shit had neglected to recharge his radio overnight, as he had done before, so now he was stuck with no way to communicate. His negligence was the spark for a tragicomic farce that was about to unfold.

The pilot and I discussed the situation on the helmet intercom. Brian was down on the ground, and our machine was once again low on fuel from circling so long in the energetic weather. The pilot suggested landing near the base of Sandy Ridge, from which I would climb 500 feet up to where we last saw Brian and lead him back to the chopper. It was the only workable plan, so he banked toward the landing. We could not have known that a U.S. Coast Guard cutter in the Bering Sea was monitoring our helicopter intercom conversation. The stormy weather broke up our words into disconnected bits, including "low on fuel," "going down," and "on the ground." Alarmed by the garbled transmissions, the Coast Guard ship radioed the Bear Lake Lodge and asked if they knew anything about a helicopter going down in the mountains to the east. The lodge owner, a veteran bush pilot, knew we were out there somewhere, immediately became worried, knowing how fast things can go to hell in the bush, and said he would look into it.

With Sasha Golikov (left) in front of the Sandy Ridge stratigraphic section.

As our rotor blades coasted to a stop and I stepped out of the machine at Sandy Ridge, I thought I heard a plane overhead, and the pilot confirmed it. It was unusual to hear a stray plane way out in the middle of nowhere. Unknown to us, it was the lodge owner in his Super Cub circling above the fog bank that wreathed Sandy Ridge, trying to see if we had crashed or needed help. In order to make this "rescue" easier on myself, I left my Remington behind and strapped on an underarm shoulder harness with a Smith & Wesson .44 Magnum pistol. I hiked uphill at a steady pace, hoping that Brian had paid attention to the landing sounds of the chopper and was climbing down toward me. But no, he was sitting where we had last seen him from the air, waiting by a small cliff that we routinely negotiated by grabbing a solidly rooted alder bush and swinging feet free for a yard over a thirty-foot drop.

"What's the problem?" I asked, out of breath from the fast climb.

"My radio doesn't work," he replied.

"Did you try both channels?

"Yes, it's completely dead," he informed me. Looking it over, there was no obvious damage.

"You didn't drop it over a cliff or something, did you?" I asked.

"No, it's been in my pack all day," he told me.

"Did you plug it into its charger last night?" I inquired. He stared at his feet in silence. The dumb shit had not recharged his radio.

"Why didn't you hike down to the helicopter when you heard us land?" I asked, anger welling up inside me.

"I didn't feel safe climbing down alone," he whined.

"But it was okay for me to climb up to you alone?" I sneered at him as I tossed his dead radio at his feet, grabbed his pack, swung back downhill over the dropoff, and headed back to the chopper, wanting to get off Sandy Ridge before another squall socked us in. I shouted over my shoulder for him to follow me or stay there all night. He eventually followed meekly behind.

The lodge owner was landing his Super Cub at the lodge just as our chopper set down, and said he was glad to see us alive. Seeing my questioning face, he related the story of his message from the Coast Guard. He had assumed that we had gone down in the mountains and he had risked his life by taking off into the storm in his tiny plane to try and locate us through a break in the fog. It was his Super Cub that I heard circling above as I labored up Sandy Ridge.

Brian's negligence had made everyone worry needlessly, made the chopper pilot and me circle around in the fog for an hour burning up fuel, raised an alarm with the Coast Guard, caused the lodge owner to circle around in violent weather in a flimsy little plane, and caused great anxiety for Anton and Sasha back at the lodge. All because he had neglected to recharge his radio overnight. Brian did not quite get that he was an ass, but I made a new rule just for him: the next time his radio "did not work," I was not going to look for him for at least twenty-four hours. He could freeze his ass off and go hungry for a day, and worry about prowling grizzlies, while the rest of us were snug and safe at the lodge. He got the point and always charged his walkie-talkie from then on, but I never invited Brian back to the wilderness. Another personnel lesson learned: never go north with people you cannot trust.

▲ ▲ ▲

I made another, more dramatic landing at Sandy Ridge with Vic, a visiting paleontologist whose average build, owlish glasses and thinning hair marked him as a lab dweller. On the day we approached Sandy Ridge, its lower slopes with the best landing spots were wreathed in fog. The pilot and I decided to land on a narrow ridge upslope, but because it was windy he would need to keep the power on to stabilize the ship against the gusts. The ridge's width was barely more than the length of the chopper's skids, so there was little space to maneuver man or machine. I stepped out and carefully closed the door and made sure it was latched, then opened and held the rear door for Vic, who would not know the drill for properly latching a helicopter door. Chopper pilots hate it if anyone slams a door, which is a fragile and expensive item, and they definitely do not want a door to pop open in flight. After latching the door, I edged rearward as far as possible until the ridge dropped off, then opened the twin thumb latches of the luggage compartment, signaling with my hands for Vic to hold the door open. The downdraft from the throbbing rotor overhead was forceful, so holding the flimsy door open was essential lest it get damaged. Pulling out our packs and Remington, I reclosed the compartment and shouted into Vic's ear, "Follow me and do only what I do!" The ridge was too steep and narrow to get a safe distance from the chopper, so I hollered at Vic to keep his head down and pulled in my own like a turtle's while extending my arm in a prearranged thumb's up to the pilot, who lifted off the ridge amid a terrific thunder of rotor blades and a whirlwind of dirt and gravel. I was pleased to be on Sandy Ridge and turned to congratulate Vic on his first chopper landing.

"That was great," I said. "Welcome to Alaska!" Vic looked back at me silently, eyes wide and jaw slack, still in his ducked-down crouch.

"What's wrong?" I inquired. I feared he had been struck by a flying rock.

"Holy shit," he said, "do you land like that all the time?"

"Oh, that. No, usually we land on a flat spot downslope and walk up here, but the fog's in today. At least we didn't have to make a one-skid landing," I informed him.

"What the hell's a one-skid landing?" he inquired, looking as if he feared the answer.

"Well, if a ridge is really narrow, the pilot just sets down on one skid, not two, while I get out in slow motion, so I don't upset the machine's balance. Usually I've got my pack and gun on my lap, so the landing goes quicker. It's a little nerve-wracking, but sometimes it's the only way to get to a particular fossil locality. I hike down to a flat spot for pick up at the end of the day." He seemed to hang on my every word.

"Remind me never to do that with you," he said, as he shouldered his pack.

"Will do," I said, feeling secretly proud to be the experienced guy unfazed by a manly one-skid landing.

All was not work and bad weather during our Sandy Ridge expedition. On days when fog or wind made flying in the mountains overly hazardous, I endeavored to keep the troops occupied, and one favorite diversion was target shooting at an outdoor range. Many visitors came to the lodge to shoot the "big three" of game animals—grizzly, moose and caribou—and the range was meant for them, but we had it to ourselves the first day we arrived in 1998 and my practice as party chief was for all geologists to demonstrate they could handle firearms safely and shoot accurately. Years in the field had taught me that the most dangerous animals in the Arctic were my fellow geologists with firearms. Some people treated the weapons too casually, even pointing loaded guns unthinkingly at other people. The ammunition we loaded for grizzlies, one-ounce Magnum lead slugs, would have easily blown off an arm or leg or killed a person outright.

On this occasion my students were Anton, Sasha, and Brian, the field assistant of uncharged-walkie-talkie fame. Anton and Sasha were familiar with firearms from many field expeditions in Siberia during their student days in Russia. Anton had since moved to America and was a firearms enthusiast and probably the best shot among us. I had brought along Remington 870 12-gauge shotguns as our main armament and a Smith & Wesson .44 Magnum revolver, Clint Eastwood's "Dirty Harry" pistol, as a back-up weapon if two men were working together. Anyone working alone carried a Remington.

Anton was first up, adeptly handling the shotgun and revolver, then shooting at a standard target from standing and seated positions with impressive accuracy. Sasha similarly went through the drill with ease. Both were good men you could count on in an emergency, a prized quality in the Alaskan bush.

Then there was Brian. He had assured me before coming to Alaska that he was familiar with both guns and helicopters, which turned out to be untrue. He was nervous around the shooting irons, so I started with the basics, first drawing him a sight picture in my field notebook so he would know how to aim at the target. I modeled how to position one's feet and body for the heavy and powerful shotgun so it would not knock him on his ass. Handing the empty gun to Brian, I watched critically as he mimicked what I had shown him and he clicked through a couple of dry fires. So far, so good. He seemed to have grasped the basics, so I inserted one round into the Remington's magazine to see how he would handle the recoil. I expected little of Brian and got less.

Brian positioned his body more or less properly, then nestled the shotgun butt against his right shoulder, but did not fire the weapon. After a few seconds he said that the position did not feel right, so he switched the gun to his left shoulder. A few more seconds went by and no "boom," then he said the left shoulder position did not feel right either. What he did next must be unique in the history of firearms, a move never performed before or since. Commenting absently, "I'll try it this way," Brian planted the butt of the shotgun squarely against the point of his chin, then stood tall on straight legs instead of bracing his legs fore and aft. The heavy weapon wobbled in a general downrange direction in his reedy arms, as Brian reached forward to pull the trigger. The shotgun round he was about to touch off was rated at 3,000 pound-feet of energy and its recoil is vicious enough to bruise a shoulder. Brian was about to shatter his jaw and scramble what brains he had. It was stupidity raised to the highest power.

I instinctively swung my right hand up and smacked him hard in the face where the shotgun butt rested on his chin. His head snapped back as if a boxer had punched him, while the butt of the weapon flew up and I grabbed the barrel, so it was not pointed at anyone, especially me. I had no idea that Sasha was filming us with his 8mm camera. In the video Brian's head snaps back, I grab the gun, then something curiously birdlike, but not a bird, wings overhead. The flying furry thing was Brian's ball cap still attached to a wig we did not know he wore, his suddenly bare head making a gleaming addition to the earth-toned landscape. Oops. Clutching the loaded weapon, I swiveled my head to stare at the rapidly disappearing rug-hat combo that plopped onto the tundra twenty feet away and cartwheeled off in the stiff breeze toward the Bering Sea. Sasha and Anton fell helplessly to the tundra in choking laughter as Brian chased his tumbling errant rug in a zigzag path among the stunted willows. He finally stomped on his self-propelled cranial appliance, and placed his cap and rug askew atop his head, which cracked us up even more until we were helplessly laughing and gasping for breath. Thank god, Sasha had filmed the whole episode, which was the funniest thing I have seen in my life. We could not stop guffawing for minutes, mimicking with our hands and ball caps the Flight of the Rug as a mortified Brian stomped off toward the lodge. I never again let him touch a firearm, but instead gave him a couple of seal bombs, giant firecrackers which fishermen toss at seals that are stealing fish from their nets. Seal bombs might not be the best grizzly protection, but the rest of us felt a lot safer around a weaponless Brian.

Anton was a firearms enthusiast who particularly favored German Luger pistols. Their tiny bullets were worthless for defense against Alaskan predators, but he liked to carry a Luger in a shoulder holster for recreational plinking; he also thought it would be useful against a small rabid mammal, rabies being epidemic in the Arctic. While working alone on Sandy Ridge one day I observed Anton and Sasha collecting fossils on the adjacent ridge 200 yards away, and I watched as a magnificent red fox, which probably had never before seen a human, approach them without fear. The men and fox observed each other for a minute, neither one afraid, when Anton decided it would be better to not have a wild animal standing ten feet from them. He slowly withdrew his Luger from its shoulder holster and fired a round in the air. I heard a faint "putt." The fox did not move. Anton fired twice more, putt-putt. Mister Fox observed them with greater interest, not realizing the fearsomeness of the weapon that had terrorized Europe in two world wars. Sasha ended the charade by chucking a rock at the fox, which strutted away with head high.

An adult grizzly ran by just as we were landing near Bear Lake.

"Say," I spoke on the walkie-talkie, "remind me to bring a Luger next time I'm in the savage wilderness. Looks like it has a calming influence on the wildlife. That might be handy around a charging half-ton grizzly."

"I think I scared the fox," radioed in Anton, "he jumped when I fired the first time."

"But the second and third shots didn't bother the fox," chimed in Sasha. "He didn't like the rock, though."

"That's it then," I said, "Anton can carry rocks in his shoulder holster from now on. We'll all feel safer if his Luger stays home."

Another defect of Anton's beloved Luger came to light when cleaning guns one evening: the thing has a million parts. I was cleaning a .44 Magnum Smith & Wesson revolver, which is basically one large part, and a Remington 870 shotgun, which breaks down into four pieces. In contrast, Anton's disassembled Luger looked like a tiny automobile junkyard that had exploded on the table in front of him. Taken apart, the Luger had a grand total of *forty* parts, including items such as "center toggle link," "firing pin spring retainer" and "recoil spring lever." Who knew you could pack so many teensy parts into such a small pistol? The German love of mechanical complexity had clearly reached its zenith in the Luger. Watching Anton pack all those tiny parts into the small gun fascinated Sasha and me. We quickly finished up our guns while Anton stayed bent over like a watchmaker, still fiddling with the "sear bar" and "mainspring guide," focusing intently to not only reassemble the teensy parts but to do so in a precise sequence. The ideal Alaskan field gun is simple, reliable, accurate and has great killing power, because it takes real punch to stop a charging grizzly. Anton's Luger, in contrast, had the complexity of a Swiss timepiece and the punching power of an anorexic waif. When we test-fired weapons at the lodge's firing range, Anton had to shoot last. If he shot his Luger first, the tiny 9 mm pinpricks in the paper target were obliterated by the larger holes we made with our .44 Magnum and 12-gauge rounds.

Heavy-caliber firearms were a necessity because grizzly bears were an ever-present danger around the Bear Lake Lodge and even a casual unarmed stroll away from the buildings was chancy. In late August, when nighttime darkness returns, it was wise to stare into the dusky twilight for a minute to see if anything was moving, before walking the fifty yards from the bunk house to the main lodge. Sometimes what looked like an alder bush was a bear rooting around for food. Now and then a glance out a lodge window revealed a large, furry head gazing back, followed a moment later by human and bear rapidly retreating. Every few days a group of one- and two-year-old grizzlies gathered on the opposite side of the Bear River from the lodge and the bolder ones clambered across a narrow walkway made of pipework, which put them within 100 yards of us. They were clumsier than adult grizzlies, but it still paid to keep an eye on them when we were going out to the chopper in the morning.

The big bears were always curious, always hungry, and this combo got one bear into memorable trouble. One morning we noticed a huge pile of grizzly turds near the mound of fuel containers by the airplane hangar and we saw that several jerry cans had been knocked off the geometric stack and one had been punctured by grizzly fangs. We estimated that the night-time bear had an eight-foot-long body, because the massive mound of shit was ten feet from the mangled fuel can. A mouthful of Jet A had evidently caused an epic colonic spasm and the startled bruin had projectile-shat a couple of feet. Another morning we discovered a lower nose window on the Jet Ranger cracked at a spot where my boots rested when flying. The pilot found grizzly hairs in the cracked plexiglass and assumed a big bear had lifted the whole machine while scratching its back during the night. He patched the crack with duct tape, then attached a strobe light to the machine and left it flashing all night from then on to keep the bears away.

On one particularly warm day at Sandy Ridge I was sunbathing in just a shirt and slacks, baking in the unaccustomed warmth during a lunch break. The three other geologists were concealed somewhere in the folds and wrinkles of the landscape. I was beguiled to hear the faint, utterly soothing rustle of melt water flowing in thin fingers from the bottoms of turquoise glaciers that jutted from jagged peaks into the unnamed river below me. I consciously breathed in air so pure it almost crackled, my sleepy eyes resting on a herd of caribou munching grass in the nameless valley. Occasionally a faint tang of sulfur tinted the air from Mount Veniaminoff, a miles-wide volcano just north of us. I felt the contentment of a man who had spent a month divining the secrets of Sandy Ridge, knowing where each rock layer and fault was, where the richest pockets of fossils were hidden, and how the grain structure of the sand beds minutely changed up- and down-section, a familiarity beyond the comprehension of a lay person who looks at the earth more casually. The intimacy of the moment allowed the vision of the beautiful artist to coalesce in my mind as a perfect accompaniment to the luscious scene before me. My feeling of connection with the earth and life and my spiritual friend was so intense that I wanted time to stop, wanted that particular moment to linger forever, but my duty as party chief interrupted my reverie and I did a radio check to make sure the others were okay. Sasha drowsily answered my inquiry with a slowly enunciated, "I am drinking in the beauty." With the greatest of ease I can imagine myself back to that moment and place, one of life's sublimely perfect days.

It would only be years later when I discovered that the river flowing by Sandy Ridge was unnamed and I went through the official process and named it the Spirit River in remembrance of that special day.

▲ ▲ ▲

Despite his fetish for Lugers, my friend Anton Oleinik was a rare find and the best field partner of my Arctic career. We had met unexpectedly in Moscow in 1990 when I was with an American delegation to meet Soviet colleagues who also studied the Ice Age history of Beringia, the parts of Siberia and Alaska on either side of the Bering Strait region. Convened in downtown Moscow, the meeting was jam-packed with well-known Russian geologists and paleontologists whose work I used and admired. Anton, being a student who did not study the Ice Ages, had not been invited. Valentina Sinelnikova was the principal worker on mollusks of the Russian Far East, and had made many expeditions to Kamchatka, the Siberian peninsula just across the Bering Sea from Alaska. The fossil mollusk faunas in Kamchatka and Alaska had many species in common, so Valentina and I had much to talk about with the help of a translator. She insisted that I visit her office in the USSR Academy of Sciences' Geological Institute, where we exchanged ideas about molluscan faunas as she paged through monographs she had written about Kamchatka mollusks.

While engaged in this spirited exchange, I noticed a grad student in the shared office who was focused on me like a hawk but who did not come over to introduce himself. At the time Anton was doing his PhD work on Eocene gastropods some fifty million years old, so he felt uncomfortable interrupting our discussion about Ice Age mollusks that were only a million years old. Taking a needed break from Valentina's torrent of rapid-fire Russian, I went over and introduced myself to the young student.

"Hello," I said and introduced myself.

"I know who you are," he replied as he shook my hand, "I've read your publications." I smiled. He certainly knew how to make friends with the visiting Amerikanski. "My name is Anton Oleinik."

"Pleased to meet you," I said. "Are you a student here?"

"Yes, but I'm also an employee of the Geological Institute," he informed me.

I saw that his workspace was crammed with books on Cenozoic mollusks.

"It looks like we both study Cenozoic shells," I commented.

"Yes," he said, "I'm studying Eocene gastropods for my PhD."

It was not every day that I ran into a fellow paleontologist who was interested in essentially the same topic that I was, in this case mollusks of the Eocene Epoch, a worldwide tropical episode that ended some thirty-three million years ago. Anton was delighted to describe his research and he was a walking encyclopedia of Cenozoic gastropods of Kamchatka, as intently focused on them as I was on mollusks of Alaska. His English was far better than the norm among Russian professors and students and we were comfortable with each other right away, so I was happy that he followed the group back to the Ice Ages meeting when lunch was over.

Once we had had more time to talk about fossils of mutual interest, I decided that Anton was too bright and talented to molder in the dying Soviet system. Even a few days in Moscow, where no meals were available in restaurants even with the full staff present, streets were empty of all but a few antiquated Eastern Block rattletraps, food markets lacked food, and everyone seemed to be dressed in shabby castoffs told me all I needed to know about the Soviet system. I had wisely followed the advice of travelers experienced in Russia and brought one entire suitcase of food, which is basically all I had to eat for a week in Moscow, while my American colleagues went underfed. Someone as bright and motivated as Anton needed to be in the West where his talent could blossom.

Once back in California I plotted to import Anton to America. The most critical task was to convince a colleague at a good university to take on an unknown doctoral student, based solely on my assurance that Anton was the genuine article. Fortunately, the professor was willing to be convinced, which opened the way for me to pay for Anton to take the U.S. Graduate Record Exam and Test of English as a Foreign Language at the American embassy in Moscow, and after two years of Soviet and American red tape, Anton winged his way to America.

Anton landed in America in 1992 and got his PhD in 1998. Brilliant but jobless, he applied for a teaching job at Florida Atlantic University along with many other bright paleontologists and came out on top. Just as I had dreamed of collecting fossils in the wilderness as a boy, Anton's boyhood was filled with a dream, equally unlikely of realization, to live where he could dive for colorful seashells in a clear, warm sea. A place such as South Florida, for instance. We would both realize our youthful yearnings, evidence that the universe really does care. Bringing Anton to America was one of the finest accomplishments of my career.

▲ ▲ ▲

Anton, Sasha and I took advantage of unusually clear weather one day to attempt flying through a narrow pass in the Aleutian Range to a fossil locality on the Pacific side that an oil company friend had recommended as having fossil shells like those at Sandy Ridge. The air was crystalline as we approached the mountainous spine of the Alaska Peninsula, but fog materialized and got denser the higher we flew. Bush pilots will fly through anything but fog, so our trip was looking dicey. I was up front with a topo map, marking our progress through the sinuous valleys bounded by precipitous rock walls, while the pilot concentrated on not hitting anything. My topo map had a scale of 1:63,360 or an inch to a mile, leaving me guessing as to our precise placement among the narrow valleys and indistinct mountains looming through the mist. We were feeling our way forward, advancing in weather that would have closed any commercial airport in the world. However, there were so few decent flying days on the Alaska Peninsula that we had to take risks to do our job.

The fog coalesced into a dense overcast, so we were able to fly through a tiny triangle of clear air between the almost-touching walls of the narrow valley and the overarching cloud ceiling. The overcast angled down toward the mountains, so that our triangle of clear air grew smaller and smaller as the pilot flew lower and lower and the walls of the valley drew closer together. I was considering turning back when we flew over a saddle and were in clear air on the Pacific side of the Peninsula, having taken off on the Bering Sea side. Sasha may have been especially happy to land, since he was always uncomfortable flying in small helicopters. In Russia, large helicopters brought geologists to field areas, then left them to hike around for a month; he was used to larger machines, which may explain what happened next.

Sasha bounded out of the Jet Ranger, hurriedly scrambled up a steep gully toward where I had put an X on our topo map for the fossil site, and disappeared into the mist wreathing the outcrops. As he vanished from sight, Anton and I heard the telltale hollow cracks of boulders bouncing against rock walls and dived for the sides of the gully to avoid the mini-avalanche that was coming. Boulders and cobbles rocketed past our heads and ricocheted against the gully walls like cannon balls as Anton and I cursed a blue streak. Trying to follow Sasha up was impossible without courting serious injury; I had had colleagues permanently injured by falling rocks and the risk was not worth it. The mini-avalanche subsided, but we could do nothing but wait; Sasha had not turned his radio on.

Enjoying a bounty of mollusk specimens lying on a rocky shelf beside me at Sandy Ridge.

While this travesty was taking place, our pilot noticed that the triangle of clear air in the mountain pass was getting smaller as the overcast lowered toward ground level. By the time Sasha reappeared with an armful of fossil shells and a shit-eating grin, we had to pile back into the chopper and head back to the lodge. On the flight home and at dinner that night, Sasha regaled us with his experience of collecting what he called "the best-preserved mollusks" he had ever seen, while Anton and I silently stewed. We had barely made it back through the fog-shrouded pass and bad weather kept us from ever again returning to the Mt. Veniaminoff fossil site.

With time left in our shortened day, however, the pilot took us on a grand tour of the inside of Veniaminoff volcano. He zoomed to the top of the 8,000-foot mountain, then dropped precipitously into the snow-filled crater, a miles-across bowl-shaped wonderland of geological outcrops curtained in snow, with a steaming conical vent at its center emitting a plume of sulfurous vapor that gave promise of a future eruption. We circled around and around the central phallic column in the bowl, like a ball in a roulette wheel, then zoomed up to the crater's lip, paused for a moment as the machine's nose tilted forward, then rocketed down the volcano's flank. The lava that had spewed from Veniaminoff was jet black and dramatically contrasted with an anastomosing patchwork of snowfields that were half-melted in the brilliant sun. Sitting in the front seat as we zoomed along at 100 miles an hour only 50 feet off the ground, I felt like a jet-propelled flea hurtling along a zebra's back, or like I was scanning a Brobdingnagian bar code at NASCAR speeds. The mesmerizing rush forever burned itself into my brain and ended only when the snowfield ran out. It was the kind of thrill that wilderness geology provided in abundance, that I had wanted since boyhood, but that rarely happens in normal life.

▲ ▲ ▲

It was a career highpoint for me to document the earliest opening of Bering Strait at 5.4-5.5 Ma, some two million years earlier than previously surmised, in *Nature*, the world's most prestigious scientific journal. In addition, *Nature* cited my paper on the front cover and chose it as the "feature of the week," meaning that a scientist in my field wrote a separate article on the significance of my work. Quite a splash for a small clam that had lain unnoticed in a museum collection for two decades.

The eureka moment seemingly had been arranged for me alone. A few colleagues would have recognized *Astarte* in the Cal Academy collection, and perhaps one or two might have known that *Astarte* dwelled only in the Arctic and North Atlantic oceans for 100,000,000 years. However, I was the only paleontologist in the world who had ever been to Sandy Ridge, knew how old the rocks there were, and that *Astarte* there was an unambiguous signal of an open Bering Strait. Experiences like this one were a reassurance that life is not simply a random arrangement of molecules moving chaotically, but has an underlying pattern.

▲ ▲ ▲

"We're going down," announced the pilot as he threaded the Jet Ranger through a ragged hole in the fog that had instantly enveloped our craft. We had just crossed the craggy volcanic spine of the Aleutian Range that divides the Alaska Peninsula into two worlds, one on the Bering Sea side, and the other on the Gulf of Alaska or Pacific Ocean side, which are connected by narrow, fog-choked mountain passes. The passes had been clear today and drawn us toward uncollected fossil beds along the Pacific coast, so the sudden coalescence of fog while flying over the sea had been a surprise.

Fog equates with death for aircraft in the wilds of Alaska; there is too much steep ground to run into when you cannot see it. Which is why our alert pilot plunged us like a stone toward *terra firma*, which turned out to be tiny uninhabited Ukolnoi Island. Glad to be on the ground, the four of us chatted in tension-relieving conversation until we had fogged over the inside of the helicopter bubble and I decided to take a walk.

"It's been fun dropping from the sky and all, but as long as we're on the ground I may as well go for a walk," I said as I opened the door of the stuffy bubble.

"The whole island is mapped as volcanic rocks, so have fun digging fossils out of the lava," commented my partner, Tony.

The published geological map did indeed show the whole island made up of volcanic rocks, but as I walked along I could not help seeing fossil shells in the rocks, which were obviously sedimentary and not volcanic. Suddenly I hit the jackpot when I spotted a distinctive species of the snail *Turritella* that was known only in Japan from rocks some fifteen million years old. I rushed back to the chopper to announce my good fortune and get my collecting gear, after which my fellow geologists Tony and Victor and the pilot stood around and watched me chip soft shells out of the hard sediments. The sun suddenly broke through as I was working and they wanted to fly to other geological localities.

"Come on, Lou, we're burnin' daylight," said Tony, the party chief.

"That's a really old John Wayne line; we're in Alaska in summer, the sun won't go down until October. I'm working as fast as I can. Besides, I feel like I'm on a county road crew: I'm digging a hole and three guys are standing around watching," I answered. "A lot of these species are new to science; I gotta collect them."

"Well," said Tony, "maybe we could leave you here and come back in a few hours. You like to work alone."

"Well, yeah," I replied, "but right now we're on an uninhabited island in the middle of nowhere that I'm not sure you can even find again. All these little islands look the same. Maybe you won't be able to find me and I'll end up as dead as the fossils. Besides, if the fog comes back and stays a week I'll be screwed."

"Yeah," said Tony, "but maybe that won't happen and we *will* find this crummy little speck of an island again; twice in one week would be cool. What's the name of this place again?"

"If it helps any," chimed in the pilot, "on my flying map this place is called the 'ass end of nowhere.'"

"Makes sense," I said, "considering the clientele."

Being basically good guys, even if they were not paleontologists, they agreed among themselves, without letting on, that we would stay on Ukolnoi Island until I had collected a representative sample of the fossils. Their silent pact gave them free rein to heckle me mercilessly while I focused on the task of collecting enough specimens to show the species' full range of variation in shape and sculpture. As a well-known warm-water species from Japan, the *Turritella* was more evidence of long-ago global warming fifteen million years ago. We were all relieved when I finished, so we could head for the mainland.

In addition to the *Turritella* I unearthed a six-inch-long amber-colored snail that was an undescribed species that I ultimately named *Tyrannoberingius rex* because I thought there should be two T. rexes in the world even if my vertebrate paleontologist colleagues did not agree. So, now there are two, one a snaggle-tooth monster and the other an elegant gastropod. Just after my publication on *T. rex* came out, a colleague from the University of Chicago called me in mock anger, because he had wanted to name a tiny clam *"Tyrannonucula rex"* and I had beaten him to the joke.

Over the decades I made many one-time visits to rich fossil localities in out-of-the-way places, but my time on those outcrops was limited by weather, helicopter fuel, or my companions' geological itinerary. If I get reincarnated as a paleontologist, I will know exactly which neglected outcrops to revisit.

One of my scary wildlife encounters on the Pacific side of the Alaska Peninsula that summer was vividly real, and another possibly imaginary, with the first being a close encounter with a wolverine on Stepovak Mountain, which consists of thousands of feet of dark-gray shale and is completely devoid of vegetation—one of the most barren and brooding places I have ever seen. I had been searching all day for shells in the eponymously named Stepovak Formation of late Oligocene age, about thirty million years old, and finding only scraps of shell. At one point when I was flying in the chopper, a geologist on the ground radioed that he was finding lots of well-preserved mollusks. We changed course for the fossil site and the other geologist in the chopper asked to borrow my Remington shotgun, since he was going to a place that we informally called "Bear City." I grudgingly handed over my shotgun, reasoning that the high slopes of Stepovak Mountain where I was going were barren of vegetation and miles from the coast and that game and predators were unlikely to hang out there. Besides, the geologist already on the ground and I would enjoy safety in numbers and he also probably had a firearm. This bad decision was about to teach me a career-long lesson.

After an hour I had accumulated a nice little pile of Oligocene snails and clams with the help of the other geologist, Buck. I was being careful to avoid knocking any rocks onto Buck, who was working *down*slope from me, when I noticed rocks tumbling toward me from *up*slope. Looking up, I beheld a fast-moving wolverine, the most vicious predator in the northern wilderness and about the size of a large dog, charging straight toward us. I had bumped into wolverines before and knew that they were mindlessly nasty, the only animal not afraid of a landing helicopter and easily capable of scaring off a grizzly bear. I stood up in my bright orange rainsuit and yelled out, "Wolverine!" and Buck got up too. Once the wolverine saw and heard us, it came to a sliding halt with its front feet dug into the talus slope, its squinty little eyes fixated on us from twenty yards away. Buck and I were motionless and not breathing as we maintained intense eyeball to eyeball contact with the animal for what seemed like a week. The creature's mouth was wide open, its gleaming fangs clearly visible and I felt naked and intensely vulnerable without my shotgun and cursed myself for loaning it away. The wolverine finally hopped sideways to our left and disappeared behind some boulders, at which point we resumed breathing.

Visiting a walrus colony at Cape Seniavin near Bear Lake.

The wolverine probably had not seen us until we stood up and surprised it. As the animal bounded away, I discovered I was cradling several large rocks in my left arm, with one in my right hand ready to toss. I was unconsciously preparing to fight for my life. Buck did have a Smith & Wesson .44 Magnum revolver, but it was at the bottom of his pack buried under bags of rocks and gear, which was foolish. But not as foolish as loaning my beautiful Remington 870 to someone else and ending up unarmed in the face of a charging wolverine. It was a mistake I never made again.

My second scary wildlife run-in that summer on the Pacific shore may or may not have happened just after I had been dropped off alone for the day on small, figure-eight shaped Korovin Island, which I was going to scour for Stepovak Formation mollusks. Once the rotor-wash sand-storm had settled I shouldered my pack and began scanning the fifty-foot cliff of gray siltstone behind the beach for fossils. I had taken only a few steps in my lug-soled leather boots when I stopped for no obvious reason and looked behind me, then scanned the cliff edge above. My finely tuned senses told me that I was not alone, that I was being observed by *something*, but I did not see any obvious hazard, although the hair on the back of my neck was standing up and I felt deeply fearful. With my intuition and senses turned to full gain, I somehow knew I was in danger and instinctively unsheathed the shotgun from its case, expecting to see a grizzly come prowling along the beach.

There was no bear, but the brooding dark cliff and narrow, black-sand beach and gently lapping waves suddenly seemed very spooky. A dozen years of Alaskan fieldwork, much of it performed alone, had honed my sixth sense to a razor's edge, and my instincts said I was in danger. I then did something I rarely allowed myself to do, because it was so unsafe: I racked the action of the shotgun to transfer a slug from the magazine to the firing chamber. Then I replaced the chambered round from my ammo supply, so I had four in the magazine and one "up the spout." I imagined a big grizzly advancing on me, from left, right or above and scanned continuously, weapon at the ready and trigger finger poised beside the trigger guard, but saw nothing. Lowering my pack to the beach, I slowly backpedaled toward the cliff from the water's edge, to keep the cliff at my back while tingling with anticipation of what would happen next.

I survived the day unscathed physically, but the episode on Korovin Island was the only time in 34 years of Arctic work that I stayed in one place all day without collecting fossils, too fearful to move. My walkie-talkie did not have enough range to recall the chopper, and I stayed on high alert the whole day, even skipping lunch for fear of being distracted at the wrong moment. No animal appeared by the time the chopper returned—to my immense relief—in the early evening, but I knew that I had done the right thing by staying rooted to one spot. ▲

OCEAN POINT,
ALASKA

Rep and I were spending the morning helicoptering along sinuous North Slope streams searching for fossil mice and voles in Pleistocene, or Ice Age, deposits about a million years old. Charles "Rep" Repenning was a distinguished USGS scientist who had used fossil rodent teeth to establish a biochronology that was useful for dating sediments of the past four million years. Finding a few rodent teeth in this previously unsearched area would allow us to date Ice Age sediments in northern Alaska to within 100,000 years or so, which is pretty fine resolution for the geological record. As usual, the tiny rodent bodies and bones would have long since rotted away and left only their diminutive teeth in the sediments as evidence that they had ever existed.

Intently focusing on a nearby grizzly while holding a Remington .375 Magnum rifle and wearing a .44 Magnum revolver in a shoulder harness.

It is difficult to see rodent teeth even when you are standing right over them, and completely impossible from a moving helicopter, but we were scouting for the thin, yellowish sand beds in which the teeth might be present. Rep, the pilot, and I peered intently to the sides as we flew low along sinuously meandering creeks west of Umiat. We landed now and then to examine sand beds and sift the sand through screens hoping to find the tiny rodent teeth, without success. As we turned back toward Umiat and home, we abandoned the stream we had been following and hopped across the treeless tundra country to the larger Ikpikpuk (ik-PIK-puk) River, which had higher bluffs and thus a greater thickness of exposed Pleistocene strata to examine.

The course of the Ikpikpuk was especially sinuous, having a fifty-foot-high bluff along one bank that exposed lots of sandy sediments, but unfortunately no yellowish sand beds that might hold a trove of mice and vole teeth. However, around the very next bend the pilot halted abruptly in midair as we stared in astonishment at a complete mammoth skeleton exposed in a bluff that had probably slumped away that morning.

"Whoa," said the pilot, "is that one of those rats you're looking for?"

"I wouldn't call it a rat; it's more like a woolly mammoth," corrected Rep with a smile.

"Well, just in case it *is* a rat," I joked, "maybe we should get out of here in case its descendants are still around."

"You're right," said the pilot," I forgot to pack mouse traps in our survival gear, so we wouldn't be safe here."

"No problem," I chimed in, "I've got a 12-gauge to terminate any and all rodent infestations."

"How about you clowns landing the ship so we can check out the mammoth and scout around for rodent teeth," interjected Rep.

From tusks to tail, the entire mammoth skeleton was exposed in a standing posture, having died from sinking into a mud bog ten or twenty thousand years ago. Rep already knew that the University of Alaska had a warehouse bulging with mammoth bones, so we gave no thought to collecting them. A new crop of bones was unearthed every spring when North Slope rivers that had been frozen solid all winder thawed and the surging currents cut into the soft bluffs where the mammoths were buried. In addition to nobody wanting the mammoth bones, Rep was equipped only with tiny vials, small artists' brushes and the sharpest of tweezers to collect and handle mice and vole teeth, not gigantic elephant bones.

Continuing the joking, I commented, "You know, Rep, you could collect a thousand mice and vole teeth, maybe fill a whole thimble, and they'd weight, what, a quarter ounce? On the other hand, a single mammoth bone would weigh more than your lifetime collection of rodent teeth and we'd be done for the day."

"Makes sense to me," added the pilot. "Plus, you'd have something to be proud of, big enough to show your friends."

"Well, *my* friends like to look at mice teeth, so let's spread out and look for a sand bed that has some in it," said Rep in an attempt to raise the level of our conversation.

Unfortunately for rodent science, our search for a sand bed bearing their teeth was in vain. Still, it is not every day that you begin by searching for mice and accidentally find a woolly mammoth, even if we did not collect it. Once we got back in the chopper, the pilot poured on the coal for Umiat, because we did not want to be late greeting an unwelcome visitor, our boss from D.C.

This was my first time as party chief and I led a multi-faceted expedition to investigate Cenozoic and Mesozoic mollusks, vertebrates and plants at outcrops spread across a 200-mile swath of the North Slope. It was a complicated undertaking, but since leading a wilderness paleontology expedition was exactly what I had dreamed about as a boy, I gloried in organizing and leading it. Unfortunately, the size of my expedition had attracted our boss's attention in far-off D.C. and he had decided at the last minute to pay us a visit.

We had hardly unloaded and fueled up the Jet Ranger from our mouse-scouting trip when a Cessna 206 with the boss inside bumped to a halt on Umiat's dirt strip. Since our chopper was about to go out to examine a Mesozoic plant locality, and there was no time like the present, I gave the boss time to pee but not to unpack before shoving him into the waiting chopper. The Jet Ranger carrying the boss had not been gone 30 minutes when the pilot radioed in that someone was injured and that he was returning to Umiat, at which point I broke out our first aid kit.

The boss had broken his leg when he slipped while crossing a creek, because his boots had crepe soles instead of heavily lugged ones, so he was an accident waiting to happen in Alaska. He had broken his leg within sixty seconds of stepping off the chopper. Welcome to Alaska, free accidents, no waiting!

There was nothing to do but fly him 300 miles to a proper doctor in Fairbanks, and I decided to stabilize his broken leg with an inflatable plastic splint, which was a clear plastic affair with a zipper along one side that enclosed the entire leg and looked like a giant Christmas chimney sock.

Propping up the boss on the steps of the "Umiat Hilton," as pilot and Umiat resident O.J. Smith referred to his headquarters hovel, I gingerly removed the boss's left boot while others supported his fractured leg. Gently slipping on the inflatable splint, I slowly zipped it up from his foot to the top of his thigh. Next came inflation, which was accomplished by blowing by mouth into a tube that arose from the top of the splint, right at my boss's crotch level. As I bent down over the splint and blew into the tube, cameras clicked furiously behind me, followed by rude comments:

"It looks like you're enjoying yourself a little too much," noted one cretin.

"So that's how you get ahead, as they say, in the paleo group," commented another churl.

"Looks like Lou's up for promotion," observed a former friend.

"I can't blame you for trying to give, I mean *get*, ahead," opined another low-life.

"Your boss sure picked the right field party to visit," slandered another loser.

I made sure the splint was blown up nice and tight the first time, so I would not have to repeat the performance in front of that particular audience. We helped the boss, now more comfortable, to O.J.'s Super Cub and waved goodbye as they disappeared southward toward the Brooks Range and a doctor in Fairbanks. We found out later that the flight turned into a hellish ordeal for the victim. I had blown up the splint as tightly as possible, but had not taken into account the drastically lower air pressure in a plane several thousand feet above the ground. The higher the Cessna got, the tighter the splint gripped the boss's leg, which soon turned purple. By the time O.J. gained enough elevation to fly over the 9,000-foot peaks of the Brooks Range, the boss was in agony, his leg in a relentless vice, his screams drowned out by the roar of the engine and unnoticed by O.J., who was hard of hearing anyway. O.J. later said he thought he heard something unusual but was not sure what it was.

▲ ▲ ▲

My main reason for being on the North Slope was to revisit the early Cenozoic mollusk beds at Ocean Point, 60 miles east of Umiat, where I had had an out-of-body experience during a life-threatening storm the previous summer. Another experienced molluscan paleontologist, Phil, and I would camp there for ten days to thoroughly collect the molluscan fauna, the first people ever to do so. The only way to get there was in O.J.'s Super Cub configured on floats for landing on the Colville River right beside the fossiliferous beds in the shoreline cliff, and I would be the first to fly out as the only person in the group who knew where the beds were.

I could not have been happier as I sat behind O.J. in his tiny Super Cub, jammed between and under bundles of survival gear. It was my first ride in a float plane, and I marveled at the silky takeoff, absent the rumble and bounce of the usual dirt airstrip, as we gently rose from the muddy Colville River. We flew low on a sunny morning and I was enthralled to spot grizzlies, wolves, and a moose during the 60-mile trip over the variegated green tundra and blue thaw lakes until the Ocean Point bluffs rose into view. It felt like a homecoming. After we circled the area for grizzlies and glided to a stop on the river, I piled my gear on shore while O.J. went back to Umiat for Phil and more gear, the second of the five trips he would make that day. After waving goodbye, I began hauling gear up the 100-foot cliff, climbing the same gully I had ascended a year ago to the tundra-covered plain where I had had my out-of-body experience.

My first order of business was to erect the heavy canvas ten-foot by ten-foot tent, for weather protection in case the sunny day turned suddenly nasty, but merely getting it to the top of the high cliff was such a chore that it taught me to use only lightweight domed nylon tents in the future. Once that monster was up and solidly staked into the permafrost, I rested on the cliff edge, feet dangling over the river, admiring the grand sweep of the muddy Colville River across the horizon-filling expanse of green tundra. Without trees or large bushes to distract my eye, while scanning the horizon I once again sensed to a degree beyond mere intellectualizing that the earth was a globe, that life was a thin, precious skein upon it and that consciousness pervaded all animals, plants and the earth itself. The vision of the slender, short-haired artist also arose in my mind and she was somehow intertwined with my life in a still-unknown way. I could not have felt happier or luckier, even if I could not fully comprehend my feelings about life or the familiar but unknown woman.

O.J.'s daughter had been kind enough to make us bag lunches before we left Umiat: thick ham sandwiches, fruit, chips and a Coke. The next Super Cub load would include Phil and more gear to lug up the cliff, so I decided to eat while I had the chance, wolfing down the two fat sandwiches while my legs dangled over the river bluff and I took in the magnificent tundra view. After he landed and we had lugged equipment up the bluff, Phil and I sat down to watch O.J. take off from the river, as I once again marveled at being in such a wondrous place. My reverie was broken when Phil took one bite of his ham sandwich then violently spit it over the cliff and yelled, "Yech, maggots!" I looked over as he held his sandwich open, revealing a swarm of maggots wiggling over the ham, the same ham I had just eaten in my two sandwiches. I am sure I turned pale, as my gorge rose and I began violently puking my guts out right then and there, the thought of ingesting two maggot sandwiches a few minutes ago too revolting for words. Had not O.J.'s daughter noticed the disgusting fly larvae infesting the ham as she sliced it, or did she have a perverse sense of humor?

Float plane landing on Colville River at Ocean Point.

It took hours for my guts to settle, and even longer for my mind to stop obsessing on maggots tartare, and in the meantime Phil and I hiked down to the the fossil beds at river level. His knowledge of Cenozoic mollusks complemented my own, but still a large portion of the fauna consisted of genera we could not identify. We both recognized genera that were supposedly restricted to older, Mesozoic faunas, but they were sitting side by side with genera supposedly known only in the Cenozoic Era. The age of the fauna was not clear, but it was satisfying to work side by side in Alaska with another paleontologist, a first for me. Up to that time I had been in field parties with regular geologists and had no opportunity to talk shop with anyone while collecting fossils. Our first day of collecting went by quickly, both of us making discovery after discovery of genera and species we had seen only in scientific journals.

Phil and I did not always work side by side, because the fossil beds extended for several hundred yards along the river and we often spread out to properly scout the area; by late afternoon I was slowly making my way along the boulder-strewn river bank back to camp. At one point I heard a distinct whoosh sound, as if someone had thrown a softball right by my head, but saw nothing unusual when I looked around. The second time it happened, the whoosh by my head was accompanied by a loud screech. Looking up, I beheld a large bald eagle swooping upward, apparently recovering from a diving attack on my head! A more distant screech alerted me to its mate circling high above and in the act of turning over into a dive. I ducked down to ground level as the ball of feathers and talons went shooting by. I scanned the cliff tops for a nest, which we always gave a wide berth to for reasons of our safety and theirs, but saw none. Maybe the big birds were merely passing by and decided to investigate me. There *were* peregrine falcon nests here and there on the cliff top, and they had been a major pain in getting permission to camp at Ocean Point. Even if the eagles were only hunting for falcons, and harassing me for fun, I still had to get the half mile to camp with my head still attached to my shoulders. I caught the eagles' attention by shooting one round from the Remington and waving it overhead, then marched back to camp with the gun carried upright on my shoulder. This awkward pose slowed down my trek to camp, but relieved any thought of an eagle talon suddenly piercing my skull. Sometimes the wildlife is a pain in the ass.

I had planned to set up our second ten-foot by ten-foot tent to shelter supplies, but abandoned the idea the next morning when the wind rose to over 50 mph and I realized it would be a fight simply to keep our single boxy canvas tent from blowing away. The tent was our only shelter against subfreezing wind chill and without it we could suffer from exposure.

As the wind picked up, it alarmingly bowed in the front wall of our tent, and the rotted canvas of the borrowed tent would not take such punishment for long. We tried stacking heavy footlockers and backpacks against the bulging tent wall, but the wind gusts simply flung them aside. Desperate to save the tent and ourselves, I assembled a center pole from our spare tent and jammed it into the sagging tent corner to hold it up, then grabbed another tent pole and supported my body upright, backing against the pulsing tent wall, by jamming the other end of the pole into the tent floor in front of me. My hasty measure kept the tent wall from bulging in dangerously, but Phil had to step in to spell me before long. We could each endure this pounding for fifteen minutes at a time, with each gust jolting us inward a foot, before we needed to rest. The storm blew fiercely all night and if the wind had ripped the canvas, our tent would have instantly inflated into a giant khaki balloon and we would have been beaten to death by our own packs, cots, footlockers, food boxes and shotguns as we cartwheeled crazily down the tundra within a canvas shroud tied up in flailing tent ropes and stakes. We were in a life-or-death fight, the Arctic having once again suddenly turned murderous.

The borrowed tent was well beyond its useful life, the canvas rotted and fragile. Four times during the gray night, grommets ripped from an outside corner of the tent, the tent rope fell slack to the ground, and the tent corner collapsed inward as the savage wind clawed at the new concavity. I rummaged in a footlocker and found a grommet repair kit that I had never used or even seen before. It was a confusing selection of round brass grommets in halves, a steel punch large enough to fit over them, and a hollow punch to pound a hole in the canvas against a wooden block. We slipped out into the clawing wind in our parkas as I tried to read the instruction card.

Our first desperate lesson in grommet repair was a nightmare in the middle of a freezing Arctic hurricane. Phil clutched tight to the maniacally flapping tent edge at chest height, while I both supported the edge from underneath with the wooden block *and* simultaneously held the hole punch above it with my left hand; my right hand held the rock hammer for hitting the punch to make a hole. The canvas flapped like mad, we were pummeled off balance by the wind, and the wooden block and hole punch spasmed up and down with the canvas, so more than half the time I unintentionally hammered my gloved left hand, but eventually I punched a round hole in the canvas.

Pocketing the hole punch, I grabbed the grommet punch and again supported the canvas with the wooden block while simultaneously pinching upper and lower grommet halves around the hole. It was maddeningly difficult to keep the grommet halves aligned with the hole while also supporting the wooden block in just the right place with only one hand. I also had to support the heavy steel grommet punch with my left hand, struggling mightily to align the wooden block, upper and lower grommet halves, and grommet punch with a hand that seemingly did not have enough fingers to properly do the job. I could not afford to miss the grommet during the brief moments when all the parts were in alignment, so switched from the light rock hammer to a four-pound sledge hammer. We shouted encouragement back and forth while we struggled to align the maddeningly flapping parts, but it was hard to understand each other over the roar of the wind and the vicious snapping of the canvas. I waited until there was a brief letup in the wind, then struck hard with the sledge, but I missed and hit my gloved hand. It took four blows to seat the grommet halves together. With the new grommet in place, we reattached the tent rope and then went around the outside of the tent pounding all the stakes back into the tundra. The surging wind had loosened them all with its constant rhythmic tugging.

Tent at Ocean Point beside the Colville River, on the same spot where I had had an out-of-body experience the year before.

Exhausted by our foray outside, we resumed jamming our backs into the bulging tent wall in fifteen-minute intervals. Unfortunately, the grommet in the same corner of the tent ripped out three more times that night and we went through the same desperate exercise to put in a new grommet while worried sick about our tent inflating like a balloon and blowing away, leaving us without protection, radioless in the middle of a freezing hurricane. The storm blew out by morning and we spent that whole day sleeping. Our tent looked like a crumpled Baggy, but it had survived and we were alive. I had learned my lesson about avoiding heavy, boxy canvas tents that would blow away and switched in the future to windproof domed nylon tents.

The fossil beds at Ocean Point were best developed right where we were camped, but I had seen from the O.J.'s Super Cub that thinner and less fossiliferous beds extended upriver for a couple of miles. There was no efficient way to get to these beds, because of the continuous talus slopes along the base of the river bluff that slowed hiking to a crawl. Fortunately, another part of my field party was camped on a Colville River gravel bar only about ten miles upstream and they had a couple of inflatable Zodiac rubber rafts with outboard motors. One of the rafts motored down to where Phil and I were camped and picked me up for a short haul to a fossil bed a couple of miles upstream from our tent, where I would spend the day alone collecting shells.

Sediments as old as those around Ocean Point, some sixty million years, would normally be as hard as regular rocks that have been buried miles deep in the earth and subjected to crushing pressures at some point in their geological history. In contrast, the Ocean Point beds had never been buried deeply and were so soft I could scratch my initials into the sandy sediments with my penknife or fingernail. Despite their softness, the sediments formed impressive 100-foot-high river bluffs because they had been saturated with groundwater and frozen solid since the start of the Ice Ages 2,000,000 years ago. The Ocean Point cliffs were frozen in place. They were fairly safe to work around in cold and cloudy weather, but became a serious landslide hazard when the 24-hour summer sun warmed them up on a cloudless day such as the one when I was dropped off from the Zodiac.

The shells were so abundant at this new site that I hardly moved fifty feet all day while filling my pack with fossils. However, as the Midnight Sun circled around to beat directly on the cliffs where I was working, the cliffs became unstable when the frozen groundwater holding the sediments together melted. I soon realized I was in a dangerous spot when landslides thundered down to the left and right of me for a mile on each side; some were the size of a dump truck load while others were the dimensions of an apartment house. It does not take a large rock to disable a person; a fellow USGS geologist was hit in the spine by a single fist-size rock in Alaska that forevermore cost him the use of his legs, while the man who discovered dinosaur bones at Ocean Point in the 1960s was killed there by a landslide the following year. Landslides were a fact of life along the Colville River, and the place where I was collecting that day had particularly weak bluffs. It was unnerving to see and hear the sun-warmed 100-foot cliffs loudly collapse into the river on both sides of me all day long.

I was relieved to hear the Zodiac clatter into sight at the end of the day and was all packed up to leave by the time the raft nosed ashore. I handed my unloaded shotgun to Marie, a geologist, and lifted my pack onto the edge of the raft for her to drag onto the floorboards. I had been standing in cold mud all day, and my calf-high rubber boots were thick with it, so I spent a few moments surveying the Zodiac to see where I could step without getting both occupants' gear muddy. As I was contemplating my next move Marie screamed, "Jump!"

I reacted without thinking, leaping without hesitation into the Zodiac, face down with arms out like a diver, and Marie grabbed my belt and pulled me aboard as the outboard burst into high-revving life. My legs from the knees down were still sticking straight out from the bow, and boulders struck my rubber boots with loud thumps as a major landslide rumbled down the 100-foot cliff and into the Colville shallows behind me. My two pals in the Zodiac had been facing shore and saw the landslide start at the top of the cliff behind me, and I am eternally grateful that Marie yelled out a warning. If one of them had not been looking in the right place, and the other had not had his hands on the outboard controls, they might have been a moment too slow to save me. Had the raft arrived a minute later, my crushed body would have lain under tons of rocks, the landslide that buried me looking just like a hundred others along the Colville. "What happened to Lou?" would have remained an unanswered question. I had been lucky to escape death by inches. It is good to be with quick-thinking friends when you are in the middle of nowhere.

Over the next week, Phil and I steadily collected hundreds of Arctic mystery mollusks, but we could not decide on their age except "late Mesozoic or early Cenozoic." In fact, Ocean Point yielded its secrets only slowly. It was not until fifteen years later that I published a comprehensive monograph on the molluscan fauna, after painstaking preparation, or cleaning, of hundreds of specimens; I spent thousands of hours in study before I inferred an age of 60 to 65 Ma, within the earliest part of the Cenozoic Era. These mollusks had lived just after dinosaurs and ancient mollusk lineages went extinct and were replaced by mammals and modern mollusks.

While preparing our Fourth of July dinner of freeze-dried packets over a propane stove one bright evening, we heard a plane coming from the direction of Prudhoe Bay, some 75 miles away. It sounded different than normal, because it was skimming just above the tundra and headed directly at us. The twin-engine Piper Apache looked like it was on a strafing run and almost blew down our tent as it blazed overhead. Now that he had our full attention, the pilot circled back and tossed something from his window as he flashed overhead and disappeared toward the horizon. We watched the object plummet to the ground fifty yards away and ran over to retrieve it. The pilot had made an ERA Aviation ball cap into a parachute, below which swung a plastic pint of bourbon and a half-dozen sparklers wrapped in a sheet of paper. Scratched in pencil on a torn notebook page was, "Lou, your girlfriend says hi."

I learned later that my girlfriend of the time had freaked out at my weeks-long disappearance into the Arctic wilderness. At that time we had no radios in field camps and were completely and blissfully out of touch with the world. My girlfriend had called all over the North Slope to track me down, eventually connecting with an ERA dispatcher in the Prudhoe Bay suburb of Deadhorse. She dictated a long-winded, emotional plea centered on her feelings of eternal love, loneliness, hope, resolve, joy at my return, and so forth. The harried radio dispatcher, who monitored three radios for traffic from half a dozen bush planes and helicopters spread across northern

Alaska, had no time for a long-winded plea from a panicked civilian in California. He abbreviated her extended monologue, which had attained the length of a Victorian novel, to the brief note dropped from the plane. More important than the note was the plastic bottle of cheap bourbon, which had unfortunately cracked open; by the time we retrieved it, half the contents had soaked into the sandy ground. Phil and I, however, appreciated the after-dinner snort when we celebrated the Glorious Fourth with sparklers that were barely visible in the glaring Midnight Sun.

After ensuing years of study, I concluded that the more-ancient Ocean Point molluscan taxa had continued to live past the Mesozoic-Cenozoic boundary extinction event by virtue of evolving in the Arctic, where they had survived months of total darkness every winter. As a result, the cloud of dust that supposedly enveloped Earth at the end of the Mesozoic, when a meteorite strike in Yucatán, Mexico, supposedly killed off the last of the dinosaurs, did not strongly affect these Arctic Ocean shells. My idea about the survival of Arctic Ocean mollusks past the Mesozoic-Cenozoic extinction event came to be widely accepted, a satisfying resolution to a mystery that took almost half my career to untangle, from first seeing Ocean Point in 1977 to publishing my monograph in 1993. All in all, our expedition to Ocean Point had been one of the most productive field trips of my life, and the world would not have known any of my conclusions if that storm had demolished our tent or the landslide had entombed me.

Collecting at Ocean Point was definitely worth the risks of falling rocks and perishing weather. The insights I had gained into the composition of the early Cenozoic Arctic Ocean molluscan fauna could not have been gained in any other way. The nature of the early Cenozoic Arctic Ocean had mostly been a matter of conjecture prior to my work at Ocean Point, and now it had a solid basis in fact and a known relationship to the world ocean. Another revelation had been the out-of-body experience during my first solo visit there, which had similarly placed my worldly life into a broader context. ▲

BARTER ISLAND, ALASKA

"Are you one of the geologists?" asked the electrician as he set his food tray across from mine in the galley of the Distant Early Warning Line (DEW Line) radar site on Barter Island, in the extreme northeastern corner of Alaska.

"Yup," I replied while chewing. I was annoyed that he had come by, since I tried to avoid the DEW Line workers, too many of whom had been onsite without a vacation for two years to build up a nest egg and in the process had gone certifiably bonkers. The lives and mental evolutions of the three dozen male civilians, plus one woman on the kitchen crew, in this microcosm, would have made a fantastic doctoral thesis for a psychiatry student.

"Are you lookin' for buried treasure?" he inquired hopefully.

"No, archaeologists do that. We look at rocks and fossils," I informed him.

My last tent camp in the Arctic, at Carter Creek in 2005; my sleeping tent is on the right. The supply tent is fifty yards from the sleeping tents in case a grizzly comes by when we are asleep.

"Did you find any dinosaurs?" he continued, expressing the universal impression that only dinosaurs turned into fossils, no other animal or plant ever did. "No. We're looking for fossil seashells, not dinosaurs," I educated him.

"Oh," he said, disappointed. "Have you run into any grizzlies?" Now he was more in his element.

"Sure," I said, "lots."

"What do you pack?" he inquired.

"Remington Model 870 12-gauges with one-ounce Sabot slugs and .44 Magnum Smith and Wesson Model 29 revolvers with 240-grain semi-jacketed hollow points," I replied, knowing he would eat up the gun and ammo lingo. There is a bewildering variety of bear-killing shotgun ammo, each of which has vociferous advocates in Alaska: plain lead slugs, rifled slugs, Sabot slugs, Brenneke slugs, and Magnum versions of all these. I could see in his rheumy eyes that I had gained points for being ammo-savvy.

"Are your .44s Magnums semi-automatic?" he asked.

"No, we use revolvers with six-inch barrels. They're more accurate. I don't think anyone makes a semi-auto .44 Magnum pistol," I answered while still trying to eat.

"Sure they do," he said, reaching into his overalls and withdrawing a huge semi-automatic .44 Magnum pistol from a shoulder holster. "I got one right here," he said, brandishing the monster gun in the air. "It's a stainless steel Auto Mag. I carry it everywhere."

"Nice," I said, setting down my fork while tensing my body and mentally preparing to grab his arm and wrestle away the pistol.

The electrician reminded me a lot of Gus, a man I had met who was living alone in the middle of nowhere at Cape Yakataga on the coast of south-central Alaska. Gus did not precisely live *nowhere*, because he had made a home of an abandoned oil tank thirty feet in diameter and two stories high, something you normally see in an oil refinery. The tank had been built in the 1930s during a minor oil boom and then abandoned with a few hundred gallons of crude oil still in it. Gus had come across it in modern times and figured it would make a comfy weather-proof home in the wilds, except for the oil inside, so he had carefully used hand tools to cut a door-size opening in the side of the tank to get rid of the oil. He wanted to torch the oil, but somebody, probably a bush pilot, would have noticed the mile-high column of oily black smoke even in the Alaskan bush, so he waited for heavy fog to set in, *then* set the tank on fire. He had industriously welded together a balcony with a stairway inside and used a cutting torch to make windows with iron shutters on both levels. It was an admirably simple solution to the bush housing question, and Gus explained over a beer that the best feature of the neighborhood was that there were no neighbors. He would have fit right in at Barter Island if he had been less of a loner.

A lot of us in the Barter Island DEW Line galley were armed, because stepping outside was always risky; polar bears wandered off the Arctic Ocean ice, only a couple of hundred yards away, to root around the garbage dump at all hours. Still, I was disconcerted to have a loaded pistol waved in my face by a wild-eyed semi-recluse whose cultural life consisted of reading comic books and jacking off in his bunkroom for the past 700 days. Once he had returned his Auto Mag to its underarm holster, the electrician related that he liked to scare incoming DEW Line military officers with exaggerated stories about polar bears and grizzlies coming onto the site and mauling people. He gleefully followed up his tall tales by strapping to his feet a couple of metal trash can lids, which he had cut into outlines of gigantic polar bear paws, then stomping in the snow or mud outside the new officers' bunkrooms. In the morning he would point out the humongous paw prints outside and caution the newbies to always be on the lookout for bears, then hang his head and walk away muttering, "I hope we don't lose these guys, too."

▲ ▲ ▲

In later years, after the DEW Line station was torn down following the Cold War, we stayed in the neighboring Eskimo village of Kaktovik at the Waldo Arms, a lodging run by the companionable Walt Audi and Merlyn Trainer. The Waldo Arms has loads of character, looks as if it had been thrown together by a slightly tipsy carpenter from old shipping containers and battered packing crates, makes no pretense of appearances on the outside, but has snug two-man rooms, a homey air, coffee and snacks always out in the kitchen, and killer meals done up by Merlyn.

It was there one year that I was shocked to learn that camping in Alaska had changed in an amazing way: even though bears still shit in the woods, people now shit into plastic bags, at least on federal lands. Recalling the Texaco camp at Driftwood in 1974, when we had nightly shit-barrel bonfires, the burning of offal has now taken its place with scaring grizzlies away from camp in a helicopter as part of the Glorious Old Days of Alaskan fieldwork. Now, not only do campers not burn shit, they cannot even bury it in the woods or tundra. This wondrous efflorescence of bureaucracy happened when I was not paying attention sometime in the early 2000s, but affected me in 2005, when I was again on the North Slope. While residing in the cushy splendor of the Waldo Arms, I had the misfortune of mentioning our next day's helicopter flight to a representative of the U.S. Fish and Wildlife Service, known to Alaska veterans as "Fish and Feathers."

"So you're heading off into the bush tomorrow?" the bureaucrat inquired as he guarded a pot of coffee and pile of raisin scones.

"Yup."

"How many in your party," he asked.

"Four."

"For how long?" he inquired further.

"Two weeks."

"Do you know about the shit bags?" he asked as he looked me directly in the eye. I had an unworthy, if justified, flash thought of the two questionable student assistants my professor friend, Anton Oleinik, had brought on our trip, but quickly suppressed it.

"Uh, shit bags, what shit bags?" I fumbled. I wondered if maybe there were nefarious characters up to no good out there in the remote bush, maybe robbers skulking about the tundra, preying on isolated campers like us.

"Real shit bags. Plastic ones. So you can haul your shit out with you," he informed me.

"With me where?" I queried.

"For when you fly back to Kaktovik," he replied directly.

"Why would I fly bags of shit to Kaktovik?" I wondered. "This place is already depressing enough without adding more crap to the scenery." As I spoke I looked out a window beside our linoleum-topped table at years-old abandoned snowmobiles, mounds of general refuse and, amazingly, considering that Kaktovik is an Eskimo village, an abandoned refrigerator.

"Well, you're supposed to," he said, "to keep the wilderness clean."

"I've been working in the Alaska wilderness for thirty years and never saw turds piled up all that deep. I mean, they would have been obvious," I commented. "Besides, all the turds I've seen are animal droppings. People always bury their shit in little holes. The animals are the only ones that leave turds on the ground, and I'm not sure how you're going to get them to crap into little plastic bags."

"The bags are only for human visitors to federal lands," he replied as if explaining something to a child, "so bacteria from The Outside don't get introduced into the wild."

"The bags are just for visitors?" I inquired, "Eskimo don't have to crap into bags?"

"Right," he said. "The Eskimos live here, they have different germs."

"But, half the village migrates to Seattle for the winter, and their kids in college come to Kaktovik for summer break from all over the U.S. The bacteria in their colons must be the same as for anyone living in the Lower 48," I explained patiently.

"I suppose so," he replied with disinterest, "but they still live here and you don't, so you have to shit into bags and they don't," he huffed with bureaucratic finality while staring directly at me. The sense that I was defeated was palpable.

"Yeah," I said, "it makes sense when you put it that way. So where do I get a supply of wilderness shit bags?" I inquired with feigned sincerity.

"I've got a bunch in my room," he brightened, leveraging his hefty bulk up from the table as he slurped down the last of his coffee, "Come on back and I'll give you some."

"Gee," I said as we stood in his tiny Waldo Arms room, "those look just like lawn and leaf bags back home."

"They are," he replied somewhat testily. "I ran out of the special bags."

"There are special shit bags," I asked in amazement, "just for, you know, shitting in the woods? I mean, if there *were* any woods around here." The closest trees to Kaktovik were 200 miles south, but I surmised that the special bags were suitable for shitting on tundra too.

"Yeah," he replied, "the special bags are biodegradable, but I ran out, so I'm asking people to use regular plastic bags."

"I thought shit bags would be smaller. Those lawn and leaf bags will balloon out like a parachute when you're taking a dump in a 40-mile-an-hour wind. I'd probably take off like a balloon and they'd see me on DEW Line radar and think I was an incoming Russian bomber or something. The shit bags aren't safe," I remonstrated.

"Well, nobody's complained yet," stated the shit-bag bureaucrat.

I suspect nobody had actually used the shit bags, though I am sure they claimed they had to placate Fish and Feathers regulators.

My mind reeled at the thought of four people in my tent camp shitting into lawn bags for two weeks, then hauling a helicopter load of turds forty miles back to Kaktovik, only to deposit our accumulated plastic-wrapped droppings in the town dump. However, two decades in federal service with the U.S. Geological Survey informed me that this was not a joke, despite appearances. I imagined that federal shit-bag committees had met for months, eco-weenie groups had been consulted, earnest-appearing lawyers had summarized prevailing shit-bag policies in First and Third World regimes, samples of shit bags had been examined and maybe even tested—the mind reels—opposing positions staked out, compromise reached, and binding shit-bag policy hammered out in bureaucratic boiler plate. In other words, I had no fallback position, and further resistance was futile. Smiling, I counted out fourteen federalized shit bags, one for each field day, commented on the wisdom of the federal policy, thanked him for his clear elucidation of the inexplicable, and retreated to my own cramped room in the Waldo Arms.

I did haul the federalized bags forty miles by helicopter to our campsite at Carter Creek, but we never used them. We did have bowel movements during the ensuing two weeks, but it was simply easier to shit into a hole in the ground—a practice probably begun by *Homo erectus* in Olduvai Gorge—than to aim one's stools toward a plastic bag and hope for the best. The reader will appreciate that wilderness elimination is not always a fair-weather deal, a zephyr-free controlled spasm beneath azure skies. All too often in the Arctic, the urge to evacuate one's bowels strikes during the foulest weather imaginable: the wind is howling along at some ungodly rate so that your tent walls flap like crazy and you are afraid the stakes will pull out and send you cartwheeling down the tundra like Barbie in a Ziploc, while a deluge of biblical proportions percusses loudly against the thin tent fabric. More often than not, my colon has held off announcing its evening plans until I had already settled in for the night, grateful to be warm and dry after another long day working in foul weather. I had taken off my rainsuit and parka, gloves and boots, pants, shirt and long johns, and hung each to dry on lines strung inside the tent dome. Just after I had slipped into my sleeping bag with a good book, I became aware of that familiar feeling of lower abdominal fullness. At which point I cursed a blue streak, enraged once again that my body had not bothered to form a stool just five minutes earlier, or subtly announced its evening itinerary before I had shucked off $2,500 worth of Danner boots and North Face clothing.

Muttering under my breath at the injustice and inconvenience of it all, I would rumple on my foul weather gear, put my Remington into its carrying bag, unzip the tent, zip it closed, and slip out into the storm, feeling sorely put upon. Usually, I saw the latrine shovel stuck in the ground fifty yards away, a Ziploc bag of TP tied to it, meaning there was nobody using the latrine area. If the shovel and TP were not there, one of my campmates was busy with them, and I impatiently hopped from foot to foot to stay warm in the lashing wind and rain while they finished.

Not much conversation took place as my fellow scientific adventurer handed the shovel and TP to me on their walk back to the tents. The latrine area was a bare patch of ground behind a hillock or in a nearby gully, not upstream from our drinking water supply and not upwind from camp. Each person dug a new hole for each colonic event. The trick during a roaring Arctic storm was to unsnap and unzip four layers of clothing as quickly as possible, while standing on your gloves to keep them from blowing away, pull your rain pants, slacks, long johns and underwear far down your legs, aim your ass at the hole you had quickly dug with the folding U.S. Army shovel, and let fly to the best of your ability, making sure that your thermals, shirt, parka and rainsuit tops were not hanging dangerously low, or your rainsuit pants, slacks, thermals and undies were not too high. The sudden smack of gale-force wind, rain and maybe sleet on your private parts was always an indignant shock, being exactly as pleasant as stepping through thin ice on a lake and plunging in up to your genitals.

Making shit happen fast was imperative, to say the least, since your bare ass was fully exposed to the polar elements. Not to mention that a grizzly, wolverine, wolf or fox could lope up at any second while you were in a full squat, which was not a position we had practiced target shooting a 12-gauge from. Finishing up was always a challenge, because it was difficult to manipulate toilet paper around the manically flapping bulk of your wind-ballooned rainsuit and parka, hobbled as you are by heavy boots, thermals, slacks and rainsuit around your ankles, all the while stomping on your gloves as the wind clawed at them. The TP instantly dissolved in the rain if you had not folded it into convenient pads ahead of time while shielding it inside your parka *before* undressing. Given the miserable conditions and awkwardness of the whole procedure, it was worth taking an extra minute before retreating through the storm to your tent, to be sure your body was truly finished, and that this indignity would not be inflicted upon you a second time that evening. Which sometimes happened anyhow.

The idea of performing this acrobatic act of elimination while clutching a government-issued shit bag that is ballooning downwind was too preposterous to consider and probably was not even feasible. Mercifully, nighttime peeing was not much of a chore, since everyone had a pee bottle in their tent. Even women geologists did this, using a wide-mouth jar, rather than hang their ass out in a storm for such a trivial reason.

If necessary, I would have filled the federalized bags with dirt to masquerade as shit if anyone from Fish and Feathers had been paying attention when we returned to Kaktovik. There being no lawns to mow or leaves to rake within 400 miles of Kaktovik, I had no use for the bags and gave them away to some Eskimo fishermen who were just heading out into the Arctic Ocean. They laughed up a storm when I described how the shit bags were for bringing federalized turds back to town.

"Check out the two grizzlies on the tundra," said Marie as she pointed to the large bears closing in on each other a third of a mile north of our camp.

I saw with binoculars that the smaller bear, weighing maybe 500 pounds, was trying to defend its kill, but an 800-pounder drove it off after several charges and swatting matches. We heard the loud roaring even from our distance, and it was fascinating to watch the huge brutes fighting.

"The small one's losing out and you never know where it might go," I said as I gathered everyone together on a small knoll near camp for safety. Three of us carried shotguns, so being together lessened the chance of someone being shot by accident. Sure enough, the juiced up smaller grizzly that was driven off the carcass hauled ass straight for us. A grizzly will not hesitate to attack a lone person, but it is unusual for one to charge a group of people; this one had not read the rules, so it came right at us. Once we were in a tight group, I lay on the rocky knoll and took aim as the grizzly thundered in at 30-plus miles an hour.

"Nobody else shoot until after my second shot, if it's still coming in," I announced.

I had been taught to not shoot a charging bear until it was within 25 yards, but that is less than two seconds away when a grizzly is running full tilt. I had also been told to shoot for the bear's legs, to immobilize it. I knew from past experience that the rule was bullshit, because the bear's legs were mostly concealed by the tundra's grassy tussocks, the bear was dodging left and right around rocks and tussocks, and rising and falling with the ground. I could not even *see* the flailing legs, much less aim at them. The dark brown bear stood out from the green tundra, a predator intent on our destruction growing larger by the second.

I fired the first one-ounce lead slug into the ground ahead of and just to the left of the rapidly enlarging fur ball. The Remington boomed, the ground ahead of the bear exploded in a burst of dirt and rocks, and the grizzly noticed not at all. My second shot hit the ground just ahead of the onrushing beast and at that point the bear turned around like it was tethered on a rubber leash. It headed away from us at full speed to the west, also avoiding the larger bear by the caribou carcass. We never saw the attacking bear again, but the bigger grizzly stayed with the kill for a couple of days to gorge on caribou meat, and its proximity made it even harder for us to fall asleep under the Midnight Sun. After all, grizzlies eat anything, plants mostly, but prefer meat such as us. I had taken the normal precaution of grouping our sleeping tents fifty yards from the supply tent storing our food, on the theory that a grizzly or polar bear would go there for food while we slept, instead of attacking one of us in our sleeping tent. Like all theories, it was flawed, because each sleeping geologist was potential grizzly food. In sad fact, while we were camped out that summer, two experienced campers were attacked by a grizzly in their sleeping tent along the Hula Hula River, just twenty miles to the east of us. The bear killed and ate the unfortunate people, and was later shot by Eskimo hunters when someone in a passing raft noticed the empty, disheveled campsite.

We had set up camp at Carter Creek, fifty miles west of Barter Island, to study rocks we called the Nuwok Beds that had been discovered at the start of the 20th century but never studied by professionals. During a brief stopover years before, I had collected samples of mollusks that I estimated to be five million years old and microfossils that implied an age of 25-35 million. To resolve the age disparity, I organized a field party with a variety of specialists in mollusks, microfossils and stratigraphy. For the first time, various experts would collect fossils and sediments at the same time from the Nuwok Beds and we would hopefully resolve the age dispute and understand the Arctic Ocean's history and paleoclimate a little better.

It was in the nature of things that my professional specialty kept me closer to the earth than other geologists and I got dirtier than anyone else on our expedition. Others may have worked harder, but they usually could eyeball rocks or chip off samples without lying full length on the ground. Despite getting muddy, I never lost the thrill of being the first human being to see a particular fossil shell. I marveled at the immensity of time it had lain there, and my luck at being the one to uncover it, remove it from its sediment burial, carefully cushion and wrap it, record its location, ship it to my office in California, and after publication send it to the Smithsonian with my name on the specimen label. This is exactly what I dreamed of doing as a boy, and I was aware not only of the shell's age, but my own arc through time from my boyhood beginning.

Like the great majority of scientific studies, ours was steady and unspectacular grunt work. The outcrops along Carter Creek extended for half a mile along a range of rounded hills, so the hours between breakfast and dinner sometimes went by while we each attended to solitary study of the rocks and fossils.

We may have lacked chairs and a table, but we needed thousands of calories a day to work in cold weather and I made sure we never suffered for lack of food in any tent camp I organized. If we were in the High Arctic—the North Slope or Arctic Canada—I brought along a couple of foam coolers filled with steaks and set them into holes chopped into the permafrost, or permanently frozen ground, to keep cool indefinitely. Once the steaks were eaten we were reduced to beef jerky and pouches of freeze-dried meals, blocks of cheese, massive jars of peanut butter, trail mix, cases of candy bars, and the ubiquitous Sailor Boy Pilot Bread unleavened and unsalted crackers that were an edible plate for whatever you piled on then. Over the years I learned to overstock every food item by thirty percent in case we ate more than expected, which usually happened, or in the event the bush plane was days late picking us up due to a weather or mechanical problem. Better safe, and well fed, than sorry.

I was startled fully awake in bright sunlight at 3 a.m. by an animal sound I did not recognize. After decades of bush adventures I thought I was familiar with every wilderness sound, but this was something new, a kind of distant mewling that grew louder as I listened while lying atop my sleeping bag in thermal underwear. I slowly unzipped my tent flap, stuck my head out and saw nothing unusual. Stepping out with shotgun at the ready, I heard the strange sound more clearly but I could not place its direction. I even looked overhead in case it was a flock of birds. Nothing. Then, looking south, every sense sharpened, I viewed an almost hallucinatory sight in the distance.

A large caribou with magnificent antlers trotted by within touching distance as I sat quietly collecting fossils.

We were camped at the base of a line of rounded hills covered in green tundra grasses, and the hills a quarter of a mile away were changing from green to brown, the effect looking like caramel sauce poured over mint ice cream. I could not comprehend why the hills were darkening. It did not make sense; there were no clouds to cast shadows. Suddenly the scene snapped into awesome clarity. I was staring at a huge caribou herd, tens of thousands of animals, their brown bodies flowing over the grassy hillsides like liquid, pouring into our campsite valley, migrating westward into Alaska from Canada. "Hey, you guys!" I shouted toward the other four tents, "Get up. You won't believe this." We stood in silent awe as the herd slowly browsed its way along, many newborn calves included. We learned later it was the annual migration of the Porcupine Herd of caribou, 150,000 strong, named for the Porcupine River in northern Alaska and Canada.

We remained transfixed as the herd covered the hills and filled the valleys between our camp and the Brooks Range Mountains to the south. The edge of the moving herd came closer and closer to us as the main mass of caribou hove into sight. Caribou appeared at the head of our campsite gully, paused to look us over for a moment, and then were propelled down the steep slope toward us by the jostling of the animals behind them. Several of the big deer ran among our tents, and we suddenly worried that one of the animals would trip over a tent rope and break a leg, thereby becoming grizzly food right in camp, so we shooed the hooved mass away as best we could.

The herd streamed by all morning and throughout the day as we attended to our scientific work, and thinned to a westward-moving trickle in the brightly lit evening. An even more primordial scene played itself out as we stood beside the supply tent at dinnertime spooning down tin plates of beans, when a caribou cow dashed out of a gully to our left going full speed only twenty-five yards from us.

"I wonder what she's doing?" asked Marie, a fellow paleontologist.

"Whatever it is, she's really hauling ass," I commented.

"Maybe she's looking for a calf," Marie speculated.

The caribou's situation resolved itself as two wolves shot out of the gully hot on her heels. The cow was making a beeline for Carter Creek, which she could cross with a few prancing steps while the wolves would have to slowly dog paddle across. The wolves needed to kill her before she reached the creek or lose their dinner. We were transfixed, spoons halted in midair as we held our collective breath. The lead wolf slowly pulled ahead and edged closer and closer to the desperate cow, finally drew even with her haunches and sank its fangs into her leg. The caribou tripped or had her hamstring severed and went down hard in a spray of dust and gravel. The other wolf sprang ahead and ripped out the cow's throat as she flailed her legs and squealed her last. We saw, heard and smelled the kill and stood transfixed for a long time before anyone spoke. We had been privileged to witness a life-and-death scene that a National Geographic cameraman would have given his left nut to film. The wolves fed on the carcass for several days, as did foxes and ravens, but we had had enough of dinner for that night.

Getting to sleep was difficult after the excitement of the caribou migration and the wolf kill, but then it was always difficult to sleep in the High Arctic. Even after a tiring day of fieldwork it was challenging to sleep under the Midnight Sun unless clouds or fog moved in. A sleep mask, or at least a towel over your face, was mandatory, but these often fell off. Summer after summer in the High Arctic, I awakened with a start every hour or so, the bright sunlight convincing my brain that I had over-slept, only to see that it was 1:30 in the morning. Waiting to fall asleep again, I sometimes heard one of the others awaken and curse the light. The Midnight Sun added a surreal cast to working on the North Slope or in the Canadian Arctic Islands. The fact that it illuminated a stark landscape where man was seemingly never meant to be reinforced the otherworldly aspect of working in the High Arctic.

Storm clouds moved in during our last afternoon at the Nuwok Beds, catching us away from camp during a final walk-through of the stratigraphic section. We five were hiking back to camp in soft rain, looking forward to dinner, when I told the others to continue without me. I needed to be alone and waited for my companions to disappear around a ridge. Once by myself, I pushed back my rainsuit and parka hoods and observed the low hills across Carter Creek through the veiling mist, then turned my face eagerly upward to feel the cool droplets caress my skin. I did not know if I would ever return to this remotest corner of America; I wanted to *feel* this place one last time, to impress it into my soul, so that in the future I could conjure up at will the mist cooling my skin, the swelling hills of tundra grass, the sinuous creek, the pressure of the ground under my booted feet, the delicious security of being suited up against the rain and cold, the feeling that I could do anything, while staring into the heavens in solitude on the northernmost edge of America.

I once again had the familiar sensation of the Earth being a comprehensible, even intimate, globe, on which all life was ineluctably connected; humans, animals, plants, even rocks seemed to partake of some aspect of consciousness that I could not grasp but clearly sensed. The feeling of connection was intense as once more I experienced the intimate and satisfying feeling that roots grew from my boots directly to the center of the earth. My lifelong vision of the tall, slender woman with short, dark hair seamlessly blended into the moment, part of a pristine future that I sensed was waiting for me but that perhaps I would never experience in this world. All was One, and I *knew* that the human mind and body were the interface between an infinite material realm expanding ever outward and an infinite, fathomless spiritual realm within. I have returned to this wealth of sensations many times during stressful episodes in life and invariably it soothes me.

The beating helicopter blades awakened us at 6:42 the next morning, much earlier than scheduled, as the machine settled onto a river gravel bar by our supply tent. The high overcast and light sprinkles were building toward a big storm, so the pilot was pulling us out early for Deadhorse, the industrial town beside Prudhoe Bay where we spent a full day boxing up fossils, rocks and gear to ship home. As always at the end of a field party, our cozy camp rapidly fragmented into bits and pieces.

My research team's study showed that the Nuwok Beds were 26-27 million years old, much older than many experts had supposed, and most surprising, that the mollusks in them had dwelled in an Arctic Ocean that was just as cold as it is today. My own studies at Ocean Point and on Ellesmere Island in Arctic Canada had shown that the Arctic Ocean marine climate in the earliest Cenozoic some 60 million years ago was ice-free and temperate. Nuwok time at 26-27 Ma evidently was when the Arctic Ocean first froze, which roughly corresponds to the development of extensive glaciation at the other end of the world in Antarctica, and the Arctic Ocean has remained continuously cold since then. Our work documented that the Arctic Ocean had cooled millions of years earlier than previously thought.

This early cooling of the Arctic Ocean was what had thrown off my age estimate of the Nuwok molluscan fauna. I had inferred an age of five million years because the fossil mollusks were nearly identical to the mollusk species living in the adjacent Arctic Ocean. In fact, the early onset of freezing ocean temperatures had slowed down evolution of the Arctic Ocean's molluscan fauna to the point where the ancient species from Nuwok time had survived almost unchanged. Modern shells from the nearby coast looked almost the same as the Nuwok shells I had collected, even though there was a 26-27 million year age difference between them. It was a satisfying realization, even if I had been wrong in my initial age estimate of the shells. ▲

ELLESMERE ISLAND, ARCTIC CANADA

"This is the place, Strathcona Fiord," I shouted over the roar of the engines to the pilots of the de Havilland Twin Otter bush plane that was overflying Ellesmere Island in northernmost Canada and pointed toward the North Pole. I held up the topo map and aerial photo I had been using to navigate, pointing out distinctive coastline features and the meandering Thalassa River that emptied into the fiord.

The two pilots carefully evaluated the lay of the land and agreed, "We're definitely at Strathcona. Now where do you want us to set down?"

That was the question. A Canadian geologist had collected intriguing fragments of Paleocene mollusks, some 60,000,000 years old, from this valley several years before, but the locality data were imprecise due to a lack of adequately detailed topo maps. We were here "on spec"; we did not *know* where the fossil shells were, but the one published report *implied* that they cropped out on the left bank of the Thalassa River. We not only had to guess where the shell beds might be, but we also had to find a landing spot as close to there as possible, because four of us were being left off for a month to work by ourselves 300 miles from our supply base at Resolute Bay.

Pointing to the exact spot on an aerial photo, where my boots are planted on the shore of Strathcona Fiord, Ellesmere Island, Canada, at nearly 80°N. Photo by Anton Oleinik, 2001.

Roy Chapman Andrews would have been disappointed by my choice of projects, because I forsook a dinosaur-collecting trip to the North Slope for a mollusk-collecting expedition to northernmost Canada. Just the year before I had given a seminar about my work on Ocean Point Paleocene mollusks to the National Academy of Sciences in Washington, D.C., and a colleague at Shell Oil, Richard Emmons, had called later to discuss my work, and as a bonus sent me a box of presumed mammoth bones from near Ocean Point that had lain in a Houston warehouse for more than two decades. My USGS colleague, Charles Repenning, had recognized the bones as being dinosaur, not mammoth, almost as soon as I had passed them on to him. By one of those flukes of fate, had I not given a National Academy presentation on my molluscan work, the North Slope dino bones—the best-preserved dino bones in the world—would still reside in a Houston warehouse, like the Ark of the Covenant in an *Indiana Jones* movie, lost to science. The exact locality from which the dino bones had come was uncertain, so I organized a North Slope expedition to find the bone beds the following summer. However, as summer approached, I was asked to join the expedition to Arctic Canada, where a colleague and I would be the first paleontologists ever to study sixty-million-year-old Paleocene Epoch mollusks at 80° north latitude, only 600 miles from the North Pole. The Ellesmere trip would be a pioneering foray into the heart of the Arctic Ocean realm to discover what the polar marine environment had been at the very beginning of the Cenozoic Era, whereas an Ocean Point visit to locate dino bones for someone else to study had an errand-boy aspect to it, so I passed off leadership of the Alaska trip to another geologist.

My childhood fascination with dinos had faded when I realized that studying them was an end in itself and provided few insights into past environments. I was interested in the present as a key to the past, which had been the mantra for geologists since the late 18th century, and the oceans are full of mollusks from which I can infer ancient paleoenvironments, but there were no living dinosaurs and so no way to use them as proxies for past environments. Passing on leadership of a trip to rummage for dino bones in Alaska was a no-brainer.

Which is how I found myself in a de Havilland DHC-6 Twin Otter descending toward either a bumpy landing or a crash on Ellesmere Island. The two pilots circled lower and lower as we all compared the coastline and mountains against topographic maps and aerial photos. It was imperative to land in the right spot, since fossil mollusks had been reported from only that one river valley in all of the vast Canadian Arctic, and we were being sent out for a month on our own. The pilots soon determined that there was no safe landing spot for their big plane along the left bank of the Thalassa River, closer to where the fossil beds cropped out. This was unfortunate, because now we would have to land on the right bank, which meant crossing an icy river every day at our peril to get to the fossil beds. The pilots were searching for hard ground that was relatively smooth and long enough for a heavily loaded bush plane to land, a particularly nerve-wracking time for all onboard. Hard or soft ground can look the same from the air, and at one point they flew at ground level and dragged the wheels in the dirt to test whether or not the ground could take the weight of the largish bush plane. If the ground was too soft, our machine would screw into the ground amid an explosion of body parts, both metal and human. They then circled around and evaluated the grooves our tires had made in the raw earth. Once satisfied at the ground's firmness, the pilots committed us to a landing while we four passengers held our breath and stared out the portholes with grim visages.

"You ready for this?" asked the pilot.

"I've made a lot of bush landings in Alaska, but this place seems to have a pretty high pucker factor, what with the boulders sticking up from the ground and all," I commented.

"Yeah, there's a pretty high pucker factor here," chimed in the co-pilot, "but nothing like one landing on Bylot Island. After that one we had to fly one of the scientists down to Montreal to have seat upholstery surgically removed from his asshole." Upon which both pilots broke into uproarious laughter. I had heard the old joke before, and felt comforted that they could joke around while making such a remote landing. Our bouncy landing was uneventful, then the pilots taxied as close as possible to the Thalassa River, our only source of drinking and cooking water for a month in the polar desert.

Strathcona Fiord was as forbidding on the ground as it had been from the air.

"This place makes the North Slope look like the Amazon rain forest," I commented to Dick, the fellow paleontologist who had organized the expedition and brought along two student assistants.

"No kidding," he replied. "I don't see *any* vegetation, just bare dirt."

"I see why they refer to these latitudes as the 'polar desert,'" I commented, having read that Ellesmere Island received less precipitation than Phoenix, Arizona, owing to the lack of evaporation from the almost perpetually ice-covered Arctic Ocean. "The North Slope looks like the 'banana belt' in comparison."

"At least we won't have to worry about plants covering up the rocks, since there don't seem to be any plants," he said.

"Those dark blotches that look like big ink spots on the ground are dwarf willows," shot back one of the pilots. "They're only an inch high and you can camp right on top of them."

"Great," I said, "no plants means no herbivores means no carnivores, so we shouldn't have to worry about bears."

"We're too far north for grizzlies, of course, but the occasional polar bear wanders in from the coast, so keep your eyes open," commented the same pilot. "You'll likely see arctic hare and foxes, and maybe wolves and musk oxen."

"That would be cool," said one of the students.

"And none of the animals are shy up here, since they haven't seen people before and aren't afraid," added the pilot.

We were all quiet after he said that, mulling over the prospect of wolves and polar bears that were not shy.

Basking in the Midnight Sun beside our supply tent at Strathcona Fiord in a photo taken—to the second—at midnight. Sleeping tents are in the background.

One of the most evocative feelings in Arctic fieldwork is to watch the bush plane roar off in a cloud of dust and wing back to civilization, leaving us alone to our fate. It had taken months to arrange the many logistical details that were vital to work and survive in the Arctic, then we had flown 300 miles from our supply base at Resolute Bay over an unforgiving and unsustaining wilderness to an island from which we could not escape by foot. Excitement was at a fever pitch for our scientific goals, but we were doing something hazardous and would be subject to all the vicissitudes of weather, wildlife and the land. It was great to be in the polar wilderness and much fun and adventure awaited, but we felt strangely abandoned. The plane's departure was a bittersweet moment, a churning mix of joy, excitement and anxiety. It was jolting to realize that standing at nearly 80° North I was farther from my home in Palo Alto, California, than if I had just landed in Ecuador.

My itinerary to Strathcona Fiord had taken me through Montreal, where I had promised to buy a box of wine for camp. I imagined that boxed wine would not be popular in a French-speaking city, but I found a liquor store that was a trove of week-old vintages in boxes of all sizes. Wanting to do the best job possible for my wilderness buddies, I staggered out with a twenty-liter box of white wine, more than five gallons. Divided by thirty days and four men, the wine would be a nice complement to dinners of freeze-dried chicken tetrazzini or peanut butter on pilot bread. Suspended from a ceiling pole of our main tent, the wine supply was even more generous than planned: imagine our delight when one of the two students declared that he never partook of alcohol. Twenty liters divided by three sounded a lot better than being divided by four, so we three tapped the box right then and toasted his commitment to clean living.

Unfortunately, our other food stores were not as abundant. This was my first field camp where I had not planned the month's food in advance, but instead relied by default on the party chief who had organized the fieldwork before I became involved. He had never worked in the Arctic and did not realize that in a strenuous work environment such as we faced at Strathcona Fiord each man consumed about 6,000 calories a day, the more fat and sugar the better, and that bringing thirty percent extra food was mandatory to account for weather emergencies that could delay our extraction. I missed the cases of candy bars, bags of beef jerky and blocks of cheese I had in my Alaska camps, while being appalled at the abundance of a canned gray paste labeled "potted meat food product." It was going to be a long month from a culinary standpoint.

After two days of searching, we discovered the fossil shell beds in what we informally called the Five Mile Hills, to commemorate the fossils being that far away from where someone had put an X on our topo map.

Getting to the fossil beds required a two-and-a-half-hour hike uphill in the morning and a downhill return journey in the evening, crossing the Thalassa River in hip waders each time. I hated hip waders because they are tricky in a fast-moving river if you are wearing a heavy backpack, because the force of the water against your legs increases geometrically as the water deepens, and soon you are performing a precarious balancing act, trying not to tip your body too far one way or another because your heavy pack will pull you over. Even worse, if the icy water overtops your boots, it fills them almost instantly and you cannot move; the waders would have become so heavy that you are trapped standing midstream in immovable boots, with a backpack and gun bag weighing you down even more. Without help you are in serious trouble; which is why I rarely used hip waders when working alone in the Arctic. Better to wear calf-high rubber boots and risk getting wet feet every now and then.

The fossils were worth the work. In short order I recognized some of the same genera and species that I was then studying from the Paleocene beds at Ocean Point in northern Alaska. I found other taxa I had read about from Paleocene faunas in the North Sea region of Europe, and yet others I had seen in museum collections from Paleocene beds in South Dakota. Strathcona Fiord is the most central of these locations, being only 600 miles from the North Pole, and the only place where Paleocene shell species from Alaska, South Dakota and Europe occur together, so it is akin to a Rosetta Stone for Arctic Ocean molluscan faunas of sixty million years ago. Taken together, the shells from Strathcona Fiord and these other regions define a distinct early Cenozoic Arctic Ocean faunal realm that had little in common with coeval faunas of the northern Atlantic or Pacific oceans. "Thank you," I whispered to the heavens, in gratitude for the rich trove of shells that lay before me at both the northern edge of North America and the leading edge of my scientific specialty.

The shells were a bitch to collect, especially the clams. Sitting in plain sight, the most abundant shell, an oval, white clam about four inches long named *Arctica*, looked whole at first glance. However, up close I saw that years of -70°F winter freezes and summer thaws had minced the specimens into hundreds of tiny fragments barely held together by gravity and inertia. The mere act of gently blowing on a specimen dismayingly exploded it into tiny pieces. To make matters worse, the shells were essentially floating in a stratum of fine, loose sand that had never become lithified or hardened in any way. The shells had lived and died in a shallow sea near land some 600,000 centuries ago, became buried thousands of feet deep in sediment over the eons, then more eons later had been uplifted by tectonic forces to become exposed at Strathcona Fiord. And all the while the enclosing sediment had amazingly remained as loose sand. Excavating whole specimens from the sandy matrix was going to be a supreme test of collecting ability.

After messing up several clams, I figured out how to collect them intact, starting by removing individual sand grains from a postage stamp-size area of the clam with a fine artist's brush, followed by the barest spritz of clear spray lacquer. When that dried, I sprayed a heavier coat of lacquer on the small area of exposed shell. Once *that* dried, I moved onto an adjacent stamp-size area and repeated the entire process with brush and lacquer several times until the whole clam shell was exposed and lightly glued together. That was the end of the beginning.

I worked on three or four specimens at a time, removing sand grains from a second clam while lacquer was drying on the first one. Once the spray lacquer had hardened, I gently brushed over the whole shell surface a coating of heavier glue that took hours to dry and I usually let it go overnight. Now that the outer surface of the clam was stabilized, I gingerly excavated around the shell with a knife until the glue-covered specimen was perched on a pedestal of loose sand that I then patiently lacquered and glued just like the specimen. After again drying overnight, I had a pillar of loose sand with a clam shell at one end that was ready to be collected. Then I sliced the base of the pillar from the ground, turned it over, and ever so gently sprayed and glued it. If everything went as planned, *mirabile dictu*, I had made a glue-box of loose sand with a shell on one face that had taken days to construct. Swaddled in cotton, toilet paper and paper towels, the priceless specimens were carefully arranged in our backpacks to survive the rough two-and-a-half-hour hike back to camp. After dinner we unwrapped the day's specimens and made sure they were dry and intact, touching them up here and there with glue before lovingly rewrapping them and packing them in barrels of powdered laundry detergent for eventual shipment home.

Confronting the alpha male wolf that boldly led his pack into our camp several times, just before I shot-to-wound it, after which the pack stopped harassing us. The low, dark plants are willows.

As tedious as this collecting might seem, I loved it. The painstaking excavation process played to my thrill of discovery, appreciation for the beauty of the shell, awe at being the first human to see a shell that had lain undisturbed for eons, pride in my collecting skills and meticulous attention to detail. I was in hog heaven.

Dressing for work on foul weather days at Strathcona Fiord before the start of our daily two-and-a-half-hour uphill hike to the fossil beds, 1984.

How I felt before the start of our long uphill (and at the end of the day, downhill) hike every day.

I trace my patience and attention to detail, as well as my sense of adventure, to my grandmothers. Like a lot of smart people, my grandparents correctly read the signs that Europe was going to hell again, so they bailed out before World War I. All four departed separately from what is now Croatia and paired up in America. My maternal grandmother, Katarina Medvedarovich, threatened to throw herself down the village well and stayed outside overnight to reinforce the point. Amidst the weeping and wailing, young Katie sprang out of hiding, safe and sound and her parents were so relieved that they let her leave for America alone at age nineteen. Not content with that escapade, the newly married Katie Stevens returned while pregnant to visit her parents in the summer of 1914, intending to return to America before giving birth, but she was trapped in Europe when the Great War broke out in August, and she gave birth to my mother, Teresa Marie Stevens, in her ancestral village of Jakovo. Not one to cool her heels, and German submarines be damned, Katie and daughter were soon back in Philadelphia. Many years later, when her marriage cooled, she uprooted herself and my future mother and moved to Los Angeles, where she parlayed her sewing skills into becoming the head seamstress for Western Costume, the largest costume company in Hollywood. She remarried and saved her nickels by walking miles to work each day and eventually had enough to buy an apartment house. I trace my own wanderlust to Granny Katie's escape from Europe and her dedicated move to California.

My paternal grandmother, Perina Vodanovich Marincovich, known to all as Nana, was seemingly less adventuresome, but like Granny Katie she liked to sew if only for pleasure. Many times while excavating fossils, especially on Ellesmere Island, I thought of her decades of dedication to handcrafting yards of exquisite needlepoint lace one stitch at a time. She was rarely without crocheting hooks in hand and I inherited her attention to detail and patience, which I needed in large measure to collect the shells at Strathcona Fiord.

Our daily hikes to and from the fossil beds often brought us within a few feet of twenty or thirty snow-white arctic hare that barely noticed us as they munched on the ground-hugging willows. I was charmed to stand still and observe the bunnies slowly browse their way from willow to willow around me, acting more like pets than wild creatures. The other snow-white wildlife was a pack of ten wolves that often lay out in the open a quarter mile from our camp. We made sure to zip the tents tight and not leave anything loose in camp when we marched out in the morning, because as soon as we left camp the wolves trotted in, presumably looking for food. We thought this was cute until one day they pulled down our twenty-foot radio antenna by tugging on the guy wires staked in the ground. The radio was our only lifeline to Resolute Bay, the logistics base 300 miles to the south and our only source of medical help or rescue. The wolves had gone too far.

"That one wolf has been sidling toward us for a while," said one of the students as we stood outside the cook tent after dinner. "Maybe it wants dessert."

"The only dessert we have is students," I joked, "but we're running low."

We watched warily as the snow-white alpha male boldly trotted to within fifty yards of us and circled our entire camp, showing more moxie than I personally was willing to put up with.

He was testing us, and when he edged even closer, I grabbed the "camp" shotgun, always loaded and within reach just inside the main tent, and cycled a round into the firing chamber.

"You three stay behind me and I'll go see what the wolf wants. None of the rest of you pick up a gun." I was the only one who had worked in the Far North before and had extensive firearms training.

I locked eyes with the wolf as he stood and watched us, then I slowly and deliberately walked toward him. I was putting *him* on the defensive and he did not like it, so he slipped to the right to outflank me, but I moved to keep myself between him and our camp. He resumed his clockwise circuit around our tents, stopped briefly about thirty yards away as if figuring out his next move, and then began circling again. I had to deter him from entering our camp, but there was no point in running after a wolf, so I carefully lined up the sights on the moving animal and pulled the trigger. The one-ounce lead slug hit exactly where I wanted—in the dirt right beside the loping wolf, and the explosion of pebbles that peppered his right flank must have hurt like hell, because he did a forward 360° flip and gave out a loud yelp, which was picked up by the other nine wolves a couple of hundred yards away. The wolf chorus was enough to raise the hairs on the back of *my* neck. The alpha male limped for a few steps then resumed moving fluidly and his pack bayed and yelped into the bright sky until he got back to them, then they suddenly went silent and skulked away, never to reappear. Our radio lifeline to Resolute Bay was once again secure.

If we were far enough away from camp we sometimes encountered herds of musk oxen, primordial bovines left over from the Ice Ages. The herd formed a defensive crescent whenever we approached, horns outward to shield the calves behind them. From a distance the oxen looked large owing to their outsized heads and chests, but from forty feet away they were remarkably small, perhaps five feet high at the shoulder. A crescent formation of eight or ten adults was formidable in appearance and we never saw the Ellesmere wolves approach them. The animals feared most throughout the Arctic, mosquitoes, were almost absent from our Thalassa River camp, the few lethargic ones we saw being laughably inactive by Alaska standards.

Collecting fossils on a particularly cold day with -5°F wind chill.

The professor and I became proficient all-terrain vehicle (ATV) riders, routinely able to wrestle the tippy three-wheelers nearly all the way up to the steep fossil outcrops by circling around on gentler ground, usually motoring together for safety. The most hazardous part of the miles-long drive was crossing the Thalassa River, since most of its braided channels were too deep for the machines. When we found a shallow enough ford, one of us crossed while the other watched from shore, ready to help if something went wrong in the icy, fast-flowing river.

One evening at a new crossing place, my partner slipped and slid his machine across water that was just a little too deep, while I stood on the riverbank ready to wade out to help. Upon reaching the far bank, Dick unaccountably zoomed off without a backward glance, violating the whole idea of the buddy system by leaving me to cross alone. Edging the three-wheeler into the river, I felt the wheels slipping on the river bottom, since I weighed fifty pounds less than he did. I tried to duplicate his path across the river, but the left rear wheel of my ATV dropped into a hole and instantly bucked me off the seat into thigh-deep water. I was suddenly standing in a hole in the river bottom facing upstream, icy water surging against my thighs with tremendous force, the ATV perched precariously above me on the upstream edge of the hole, my gloved hands clutching the handlebars in a death grip. The engine was still in gear, spinning the tires against the slippery bottom and driving the weight of the ATV against me. The machine and I formed an inverted V: I grasped the handlebars over my head while the machine rested heavily on the edge of the hole, its weight and spinning tires acting to drive me under-water. Besides the machine and the river conspiring to push me back-ward, a full-frame backpack loaded with fossils and my shotgun dragged back on my shoulders.

Thinking dropped away. I would live past the next few moments on sheer bodily strength and will. I was in the best shape of my life, my forty-year-old body hardened by weeks of strenuous fieldwork, every iota of my being straining with ferocious exertion to force the heavy machine upstream. The thought of dying stupidly was intolerable; time stood still as I was locked in an unyielding iron triangle pushing upward with all my might against the ATV's handlebars, the surging river and the weight of my backpack. Had I weakened even for an eye blink, had I even *thought* of failing, the heavy machine would have crushed me backward into the river and pinned me to the bottom to drown in ice water.

Hope surged through me, joy filled my heart, when I felt the machine yield by a millimeter, and my life force triumphed against death as the handlebars arced upstream and downward. My right hand was wrenched from the handlebar when the front tire bounced off the river bottom while my body was stretched prone across the seat, but with my left hand I steered the machine through the freezing water to the far bank and collapsed in the mud for a few minutes, exhausted and grateful to be alive, before racing to camp. Shivering in my sleeping bag a few minutes later after putting on dry clothes, I realized once again that the razor-thin margin between adventure and sudden death in the Arctic depended as much on partners as on preparation. And I was with the wrong partner. While shaking in my sleeping bag, my first thought was to confront my partner about letting me almost perish due to his negligence—until I realized I was shaking with rage as much as from the cold. I had a flash thought of beating up the roustabout in Africa in a murderous rage more than a decade earlier, and began to savor doing the same to my field partner. My instinct was to kill the fucker. Fortunately for both of us, my thinking brain slowly took command of my emotions and I did not waste energy confronting him then or later. I already knew I would never trust him again.

Sparky, one of the students, and I were scouting for new fossil localities one day, having hiked miles and found nearly nothing when we became aware of gurgling water sounds ahead and were delighted to discover a narrow but deep creek flowing with cool, clear fresh water. We lay down on the creek bank and plunged our faces underwater, partaking deeply of nature's bounty. Nothing, absolutely nothing, tastes as good as natural river water in the Arctic. The crystal clear liquid burbled over clean cobbles and gravel, too cold to support the unhealthy microbes found in middle- and low-latitude watercourses. Drinking from streams was one of the delights of northern fieldwork and, sated, we followed the stream toward its headwaters. We had gone half a mile uphill, occasionally reaching down to scoop up a handful of refreshing branch water when we reached a meadow where the creek widened into a pool. To our disgust, lying in the middle of the pool was a very dead musk ox, which had keeled over a long time ago, based on the abundant crop of slimy greenery sprouting from its carcass. The pool of water around the carrion was a thriving megalopolis of bacteria that flowed downstream in thin, greasy stringers toward where we had drunk so deeply.

"Goddam," said Sparky, "we just drank dead musk ox piss."

"Yeah," I replied weakly. "Something to tell your grandchildren about, at least if you live to have any."

We trudged back downstream and back to camp, where we were almost too sickened to eat dinner. We brushed our teeth vigorously and gargled for a long time before crawling into our sleeping bags.

Halfway through the month we moved camp to the other side of Strathcona Fiord to search for fossils there, which was about the time our radio began to die. The Twin Otter that brought in a new radio also carried several barrels of drinking water, since our new campsite was miles from any source of water in the polar desert. Unfortunately, we began to run out of water a few days before our expedition was set to wind down. Even using water sparingly, we ran out, and rather than call in another expensive plane flight, we precariously clambered onto the fragmented frozen sea ice in Strathcona Fiord to chop off blocks of blue sea ice, which is lower in salinity than white ice, then melt them on our stove for drinking and cooking water.

I began to dream of hot showers as the end of our month at Strathcona Fiord approached, and once assigned a bunkroom at Resolute Bay I immediately shucked the clothes I had worn the whole time and headed for the showers. My face and hands were weathered brown from the constant beating of the cold, dry wind and twenty-four hour sunshine, while the rest of my body was as soft and pink as a newborn baby's from being protected by my clothing and marinated in my own body oils for a

261

month. Washed and smiling after my luxurious shower, I gagged on an awful odor as I reentered my bunkroom. The stench was coming from my clothes. I had lived in them continuously for thirty days; sweated copiously during our strenuous five-hour daily hikes; lain in them hour after hour while excavating fossils amid windblown grit; sprayed bug dope on them daily for mosquito protection; and used them as a utensil wipe during meals. They reeked so badly that I could not bear to be around them long enough to find a laundry, so I tossed my duds into the community incinerator. They had served me well, but our relationship was over.

Loading de Havilland Twin Otter bush plane after a month on Ellesmere Island.

The vicissitudes of fieldwork at almost 80° North for a month had been worth it. The Strathcona Fiord mollusks, once cleaned and identified, shared species and genera with Paleocene faunas as far distant as northern Alaska, South Dakota and the London Basin in England. Taken together, they clearly differentiated a separate Arctic Ocean faunal realm that had little in common with the North Atlantic Ocean and nothing at all with the Pacific Ocean area. In addition, the molluscan fauna clearly implied that the ice-free Arctic Ocean had an average temperature of around 55°F compared to 20°F today. There are no Paleocene mollusks farther north than Strathcona Fiord, which made our pioneering paleo work there even more satisfying. I had made the right choice in forsaking a dinosaur-collecting trip to the North Slope for the expedition to Ellesmere Island.

The Canadian Arctic Islands are one of the most barren spots on earth, but my research there led to some of my most important scientific discoveries, and those polar islands will always occupy a warm place in my heart. ▲

SEA OF OKHOTSK, SIBERIA

As a youngster in San Pedro I loved to play a board game based on a map of the world that you moved across by tossing dice. I was fascinated by exotic names such as Batavia and Hakodate, although the most intriguing name was not a destination but merely a space-filler on the map: the Sea of Okhotsk. It was at the far eastern end of Siberia, wedged between the Asian mainland and a peninsula called Kamchatka, with no game destinations close by, but for some reason the name lodged in my mind.

As if by a miracle, half a century later I found myself excitedly peering out the window of a Russian Mi-8 helicopter as the Sea of Okhotsk shoreline glided by, on my way to collect fossil mollusks on Kamchatka. This particular miracle had taken quite a lot of work to effect, because our uninhabited field site of Rekinniki at the mouth of the Valuvayam River was as remote a location as exists on the planet and very difficult to access both geographically and bureaucratically. I was headed into the Arctic wilderness once again with my friends Anton and Sasha, with whom I had resolved Bering Strait's age and documented a climatic warming event in Alaska fifteen million years ago. Now we were searching for similar warm-water paleofaunas on the other side of the North Pacific, to learn if the ancient warming episode was a North Pacific-wide event or confined only to Alaska.

Posing in the Valuvayam River, Kamchatka, Siberia with mosquito netting.

265

Russian paleontologists had published papers suggesting that mollusks typical of a past warming event were present in Kamchatka, but the mollusk illustrations in their Soviet-era publications were so murky that nobody was sure of their conclusions. We needed to collect our own shell specimens from verified localities, and we also needed mollusk specimens to analyze for oxygen isotopic paleotemperatures to reinforce our climatic interpretations based on faunal composition. However, access to the Russian Far East was impossible until a dozen years had gone by after the Evil Empire had fallen, because Kamchatka was at the small end of the long information pipeline from Moscow.

Kamchatka is only four time zones west of Alaska and it looks like an easy flight from Anchorage, but the Russians insisted that I fly for twenty hours from San Francisco through Moscow to the city of Petropavlovsk-Kamchatsky (PPK) in Kamchatka. It would have cost your life to get into the infamous submarine base during the Cold War, but what Anton, Sasha, field assistant Arkady and I observed was a decrepit port city crammed with rusting hulks in the backwater of a defunct empire. There was nothing graceful, attractive or charming about PPK, its shabbiness comparable to towns I had seen in West Africa: people living in cracked, crumbling, unmaintained, Soviet-era cement-block tenements, the main streets potholed like they had spent a day under the B-52s, dirt side streets with litter and discarded junk everywhere. People on the street were surprisingly well dressed, however, especially young women in fashionably short skirts and high heels; the citizens could not do much about what the state had done to them, yet maintained a sense of personal dignity. The only objects of beauty were the renowned snow-capped volcanoes surrounding the city, which were worth a visit all by themselves. One peak continuously spewed vapor from its crest and all were impressively massive and picturesquely snow-topped.

Petropavlovsk-Kamchatsky was our jumping-off point for the village of Korf, 600 miles north on the Bering Sea coast of Kamchatka, where we would meet our helicopter to take us into the field. As soon as our small jet set down in Korf, we transferred our gear to a large Mi-8 helicopter that would haul us 150 miles that same day to Rekinniki, a mere place name on the Sea of Okhotsk coast that would have lots of fossils but no inhabitants.

The dozen Mi-8 helicopters at Korf were poorly maintained compared to the immaculate machines I was used to in Alaska, the most obvious flaw being a fat streak of soot coating the fuselage aft of the exhaust pipe along the whole left side. I wondered if the twin-turbine engines had a problem, if the fuel was tainted, or if the mechanics did not care about cleanliness—not thoughts I wanted to have about a machine that was going to carry me a long way into the Siberian wilds. My thoughts turned more morbid when Anton announced that ours was the only flyable Mi-8 at Korf. The other eleven machines were inoperable owing to a lack of repair and maintenance parts and were used only for scrounging parts to keep our Mi-8 flying. Great, a helicopter put together from recycled parts. Recycled *Soviet* parts. I already thought of helicopters as 10,000 parts flying in loose formation and now I would be in a machine patched together from used Soviet parts. Too late to update my life insurance.

The cavernous interior of the Mi-8 easily swallowed our entire field camp with plenty of room to walk around, in stark contrast to the small choppers in Alaska where sitting in a confining seat was the only option. The Alaskan machines were for civilian uses in which efficiency was important, whereas the Mi-8 was a military model where carrying capacity and performance meant everything. Our Mi-8 had been fitted with an extra 100-gallon plastic fuel tank mounted inside the passenger compartment and from there a worrisomely exposed rubber fuel line snaked its way across the floor and up a wall to the engines. For someone used to the strict safety standards for U.S. helicopters, the potential incendiary bomb in the passenger compartment, combined with the filthy outside of the Mi-8 and its recycled Soviet parts inside, made me nervous—especially when all three of the flight crew lit up cigarettes just before takeoff. I have never been religious, but that moment was worth a silent prayer.

Disheveled they may have been, but the crew knew their business, lifting off smoothly and ascending to a thousand feet, giving us an unmatched tour of the Kamchatka countryside. The well-vegetated rolling hills and extensive boggy flats were reminiscent of the North Slope or the lowlands of the Alaska Peninsula, with dense patches of alder and willow in a sea of lighter green grass. We spooked one grizzly from a salmon-berry patch and watched it streak as fast as a thoroughbred horse across the tundra.

It was worrisome to fly 150 miles into Siberia in this shabby-looking Russian helicopter.

Our flight path west from Korf took us across the narrow neck of the Kamchatka Peninsula to the Sea of Okhotsk, a placid-looking body of water tightly squeezed between the Asian mainland and Kamchatka. Among all the "seas" of the world, this is surely the most obscure, the Andaman Sea and the Kara Sea being tourist hot spots by comparison. However, as an example of life's synchronicity, the Sea of Okhotsk is hard to beat, since I had first seen the odd and unpronounceable name on a board game as a child and marked it down mentally, and now, five decades later, I eagerly gazed out the Mi-8's porthole window as the Sea itself hove into view. It felt like the closing of a circle, and even though the coastline was bleak, like many Arctic beaches, it was a lifetime thrill to gaze upon after half a century of anticipation. The same boyhood years witnessed my urge to become a paleontologist and find fossils and adventure in the wilderness, so arriving here was a major marker along my seemingly fated lifetime path. I smiled continuously as we banked right and followed the Kamchatka coastline northward, my long-imagined sea on our left.

Anton and Sasha broke out aerial photos and began searching for the one headland among many in this region that marked our target location, Rekinniki, an uninhabited spot at the mouth of the Valuvayam River with rock layers rich in fifteen-million-year-old warm-water fossil shells, we hoped. They conversed in Russian as they evaluated various coastal features while moving their fingers across the photos, and even though I am skilled in reading air photos, this was their homeland, not mine, so I stayed out of their way. As events would play out, this was by far the worst decision I have made in my Arctic career. After much gesticulating, discussion and map waving, the guys decided we were "there" and the pilots set us down lightly on a broad sandy beach beside a stream that was backed by a 100-foot cliff. We unloaded 800 pounds of food and gear for our two-week stay, and after shaking hands all around, the Mi-8 crew lifted off for the 150-mile return flight to Korf. This being Russia, I worried that the aircrew would leave us to rot in the wilderness, but Anton was well ahead of the game by insisting he would pay for our round trip only when the crew returned for us 15 days later. It pays to be with the right people in the middle of nowhere.

My first act at Rekinniki was to wade barefoot into the Sea of Okhotsk to culminate my boyhood vision, dwelling for a few minutes on the multitude of factors that had to fall into place exactly right for me to be standing there smiling. By 11:00 p.m. we had moved our mountain of gear 200 yards up a coastal gully to be above what we thought was the high-tide line, staked out our tents, wolfed down a makeshift dinner and slipped into our sleeping bags at the end of a metaphorically and physically fulfilling day. Unfortunately, the cockles of my heart were not going to remain warm for long.

"Lou, the river is only fifty meters from you," said Sasha as he reached into my tent to shake me awake at 6:30 a.m. Fifty meters? More than half a football field away? Nothing to worry about there, so I rolled over and resumed snoozing.

"Lou, the river is only five meters away," was what I heard Sasha say next as woke me up a second time. I knew that words like "half," "five," "fifteen," and "fifty" sounded similar in languages I had studied, so I thought the river had not moved any closer and went back to snoozing.

"Lou, please get up, the river is only fifty centimeters from your tent," bellowed Sasha in my next waking moment. Centimeters? I stuck my head out the tent flap and saw that the ocean had risen at least forty feet. The narrow trickle of a river from the night before was now a surging, churning tidal lagoon jammed with huge jostling logs that almost touched my tent. I quickly tossed my gear out to Sasha, who threw it higher on the hillside, and then I dragged my tent away in one pull, stakes and all, as water seeped into the spot where my body had lain overnight. We four worked like demons to move 800 pounds of gear and food upslope to keep it from being inundated. Not the way I would have wished to begin my first field day in Siberia. We had learned a hard lesson about the huge daily tidal range in the Sea of Okhotsk, one that my boyhood fascination with the place had not informed me of. I had long dreamed of standing beside this wild sea, not drowning in it.

Worse was to come. During the bright Arctic night Sasha and Arkady, feeling uneasy about where the helicopter had set us down,

hiked along the coast to the next valley to get their geographical bear-
ings. To their dismay and embarrassment, they discovered that this next
valley and headland, three miles from where we were camped, was the
spot with the fossils, where we were supposed to be. Damn. So much for
my not asking to read the aerial photos, a skill I had developed to a high
degree, when we were in the air. We lacked both the radio and money to
recall the Mi-8 back to move our camp three miles, leaving us no choice
but to hump four-tenths of a ton of food and gear across three miles of
beach sand to our new campsite. A steep price to pay for misreading an
air photo.

We began hauling without enthusiasm after lunch, loading our backpacks as full as possible considering the distance we had to hike and the
difficulty of hiking on beach sand of the two-steps-forward, one-step-
back variety. The canned goods were the most difficult and awkward to
carry, since no amount of careful positioning kept the sharp edges from
digging into our backs. We eventually set up two intermediate supply
dumps along the three-mile stretch, to limit our lugging of the heavy
loads to a distance of just a mile before returning with an empty pack to
the original camp. I carried three loads to the new location, hiking a total
of 15 miles over beach sand that day, while Anton, Sasha and Arkady, by
virtue of being twenty years younger than my 60 years, carried four loads
and walked 21 miles. Even so, we had left behind a large canvas tent and
much of our food, but no one was up for more backbreaking loads that
day. I would have felt a lot of pride in accomplishing this feat of strength
and endurance at my age, had I not been too tired to think. We set up
our tents at the new site on the Valuvayam River, snacked on what we
could find among our jumbled supplies, and slept the sleep of the dead.
Nobody would have noticed if the tide rose and flooded our tents that
night. Comparing notes in the morning, Anton had hurt his left elbow,
Sasha twisted his right knee, Arkady had dropped something on his foot,
and my lower back was throbbing.

Russian-style geological camping was an improvement in many ways over the American version, especially the abundance of shoreline driftwood that we sawed and nailed into a table and chairs, so we could eat in a more dignified manner than squatting on the ground as in Alaska. Saws, nails, hammers and axes were absent from my North American Arctic tent camps, since there was no driftwood along the treeless shores. The driftwood also made for roaring fires to cook on and sit around, unlike in Alaska or Arctic Canada where we used propane stoves for lack of wood. Another welcome change was a diet devoid of freeze-dried food, replaced by large helpings of *kasha*, or buckwheat, which we boiled up for all meals and spooned down with a lavish frosting of canned condensed milk. Canned beef and chicken, plus canned veggies and a powdered orange drink completed most meals, with enough vodka and bourbon to enliven our evening campfire conversations. Life can hardly be more satisfying than telling stories around a campfire in the remote wilderness with pleasant companions, 100-plus miles from anywhere, enjoying a drink after a hard day's work, firearms handy nearby, the tingle of danger ever present, on a full stomach.

We soon discovered that the Ilinskaya Formation from which we were collecting fossils contained the same warm-water shells as did the Bear Lake Formation in Alaska that were indicators of global warming fifteen million years ago. These finds reinforced our theory that the climatic warming event that happened in Alaska at that time also influenced the opposite side of the North Pacific in Kamchatka, and we later published these conclusions, doing our part toward piecing together the past climate of the earth. We had accomplished our scientific mission, to show that the global warming of fifteen million years ago was evidenced throughout the North Pacific by warm-water mollusks that had migrated north from the tropics as the ocean heated up. Most of the earth had experienced this climatic event, but it had not been documented for the high-latitude North Pacific realm until we did so.

Camp on the Valuvayam River at Rekinniki, Kamchatka.

The situation was looking good for our research project, but the Gods of Arctic Geology did not benignly allow us to work safely and happily for long. A life-threatening hazard revealed itself on the first sunny day, when the bright sunshine melted the permafrost-underlain tundra that topped the cliffs. The meltwater from the defrosted permafrost undermined the otherwise solid cliffs, which suddenly and frighteningly crashed down with alarming frequency. One house-size slide I witnessed from a distance flung debris across the wide beach and more than a hundred yards offshore. That one would have killed us all. We adopted a system of one man collecting fossils at the cliff face while another man stood well back near the water's edge and warned the first guy of an impending land-slide, which was always preceded by an initial dribble of rocks high on the cliff. It made for tense fossil collecting and reminded me of my first USGS field summer twenty-eight years earlier at Lituya Bay when an assistant

273

and I worked along a 200-foot-high cliff beside Fairweather Glacier that rained rocks upon us all day and required hard hats for safety.

After our first dinner at Rekinniki, Anton strolled upstream for exercise and to check out the rocks, but came running back half an hour later, presumably well exercised, trailed by two adult grizzlies. Arkady fired his 12-gauge shotgun to scare the bears away, but they hung around 200 or 300 meters from camp for hours until we built a "defensive campfire" 50 meters upstream and the bears stayed away. Later in the evening Anton and I walked the three miles back to our first camp to retrieve the last of the canned goods, and on our way home ran into Sasha and Arkady who were going to recover the final item, a large canvas tent. The other two arrived back at camp around 11:00 p.m., everyone having put in another six miles before hitting the sack. No rest for the weary.

The fossil fauna at Rekinniki was as rich as we had hoped, but I clearly felt my interest in fieldwork waning after thirty-plus years of doing it. Paleontology had been my passion for fifty years, and fieldwork had been the most enjoyable and adventuresome part of my profession, but something was shifting inside; a new lodestone was drawing me in an unaccustomed direction. I had left an unhappy relationship just before coming to Kamchatka, which had opened my spirit to new possibilities. I knew that life was shifting, that something new was opening up, but had no idea what was coming or when. Emblematic of that shift into the unknown was the vision of the tall, slender artist that frequently entered my thoughts in quiet moments at Rekinniki. Her visage was more substantive than in past years and decades, and she somehow seemed closer, but I still had no idea who she was or what she meant in my life, if indeed she existed in the world at all.

We finished our studies a day earlier than planned, and when the next morning was bright and clear Anton jumped on the satellite phone and had the Mi-8 pick us up that day. The basic Arctic rule is, once your work is done get out as fast as you can, because tomorrow's weather might be unflyable crap that settles in for a week. We tore down the camp in record time and the Mi-8 guys arrived on schedule at 5:30 p.m., wearing the smiles of men who were about to get paid. As we lifted off from Rekinniki, Sasha commented that I was probably the first American ever to be there, and almost certainly the last. We dipped low over a large grizzly halfway to Korf, and landed in that ratty little village at 7:00 p.m.

We checked into the Korf Hotel, the absolute worst dump imaginable, like something that had floated up from a Third World cesspool. The scabrous pale green paint on the outside of the two-story Stalin-era, clapboard building was matched by the peeling paint of the same color in every room. Anton and I shared a room with two prison-appropriate metalframe beds, and the wire mesh under the inch-thick cotton mattresses was so stretchy that when I sat on the bed my ass hit the floor a foot below. I could not stop the belly laugh that erupted because of the absurdity of the situation. Sasha and Arkady's room was worse, because two men who looked like vagrants were already in it and were not about to leave. The situation was preposterous: the shithole hotel, in a forgotten town without a breath of tourism, located at the crumbling edge of a defunct empire, was all booked up. A great deal of Cyrillic shouting later, Sasha and Arkady were masters of the same kind of crappy room as Anton and I had. We soon discovered that the eighty(!) guests in the Korf Hotel were served by an unspeakable one-hole shitter, a ceramic-lined hole in a water closet with a continuously running stream of water to squat over. At least it was indoors, even if it had run out of TP during the October Revolution of 1917. Last cleaned by a heroic Soviet worker sometime before Khrushchev died, the shitter backed up while we were guests at Chateau Korf, leaving us and seventy-six other guests shit out of luck.

Mercifully, Anton negotiated with a guy at the airport to rent his mother's apartment while she was away, and after one long night in the Korf Hotel, which gratefully passed without the need for a bowel movement, we moved into her comfortable dwelling. We celebrated our move with the owner's son in traditional Russian fashion with lots of vodka. I had already drunk plenty of vodka while sliding down the razor blade of life in Russia, but the Topaz brand on offer was impotable and smelled remarkably like witch hazel. Thankful to be seated outside the circle of Russian-speakers in the living room, I sneakily poured every glass into a potted plant. Anton later told me that Topaz was the best vodka available in Korf, as if people living there did not have enough other reasons to suffer.

For reasons I never learned, we stayed in Korf three days, and one afternoon we were seated around a table while snacking in a corner market when an obviously drunken fellow wobbled in and bought a bottle of vodka. He came over to ask our help pushing the container up his coat sleeve, which was difficult given the generous size of the bottle.

"Why is he putting a bottle up his sleeve?" I inquired.

"He doesn't want to be embarrassed," replied Anton.

"About what?" I asked.

"He doesn't want people to know he drinks," answered Anton with a straight face followed by a huge grin.

"They can probably guess from how he walks," I observed.

"We all have our little foibles," winked Anton as the drunk bowed toward us in thanks, almost toppled over, then turned around so fast he had to steady himself against the wall before cartoon-stepping to the shop door, which he left open. "No way anyone will guess he's drunk," I commented.

Korf was abandoned two years after we left, and all buildings including the Korf Hotel were given over to the elements, an occasion that might be worth toasting even with Topaz vodka. Seeing the decaying fringes of the Soviet Empire made me extra grateful that I had met Anton and had gotten him out of that rotting carcass of a country a dozen years before. The end of the Cold War also profoundly affected the USGS, and what had been a tightly focused research institution for more than a

century went through a wrenching series of reorganizations that reori-
ented it from conducting cutting-edge geological research to performing
"public outreach." With funding for paleontological research in Alaska no
longer forthcoming, I departed for the California Academy of Sciences in
San Francisco.

The USGS had been that rarest of government organizations, an
aspirational center of excellence that drew scientists trained at the best
schools in the country. I came to regard the USGS complex in Menlo
Park, California, as the finest concentration of top-rate researchers in the
history of geology. The answer to a question about the geology and paleontology of any part of the world was merely a walk down the hallway.
And then the aspirational aspect of the organization that had prevailed
for more than 120 years was gone in the blink of a bureaucratic eye,
including paleo research on Alaska.

Until then I had never considered that I was part of a historical
period of Arctic endeavor, that research geologists would not always be
exploring Alaska to discover new wonders in a state two-and-a-half times
the size of Texas. Alaskan fieldwork in particular had gone out of fashion:
too expensive, too hard on the body, people getting killed or mangled for
life, impossible logistics, and atrocious weather. The first U.S. government scientists to study Cenozoic marine mollusks in Alaska had been
part of the Harriman Alaska Expedition in 1899, which included many
notable Smithsonian and USGS scholars such as the molluscan specialist
William Dall as well as the naturalist John Muir. They collected Cenozoic shells mainly on the Alaska Peninsula, including at Sand Point on
Popof Island, where my final collecting trip took place in 2007, so the
study of Cenozoic mollusks in Alaska had in a way come full circle. I
was the one fortunate paleontologist who spent his entire Survey career
elucidating the Cenozoic marine molluscan faunas of the Arctic, and
thereby fulfilled my boyhood dream of a life of science and adventure in
the wilderness. A century of steady progress in understanding Cenozoic

faunas and paleoenvironments ended when the USGS abandoned frontier paleontology. As a result, summers in the Arctic are quieter these days, undisturbed by the tap of paleontologists' hammers pecking out fossils, the clank of sledge hammer against chisel and the crack of bursting rocks, or the tumble of rock chips down a talus slope. No more the welcome thump of helicopter blades beating into the wind as the machine gingerly descends to pluck me, all smiles, off the tundra at the end of a particularly cold and soggy but productive and happy day. ▲

With Karen in Kyoto, Japan, 2007.

HOME

"Never sell this car!" joyfully exclaimed the beautiful dark-haired artist beside me in my 1967 Corvette convertible as she raised her arms high in the air.

"Never!" I shouted gleefully back as I lifted an arm to the sky.

"This is the most romantic car in the world. I love it."

"Then I guess I'll keep it," I smiled back.

We were zooming down the road in my vintage Vette on our way to the automobile world's ultimate yearly gathering, Car Week in Monterey, California. I looked at Karen and marveled that the finest thing that had ever happened to me was happening right now.

Fate had begun to pull us together just a dozen days earlier during my final Arctic tent camp, in remote northeastern Alaska in the same meadow where I had studied the Oligocene Nuwok Beds seventeen years earlier. However, just as you can never step into the same river twice, a lot had changed since I had last stepped from a helicopter onto the tundra grasses beside Carter Creek. My field party would accumulate a fine collection of fossils, but the shells brought me little satisfaction; in my heart I knew I was done adventuring in the Arctic, that even though I was still up to the hazards and discomforts of fieldwork, the spiritual shift that had begun in Siberia two years earlier was in full swing. Something new was beckoning, but at the time I sensed only the ebb of my life's familiar flood tide, not the impending swell of a new one.

Scouting atop a ridge miles from my field partners, I paused to gaze for long minutes at the Arctic Ocean a couple of miles away: frozen, barren, isolated, to all appearances lifeless. Turning, I assayed the tundra beyond our camp: lumpy tussocks of grass rooted in near-frozen mud lying atop earth frozen solid to half a mile deep. The forbidding landscape was an apt metaphor for my life: isolated and devoid of the warmth I craved but had rarely known. Always alone, I was seemingly fated to live and perish apart from my fellow beings, never having known love, if such a thing even existed. Satisfied with my scientific accomplishments and a life over-flowing with adventure, I was dismayed at finding only unlovable women along the way. As a youth in Hollywood I had asked the universe for a life of strong emotions, and gotten it in spades, but I had somehow missed out on the most profound emotion of all. Lost in the moment atop that barren ridge, the thought coalesced: I just *have* to meet the right woman.

I was yearning for love, but had no idea what exact thing to ask for. I thought I had been in love at times, but those experiences had been less intense than my awe at wild nature, relief at surviving a helicopter crash or rage at a thief. I had made important scientific discoveries, parsed ancient climates back to sixty million years ago, deciphered the age of Bering Strait, named new species, discovered an unnamed river, cheated death many times, and been terrified out of my body only to discover a realm beyond everyday experience—but I had never known love. True love, if it existed at all outside the illusions of art and literature, had gone missing; I was asking for it now in the form of an idealized woman who probably did not exist, and if she existed was unfindable in my emotion-ally sterile world. I longed for a relationship with more than shared inter-ests, equivalent education, physical compatibility, and all the duplicate likes and dislikes of pairing up. I needed to *know* that the universe meant for us to be together, had put us together for a *purpose*, that she and I would savor completion like no man and woman ever had. I desired a consuming intensity beyond any I had known—except in the wilderness in moments of rapture or life-threatening danger—or even knew existed. Probably I was asking for too much.

The moment passed and I snapped back to the geological task at hand, but the foundations of my life were shifting with the force of a slow, silent earthquake. The next few days dragged slowly until the chopper hauled us back to the Eskimo village of Kaktovik and we returned to Fairbanks. Usually I spent a day or two in Alaska's small cities to transition from the wilderness to the bustle of The Outside, but this time I had an unusually strong urge to be home and departed early for the Lower 48.

▲ ▲ ▲

"Karen, hello. I'm Lou," I said to the woman who now turned around to face me on a street corner in Palo Alto, just nine hours after we had "met" online. I had popped wide-awake at two that morning, unusual for me, and bounded enthusiastically over to my computer to see if any woman had noticed me. Nope. Home from Alaska, I gave in to the modern age and joined an online dating site, posted my profile and photos and went to bed, wondering if internet dating even worked. I stared at the screen blankly, thinking of going back to bed even though I was inexplicably wide-awake, and then a "Hi" pinged in from "MsWright226." Ms. Wright? The *Right* Woman?

Her pictures rang a loud bell: a beautiful artist who was tall, slender, elegant and had short, dark hair. The universe had awakened me at 2:00 a.m. so I would see her message as soon as it arrived. Karen later told me that she had also uncharacteristically awakened at 2:00 a.m.—the precise moment I had—and decided to sign *off* the dating site, because she was so popular she no longer needed the service. However, as long as she was awake anyhow, she made one final search before signing off forever, and my profile popped up.

Here, standing before me, was the woman of my countless dreams, whose vision had enchanted and mystified me for my entire life. Over time I became convinced that the visionary woman existed somewhere, in some dimension, and even wondered if she could see me, or if I was just a thought to her, as she was to me. Now I wondered no more.

"Hi, Lou. I'm Karen," she replied. We could do no more than smile and giggle as we lightly shook hands and first looked into each other's eyes, consumed in an instant with the same liberating realization, that we were meeting our soulmate at last and life from now on was a slam dunk. The silent earthquake that had been set in motion the week before on a desolate ridge in Alaska now shook our lives in one of my life's genuinely transformative moments, akin to the scene in the *Wizard of Oz* when the black-and-white film shifts to Technicolor and everything is the same but all is gloriously new.

We flirted madly while wandering in a daze up and down the aisles of the store where she had dropped off her camera.

"I was thinking of driving to the coast for lunch at my favorite restaurant, Duarte's in Pescadero. I know we only just met, but I'd be delighted if you would join me," I said.

"Duarte's! That's my favorite restaurant too!" she enthusiastically announced. "I'd love to go."

As a lifetime car enthusiast I always know where my car is parked, but I was so flustered at meeting Karen that we had to search several parking lots before I found it. Our conversation swirled during the hour ride to the coast, learning how much alike we were and, more importantly, enjoying the glow of a deep emotional connection. Lunch was joyful and over all too soon, so back we headed, stopping at a farm for a flat of strawberries to munch on the way back.

"I can't tell you how much I enjoyed myself," I said while wearing a big smile and standing beside her car in Palo Alto. "I'd like to see you again."

Smiling herself, Karen stepped forward and lightly kissed me on the lips, saying "I just had to do that."

"Thank you," I enthused, "I wanted to kiss you too, but as a guy I couldn't be so bold." She smiled and was gone.

A few days later I unlocked the door to my house and stood aside to let her in when I impetuously, without a moment's forethought, scooped Karen up in my arms and carried her over the threshold. I took a step back as she stood there in a bit of a daze.

She flashed a big smile but said nothing.

"I guess I'm impetuous. Welcome to my happy home," I said. "What do you think of it?"

After a thoughtful appraisal, she commented, "Umm, it feels sort of like a dentist's waiting room." Even as she correctly described my bachelor-level decorating scheme, I knew that the cozy home of my visions was exactly what *our* safe haven would look like once we had filled it with art she had made, curios, books and artifacts of our lifetime voyages. The fact that I visualized a particular woman through my entire life, asked for her in the Alaska wilderness, then met her a few days later, speaks directly to the mystery of life, for it means that there is a oneness to the universe. Along with my out-of-body experience, the way I met Karen is clear evidence that there is far more to existence than the everyday material realm.

▲　▲　▲

My face winced into a tense fist as I said, "You're toast, baby. That was a cop on the median strip pointing a radar gun right at us. How fast are we going?"

"Not quite 100," she answered while tossing me a quick sideways glance and a wan smile while downshifting my 2007 Corvette so we would coast down to the speed limit.

Amazingly, the cop blasted into traffic and nabbed some little red car that must have been doing a more flagrant act than trashing the speed limit. It was one more adventure on our first road trip together. She had never been around car enthusiasts in her earlier life, but she took to sports cars with joy, joining me when I competed in autocrosses in my 1967 Corvette, gleefully taking part in races, social events, car shows and road trips with new friends in the Santa Clara Corvettes club. As soon as I discovered she had never been on a Great American Road Trip we took off for Oregon in my 2007 Corvette coupe, sharing driving chores, and she loved the thrill of driving a powerful, sleek sports car either bulleting down the highway or carving along mountain roads. Hardly pausing to repack once home, we headed out for two weeks on storied Route 66 in California, Arizona and Utah. I have almost never let anyone else drive my Corvettes, but with Karen I could snooze in the passenger seat when we switched off driving duties. She could not wait to buy her own sports car, a new Mazda Miata that she drove in almost any weather with the top down. Once the engine was properly broken in, she went to autocross school and thrillingly learned how to carve a perfect path through a sea of orange cones and "be as one" with her machine. Not only did we love each other, we both loved cars.

One day we were basking in our sunlit garden on a spring day, flicking peanuts to Stellar's Jays and towhees when I told her about my out-of-body experience.

"The Arctic is more than a scientific stomping ground for me, it's a spiritual landscape."

"You mean you feel close to nature there?" she inquired.

"More than close. I somehow partook of a oneness with nature that I didn't really know existed before I went north. It felt like roots grew from my feet through my boots down to the center of the earth. At times I sensed that all living things, even the rocks, were somehow conscious but to different degrees."

"I try to get into that state when I meditate," she commented.

"Well, I don't meditate, but when I was alone once in a ferocious storm and thought I might die, my spirit popped out of my body and it was hanging 200 feet in the air looking back at my terrified body. It was more real than everyday reality. It's been 28 years and I haven't told anyone else before."

"It sounds like you had an out-of-body experience, the first part of a near-death experience when people who've died report going up a tunnel to a heavenly place filled with light. I read a book about it by a doctor named Raymond Moody."

I did not know anything about near-death experiences, but the darkness I stared into from the top of the cliff at Ocean Point may as well have been a tunnel, and the dissipation of the dark clouds and sudden brightness when I left my body had always puzzled me. Finally and at last, I felt safe enough with another person to reveal my secret.

Karen Meisenger of Port Washington, New York, was born to be an artist: two of her stained glass panels grace our living room, as does a large folio of her drawings of women's fashions used to illustrate a column she wrote for the Carmel, California, newspaper. As a voice actress she made radio commercials and took voice lessons for the pure pleasure of singing, and as a model for an exclusive hat shop her uniquely beautiful face made any hat look good. She moved through life with such unaffected, fluid grace that the ladies with whom she worked said she had a "model walk." Had we met early in life she could have followed her wandering muse, but in her fifties she earned a master's degree to bolster her counseling career.

I had never known love before. Poems, novels and movies had all failed to capture the sublime intensity of effortlessly blending with another human being with inexplicable intimacy after only a few words of conversation upon first meeting. Delighting each other was as easy as breathing. Each of us was the welcoming spirit for the other, for whom we had searched our entire lives. Meeting Karen meant that I did not have to settle for the ordinary, did not have to merely keep myself occupied until I vanished into history. Being with her was like warming myself before an eternal flame I had always imagined existing but had never experienced.

She was one of those people who always made you feel like you were special. She always had a smile and a glow about her that added warmth and a sense of presence to any gathering. I felt her radiant warmth the moment we met, I have felt it every day since then, and I feel it now.

Love had won out over science: I had no desire to return to the Arctic after I met Karen. Unfortunately, a project obligation meant a final trip north, in 2007 with Anton to Popof Island where we collected Oligocene shells to decipher the climate back then, although bronchitis laid me up soon after we arrived at Sand Point and Anton did most of the work. Midway during the week-long trip I got a phone call from the U.S. Coast Guard that Karen was worried sick about me back in California. Atmospheric conditions had prevented me from calling her, and the Coast Guard message came over an emergency radiotelephone system that Karen had pleaded for them to use. Her worry about my absence was one more reason for me to put the Arctic in my past.

Still, I experienced joy mixed with sadness when the airliner lifted off from Alaska for home for the final time, at the point where this story begins. I was glad to be heading home to Karen, but sad to think that I had trod my final boot print in the Arctic wilderness. However, my three decades of boot prints had been left in mostly frigid ground where I labored alone, while my new life would be one of warmth and delirious joy with my soulmate.

Karen and I were together for three-and-a-half years. She had undergone cancer surgery before we met, but the surgeon missed some cancerous cells, so she was doomed to die even before we met. I believe with all my heart that we were fated to meet so that her final years would be her happiest. We were married in a nursing home on Christmas Eve 2008 and spent our final weeks together looking at romances and comedies in her room, holding hands as the warm and funny scenes flickered across the screen. Her last meals were chicken soup I made for her.

The mystical way in which Karen and I had met and my own out-of-body experience prompted me to investigate the literature on death and consciousness. I reread Elisabeth Kübler-Ross's *On Death and Dying*, which led me to books on the near-death experience, or NDE. Karen and I believed in life after death, that we continue to exist as spiritual beings once our material life is over, but neither of us had ever seriously looked into the subject. Now, discovering the volume of NDE literature, much of it authored by scholars and medical doctors such as William James, Raymond Moody, Kenneth Ring, Bruce Greyson and Pim van Lommel, was a heartening surprise. I learned that the NDE experience rests upon data as solid as that underpinning any competent scientific study, including my own. I pored over books and web sites that described veridical accounts of well-investigated NDEs. I was equally surprised and delighted to discover scientific works on the diverse realms of consciousness by Dean Radin and others at the Institute of Noetic Sciences in California and Bruce Greyson at the University of Virginia. Their ideas that consciousness is vaster than the human brain was backed up by not only a mountain of hard scientific data but, importantly for me, by my own experience. Learning about a century and more of well-crafted studies reinforced Karen's and my belief that we would be together in another realm of existence.

Karen passed away on Valentine's Day 2009, ten days before her sixty-third birthday. The hospice nurse had seen hundreds of people pass away and could predict almost to the hour how long a patient would survive; she gently cautioned me that Karen was going to die on February 13, a Friday. She did not know that Karen's whole life had been about love and that her unconquerable will would cling hard to life itself until Valentine's Day, when she passed away with a final sigh as I held her hand. Some things are truly unspeakable, and such was my grief. My will to live was minimal and my own death would have been a welcome relief from the years of blackness that followed.

Karen asked me to write this memoir on June 15, 2008, as a way to pass along the adventure stories she loved to hear, and I began writing that very day. I never could refuse my soulmate anything. After she was gone, and with my research life behind me, I learned that memoir writing is a solitary endeavor, and three-and-a-half years after Karen passed away I remembered how easily we had met online. I wondered if such a wondrous connection could happen again.

Probably not. But, at least I had grieved to the point where I could contemplate meeting a woman again, but disappointing coffee dates only confirmed the obvious, that happiness only strikes once. I stopped looking at women's profiles, intending to let the service lapse. Mere sensation had no appeal; I wanted another onramp to the Yellow Brick Road. I contented myself in the thought that I had had an extraordinary life and been loved by a magical woman and that asking for more was unreasonable.

The unreasonable happened when "Betsy" said "Hi" online. She was an attractive artist like Karen, and we met at a coffee shop and hit it off immediately. More than "hit it off," actually. We were *fascinated* by each other. It felt so good to be basking in the radiance of a bright and beautiful woman again. We went on our second date that same evening and we have shared hundreds of dinners since. Once again I was with a woman I felt I had known in a past life, as if meeting was the culmination of a spiritual connection.

I could never have imagined the adult life I actually lived, when I was a bored grade schooler on my family's back stoop in San Pedro, or have prepared for what life had in store when, at the end of high school in Hollywood, I yearned for a life of strong emotions.

I wanted one kind of world, but found another. I had longed for the scientific discovery, adventure and romance that reading *All About Dinosaurs* had ignited within me. I had found all of these things, but more importantly I had found true love and a spiritual connection to nature and a world beyond.

The land that passed beneath the airliner's wings when I departed Alaska for the final time in 2007 had given me more than I had asked of it. ▲

ACKNOWLEDGEMENTS

In the nearly nine years it took to write this book, I discovered that memoir-writing is a thankless task, at least until the very end. Now that the memoir is written, I thank my wife Karen for asking me to write it *for her*. My fortunate life combining both intellectual and wilderness adventures had given me many stories with which I enjoyed entertaining friends, who sometimes asked me to write down my experiences. I demurred until my beloved wife Karen asked me to do so in June 2008, eight months before she passed away. What you are reading is a labor of love devoted to her.

I heartily thank my 1974 campmates at Driftwood: Alex Feucht, Don Oltz, Jim Molnar and Mike Simmons, for sharing their remembrances of our North Slope adventures. That trip was my first foray into the world of wilderness paleontology and it was made all the more special by being with admirable men. Another Texaco colleague from those days, Harry Quinn, who was a passenger in the plane that crashed on takeoff at Itkillik, cleared up some details of that hard landing.

Anton Oleinik, my boon companion of many an Arctic adventure and indefatigable field companion and scientific collaborator, refreshed my memory about details of our many wilderness trips in Alaska, Canada and Siberia. He kindly made the maps for this book when my software skills fell short once again.

The completion of this book owes much to my life partner, Betsy Franco, who steadfastly encouraged me to forge ahead in writing and supported my flagging spirits during particularly fraught episodes when my muse went on vacation. She also is largely responsible for eliminating a couple of hundred manuscript pages, which I think had great adventure stories on them but that she thought did not "move the story along." She was right. Karen got the memoir ball rolling and Betsy kept it rolling up the long uphill slope to the finish. I have been blessed to have two transcendent women in my life. ▲

ABOUT THE AUTHOR

Lou Marincovich, PhD, is a paleontologist who specializes in studying Cenozoic marine mollusks of the North Pacific and Arctic oceans. He is the only scientist fortunate enough to have focused on this topic for an entire career.

During his career with the U.S. Geological Survey and the California Academy of Sciences, he has documented the changing climate of the Arctic over sixty million years as evidenced in the shifting migration of mollusk species between Asia and North America. He was the first to show that ancient lineages of mollusks considered extinct at the end-Mesozoic extinction some 65 million years ago continued to dwell for millions of years in the Arctic Ocean beside newly evolved Cenozoic species. And his fortuitous find of a fossil clam specimen in a museum collection led him to solve the mystery of Bering Strait's age.

Dr. Marincovich has authored more than 100 scientific articles and books. He is a Research Associate in Geology at the California Academy of Sciences in San Francisco, California.

As a child, he was inspired to become a paleontologist by a children's book on fossils, and he hopes to pass along this lifelong inspiration through the pages of *True North: Hunting Fossils Under the Midnight Sun*.

Visit the author online at www.loumarincovich.com.

Made in the USA
San Bernardino, CA
15 November 2018